Apple
Machine Language

Don Inman   Kurt Inman

Reston Publishing Company, Inc.
A Prentice-Hall Company
Reston, Virginia

Library of Congress Cataloging in Publication Data

Inman, Don.
    Apple machine language.
    Includes index.
    1. Apple computer—Programming. 2. Basic
(Computer program language) I. Inman, Kurt, joint
author. II. Title.
QA76.8.A66156   001.65'2   80-20083
ISBN 0-8359-0231-5
        0-8359-0230-7   pbk.

© 1981 by Reston Publishing Company, Inc.
A Prentice-Hall Company
Reston, Virginia 22090

10   9   8   7   6   5   4   3   2   1

Printed in the United States

Contents

3.   `SM`   Introduced in Chap. 8. Machine language programs are hand-assembled and entered directly from the Apple System Monitor.

4.   `MA`   Introduced in Chap. 11. Machine language programs are assembled by the Apple Mini-Assembler.

The `BASIC` , `BOS` , `SM` , and `MA` logos appear in the table of contents and in the appropriate chapter headings where they are used.

Preface

The purpose of this book is to introduce Apple computer users, who have a knowledge of BASIC language, to machine language programming. The transition from BASIC is made in small, easy steps. Color, graphics, and sound are used early in the book to make the demonstration programs interesting and action-packed. Each new instruction is explained, and the demonstration programs are discussed step-by-step in functional sections.

The reader first uses the BASIC statements POKE, PEEK, and CALL to enter and execute machine language programs from within a BASIC language program. A BASIC Operating System is then developed from which machine language programs can be entered and executed.

The introduction from BASIC, a language the reader already knows, provides a natural approach that leads to the use of the Apple System Monitor. The System Monitor allows the reader to enter, examine, and execute machine language programs directly. The time used by the computer to interpret BASIC statements is thus eliminated.

The final step in the transition is to the Apple's Mini-Assembler, which relieves the programmer of many of the tedious details involved with direct machine language programming.

Approaching machine language through BASIC provides a means for the reader to use his or her previous knowledge as a stepping stone to explore a new area.

You will proceed through this book in four definite stages. Machine language programs are entered and executed by four distinct methods. One method is introduced at each stage of the book.

1. |BASIC| Introduced in Chap. 1. Machine language programs are under full control of BASIC, using the instructions POKE, CALL, and PEEK.

2. |BOS| Introduced in Chap. 2. Machine language programs are controlled by a BASIC Operating System.

Chapter 1

Review of Applesoft II Basic

| BASIC |

Several assumptions are made in writing this book. The authors felt this to be necessary because of the numerous versions of Apple computers presently in use.

1. You have made the necessary hardware connections. If not, see the reference manuals provided with your Apple computer.
2. The authors have used a version of the Apple that has:
     a. Applesoft II BASIC on a plug-in ROM printed circuit card.
     b. A switch on the card to select either Applesoft II or Integer BASIC.
3. You will read and use the Apple manuals pertinent to your particular machine.
4. You know how to switch back and forth between the programming languages available to you.

The Apple computer can speak several languages. The prompt character indicates which language your Apple is currently ready to understand. The asterisk (*) indicates that you are in the machine language mode. This language is always in the computer and does not have to be "loaded" (entered from an external source) from a cassette or diskette. The machine language monitor that controls the use of this language is discussed in the latter part of this book (from Chap. 8 on).

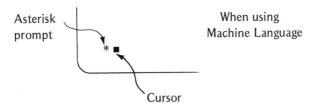

If your Applesoft is on the plug-in ROM pc card, your Apple also contains a high-level English-oriented language called Integer BASIC* stored permanently

---

*BASIC was developed at Dartmouth College by John Kemeny and Thomas Kurtz as an all-purpose computer language suitable for beginning programmers with diverse educational backgrounds.

in its ROM memory. ROM, which is an abbreviation for *Read Only Memory*, can be "read" (used by your programs), but cannot be "written into" (changed by you). The prompt character for Integer BASIC is a right facing arrow (>). Integer BASIC is *not* discussed in this book. For more information, see the Apple II BASIC Programming Manual (Apple product #A2L005X).

Applesoft II is Apple's extended BASIC language. The prompt character of Applesoft II is a right square bracket ( ]). This extended BASIC is now available in three forms:

1. The Apple II Plus System with the Autostart Monitor ROM
2. The Applesoft plug-in interface card
3. The Apple Language System

The Apple II Plus System has Applesoft II BASIC in ROM. Therefore, the Apple Mini-Assembler, the Floating Point Package, and the SWEET-16 interpreter (which are stored in the Integer BASIC ROMs) are not available on the Apple II Plus system.

Since we will be using the Mini-Assembler later in the book, we will focus on the system containing the Applesoft II ROM card rather than the Apple II Plus system.

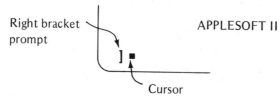

This book is designed to provide a bridge over which the reader may cross from programming in BASIC to programming in the computer's native machine language. While the book assumes a background knowledge of Applesoft II BASIC, a brief review of BASIC statements used by the Apple computer is presented in this chapter. If you feel confident of your knowledge of Applesoft II BASIC, feel free to move on to Chap. 2. However, if your BASIC is rusty, spend some time reviewing the material here.

Although this material is not a complete discussion of Applesoft capabilities, all those statements and commands necessary for understanding the remaining chapters of the book are given. An Apple computer with 16K of RAM, a tape recorder or disk drive, and Applesoft II BASIC are all that are necessary to perform the demonstrations and exercises presented.

COMMANDS

Certain fundamental commands are necessary in preparing, debugging, and executing a program. Those discussed here are NEW, LIST, RUN, TEXT, GRaphics, LOAD, SAVE, CONTinue, TRACE, and NOTRACE.

COMMANDER

NEW — This erases any old program that may be in the computer's memory. It not only deletes the current program, but also clears all variables that may have been set by this program. It is used *before* a new program is entered.

Example:

```
10 LET M = 50
20 PRINT M
30 LET M = M+1
40 IF M<60 THEN GOTO 20
50 END

]NEW
```

When you type this and press the RETURN key.

PRESTO! EVERYTHING IS GONE!

```
]
```

LIST — This causes the current program to be displayed on the video screen. Several versions of this command are shown in the examples. All assume that you have a program in the computer.

Examples:

1. Type: LIST and press the RETURN key.
   The whole program will be displayed. If the program is very long, the display will scroll upwards after the screen is filled.
2. Type: LIST 20,100
   or
   LIST 20-100 and press the RETURN key.
   This will display lines 20 through 100 of the program.

3. Type: LIST -150 and press the RETURN key.
   This will display all lines from the beginning of the program through line 150.

4. Type: LIST 150- and press the RETURN key.
   This will display all lines from line 150 through the end of the program.

5. Type: LIST 150 and press the RETURN key.
   This will display only line 150.

To stop the listing temporarily at some point, hold down the CTRL (control) key and press the letter S. Use CTRL S again to resume the listing. This will allow you to examine parts of the desired listing. A listing is aborted by a CTRL C, but the listing cannot be continued from the point at which it is aborted unless you note where the listing was stopped and continue from that point with the LIST command.

RUN — This causes the computer to RUN (or execute) the program that is currently stored in its memory. All variables are cleared and execution begins at the lowest numbered line in the program (unless a beginning line number follows the word RUN, as in Example 2).

Examples:

1. Type: RUN and press the RETURN key.
   The program is executed from the lowest line number.

2. Type: RUN 200 and press the RETURN key.
   The program is executed beginning with line 200.

TEXT — This command sets the video screen format to display a full screen of text with a maximum of 40 characters per line and 24 lines. This is the normal format used when Applesoft II BASIC is accessed. This command is used when returning from a Graphics mode to display a full screen of text. It can also be used as a statement within a program to change from Graphics to Text format.

Example:

Type: TEXT and press RETURN

GR — This command sets the low resolution graphics format for screen display. With this command, a 40 by 40 grid is available for graphics. The screen is cleared with a black background, and the cursor is moved to the beginning of a 4-line text window at the bottom of the screen. The color to be used for graphics is automatically set to black (COLOR = 0). Some other COLOR value must be given to display graphics (black on black doesn't show up too well).

Example:

Type: GR and press RETURN

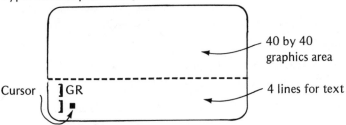

Cursor

40 by 40 graphics area

4 lines for text

LOAD — This command causes the computer to read an Apple program from a cassette tape into the computer's memory. The user must have the recorder ready (set to the beginning of the desired program and in the PLAY mode) *before* the LOAD command is given. A "beep" is sounded when the Apple has found the information on the tape. A second beep will sound when the program on tape has been successfully LOADed. The Applesoft prompt will appear on the screen at that time. A LOAD may only be interrupted by pressing the RESET key or turning off the power.

Example:

Ready your recorder, then
Type: LOAD and press RETURN.
When finished, the display will show:

]LOAD — Indicates successfully LOADed program

] ◼ ◄

SAVE — This stores the program currently in the computer's memory on cassette tape. The user must press the RECORD and PLAY buttons on the tape recorder *before* SAVE is executed. Beeps signal the beginning and end of the SAVE procedure.

Example:

Ready your recorder, then
Type: SAVE and press RETURN.

CONT — If the execution of a program has been halted by a STOP, END, or CTRL C, this command causes execution to resume at the next instruction following the halt. Nothing is cleared. CONT cannot be used if you have (1) modified, added, or deleted any program line or (2) received an error message since stopping execution.

Example:

Type: CONT and press RETURN

5

TRACE — This is used in debugging programs. It causes line numbers to be displayed on the screen as the lines are executed. You can then see if the program is performing the desired sequence of operations. The TRACE feature is turned off by the command NOTRACE.

Example:

Type: TRACE and press RETURN
Then type RUN to see the sequence of line execution.

NOTRACE — This turns off the TRACE feature discussed above.

Example:

Type: NOTRACE and press RETURN
When the program is RUN again, no line numbers will be printed.

ASSIGNMENT STATEMENTS

There are several ways that data (both numeric and string) may be assigned to variables. Instructions used for this purpose in this section are LET, INPUT, READ, and GET. DATA and RESTORE instructions are also discussed; they are used in conjunction with the READ instruction.

LET — This statement *may* be used to assign values to variables. The word LET is optional, as seen in the example at lines 50 and 60.

Examples:

10 LET M = 50	◄———— Assign a numeric value to M
20 FOR X = 1 TO 9	
30 LET A$ = "APPLES"	◄———— Assign the string APPLES to A$
40 LET M = M+1	◄———— Alter a variable's value
50 B=1	The word LET does not have to
60 B$ = " PER CARTON "	be used. It is optional.
70 PRINT M;A$,B;B$	
80 NEXT X	

INPUT — This instruction is used to assign a value to a variable during execution of a program. When the computer reaches this instruction, it stops and waits for the user to type in the value to be assigned to the variable.

Examples:

50 INPUT A

? ■

The execution of this statement displays a question mark and waits for the user to type in the value and press RETURN.

70 INPUT A,B,C

More than one variable can be assigned by one INPUT statement. The values are typed in, separated by a comma.

6

80 INPUT "PLEASE TYPE YOUR NAME"; C$

A message may be printed to tell you what INPUT is desired. The message is typed in quotes. The variable C$ calls for a string INPUT. A question mark is *not* printed with this format.

PLEASE TYPE YOUR NAME■

90 INPUT A$

No message this time. Display will show a question mark when this instruction is executed.

?■

100 INPUT "WHAT IS THE VALUE OF A?"; A

If you want a question mark when quotes are used in a message, include the question mark inside the quote.

WHAT IS THE VALUE OF A?■

READ — This instructs the computer to READ a value from a DATA list and assign that value to a variable. The first time a READ is executed, the first item in the first DATA list will be used. The second time, the second item from the DATA list will be used, etc. (See DATA for example.)

DATA — This lets you store DATA inside your program. The items will be read sequentially. More than one DATA statement may be used in a program. Items will be READ from the first DATA statement until all its items have been READ. Then items will be read from the next DATA statement, etc.

Example:
```
110 FOR X = 1 TO 10
120    READ Y          ◄────── Reads DATA in this order:
130 NEXT X                10
140 DATA 10,30,20,40,50   30
150 DATA 60,80,90,70,100  20
                          40
                          50
                          60
                          80
                          90
                          70
                          100
```

7

RESTORE — This causes the next READ statement executed to start from the first item in the first DATA list.

Example:

```
100 FOR X = 1 TO 5
110   READ Y: PRINT Y  ←——— Reads and prints
120 NEXT X                      10,30,50,20,40
130 RESTORE           ←——— Go back to start of DATA list
140 FOR Z = 1 TO 10
150   READ W: PRINT W ←——— Reads and prints
160 NEXT Z                      10,30,50,20,40,60,80,100,70,90
170 DATA 10,30,50,20,40
180 DATA 60,80,100,70,90
```

RESTORE

GET — This gets (or reads) a single character from the keyboard. The computer waits for a key to be pressed, as in an INPUT statement. The character *is not* displayed and *does not* require that the RETURN key be pressed.

Example:

```
200 GET H$
210 IF H$ = "Y" THEN GOTO 500
220 GOTO 100
```

Line 200 would wait for a key to be pressed. The typed character would be stored as the variable H$. If the typed character is a Y, line 500 would be executed after line 210. If not, line 220 would return execution to line 100.

DISPLAY STATEMENTS

The PRINT statement is used in many forms to display data on the video screen. The display can also be changed from white on black to black on white by the INVERSE statement. You can also alternate these two formats by using the FLASH statement. The NORMAL statement returns the display to the normal white-on-black format. HOME is used to clear the video screen. SPC is used to format print statements.

Examples:

320 PRINT   The word PRINT used by itself causes a line feed and return to be

5 310 PRINT A

executed on the screen. (See line 320 in example below.)

Prints the value of A and causes a line feed and return. (See line 310 in the example below.)

300 A = 5: B = 6
310 PRINT A
320 PRINT
330 PRINT B

Display when these lines are executed:

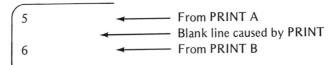

5 ←——————— From PRINT A
←——————— Blank line caused by PRINT
6 ←——————— From PRINT B

400 PRINT "A STRING"

Prints the words A STRING, and moves to the next line.

A STRING

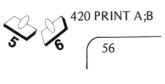

410 PRINT A,B

IF A = 5 and B = 6, this will cause the two values to be printed on the same line spaced far apart.

5   6

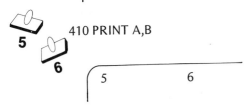

420 PRINT A;B

This time the values will be printed on the same line but close together.

56

430 PRINT A$;A

If A$="A=" and A=5, this will print the string, A=, and the value of A.

A= 5

440 PRINT A$;A,
450 PRINT B$;B

If A$="A= " and B$="B= " with A=5 and B=6, the comma keeps the display on the same line. The result of these two lines will be as shown.

A= 5   B= 6

500 PRINT TAB(10)A$;A

The TAB function moves the printed display over to the stated print position. (Print positions on a given line are 1 through 40.)

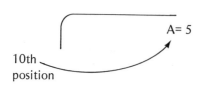

10th position

FLASH — This statement sets the video mode to flashing. The output is alternately shown as white on black and black on white. Use the NORMAL statement to return to a nonflashing white-on-black mode.

Example:

70 FLASH
80 PRINT "FLASHING" ◄——— The word FLASHING will flash back and forth.

INVERSE — This sets the video mode so that the computer's output is displayed as black letters on a white background.

 Example:

100 INVERSE
100 PRINT "INVERTED" ◄——— The word INVERTED will appear in black letters on a white background.

NORMAL — This sets the video mode back to the usual display of white letters on a black background with no flashing and no inversion.

Example:

70 FLASH
80 PRINT "FLASHING" ◄——— The word FLASHING will FLASH and remain flashing
100 INVERSE
110 PRINT "INVERTED" ◄——— The word INVERTED will appear as black on white and will stay that way
120 NORMAL
130 PRINT "NORMAL" ◄——— The word NORMAL and all future printed material will be in the normal mode (unless changed by FLASH or INVERSE again).

HOME — This statement moves the cursor to the upper left screen position within the text window. It also clears all text within the text window. HOME may be used in the TEXT or GRaphics mode.

SPC(X) — This provides for *X* number of blank spaces to be inserted between the last item printed and the next item printed if semicolons precede and follow the SPC statement. It is *only* used within a PRINT statement.

Example:

400 PRINT A; SPC(2); B

If A = 768 and B = 5, line 400 (when executed) would display:

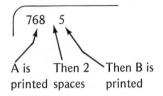

A is   Then 2   Then B is
printed   spaces   printed

LOOP STATEMENTS AND SUBROUTINES

Portions of a program may be repeated by several BASIC statements such as GOTO, ON. . .GOTO, IF-THEN, and FOR-NEXT. Subroutines may be performed by GOSUB and RETURN.

GOTO — This statement causes the program to branch from the line where the GOTO is located to the line that is specified following the word GOTO.

Examples:

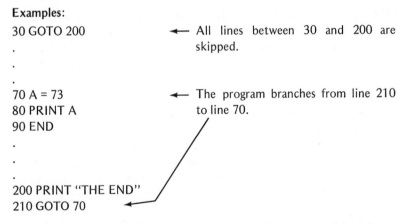

30 GOTO 200   ◄— All lines between 30 and 200 are
  .   skipped.
  .
  .

70 A = 73   ◄— The program branches from line 210
80 PRINT A   to line 70.
90 END
  .
  .
  .
200 PRINT "THE END"
210 GOTO 70

ON . . . GOTO 100,200,300 . . . — This statement evaluates the arithmetic expression following the word ON. It then branches to the line number (100,200,300, . . .) corresponding to the result of the evaluation. 100, 200,300, etc., must be valid line numbers in the program.

Example:

.

.

150 ON INT(B/100) GOTO 200,300,400
160 PRINT "INT(B/100) is 0 or >3"

.

.

The expression INT(B/100) is evaluated. Then,
a. If the value = 1, line 200 will be executed following line 150.
b. If the value = 2, line 300 will be executed following line 150.
c. If the value = 3, line 400 will be executed following line 150.
d. If the value = 0 or is >3, line 160 will be executed following line 150.

IF-THEN — If the condition stated between the words IF and THEN is true, then the instruction following the word THEN is executed. Otherwise, the instruction following the word THEN is ignored.

Examples:

200 IF X>5 THEN GOTO 400 ←Branches to line 400 if, and only if, X>5

210 IF X <=5 THEN PRINT "X IS NOT >5"
220 X = X+1 ⟍If X<=5, then the words X IS NOT >5 are printed, then line 220 is executed.
⟍Otherwise, the words are *not* printed. Line 220 is then executed.

FOR-NEXT — This is a combination of two statements. It allows you to "loop through" a set of statements between the FOR statement and the NEXT statement a specified number of times.

Examples:

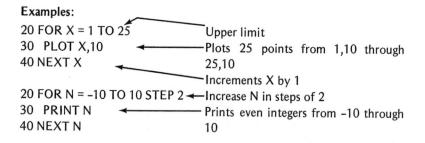

20 FOR X = 1 TO 25   Upper limit
30 PLOT X,10   ←————————Plots 25 points from 1,10 through
40 NEXT X   ←   25,10
                          Increments X by 1
20 FOR N = -10 TO 10 STEP 2←Increase N in steps of 2
30 PRINT N   ←———————— Prints even integers from -10 through
40 NEXT N   10

GOSUB — This causes the program to branch to a subroutine which you have written at the specified line number. When the subroutine is completed, a RETURN statement in the subroutine will return to execution of the program at the line following the most recently used GOSUB statement.

Example:

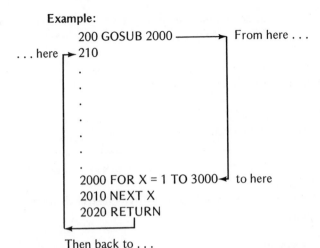

200 GOSUB 2000 ⟶ From here . . .

. . . here ➤ 210
.
.
.
.
.
.
.
2000 FOR X = 1 TO 3000 ◄ to here
2010 NEXT X
2020 RETURN

Then back to . . .

RETURN — This statement is used at the end of a subroutine to return to the statement immediately following the most recently executed GOSUB. (See example above.)

GRAPHIC STATEMENTS

Graphic statements shown here are GRaphics, COLOR, PLOT, HLIN, VLIN, PDL, and TEXT. The Graphics mode presents a display that is quite different from the TEXT mode. You must be able to change from one mode to the other.

GR — This statement sets the low resolution Graphics mode. (See GR under "Commands" section.)

COLOR — This sets the color for plotting in the low resolution Graphics mode. Color is set to black (0) by the GR statement. The color values used are:

0 black	4 dark green	8 brown	12 green
1 magenta	5 grey	9 orange	13 yellow
2 dark blue	6 medium blue	10 grey	14 aqua
3 purple	7 light blue	11 pink	15 white

PLOT — This turns on one of the 40 by 40 low resolution dots in the graphics area at the column and row specified. The dot will be of the color selected by the COLOR statement. The three statements are used together.

Example:

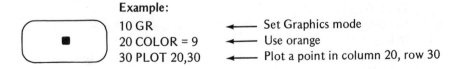

10 GR ◄—— Set Graphics mode
20 COLOR = 9 ◄—— Use orange
30 PLOT 20,30 ◄—— Plot a point in column 20, row 30

HLIN — This statement is used to draw a horizontal line. Included in the statement are the beginning and ending columns, as well as the row where the line is to be drawn.

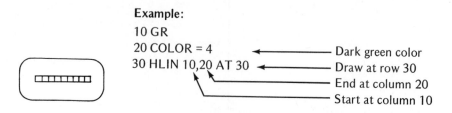

Example:
10 GR
20 COLOR = 4 ←————————— Dark green color
30 HLIN 10,20 AT 30 ←———————— Draw at row 30
————————————————————— End at column 20
————————————————————— Start at column 10

VLIN — This command is used to draw a vertical line from one row to another at the specified column.

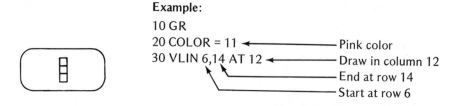

Example:
10 GR
20 COLOR = 11 ←————————— Pink color
30 VLIN 6,14 AT 12 ←———————— Draw in column 12
————————————————————— End at row 14
————————————————————— Start at row 6

PDL(0) or PDL(1) — This reads the current value of one of the game controls (a number from 0 through 255). The paddles (game controls) can be used to plot points in the low resolution Graphics mode, as shown below. (They can also be used with high resolution graphics.)

Example:
10 GR
20 COLOR = 14
30 PLOT PDL(0)/7, PDL(1)/7
——————— Row
——————————————— Column

TEXT — This statement is used to return to the TEXT mode following the use of high or low resolution graphics.

Example:
10 GR
20 COLOR = 14
30 VLIN 6,14 AT 12
40 FOR X = 1 TO 3000 ⎫
50 NEXT X   ⎬ ←——— Delay to view the color bar
60 TEXT ←——————————— Return to the TEXT mode
70 HOME ←——————————— Home the cursor

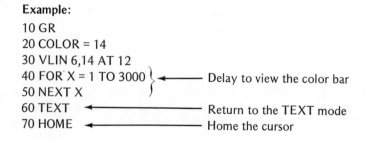

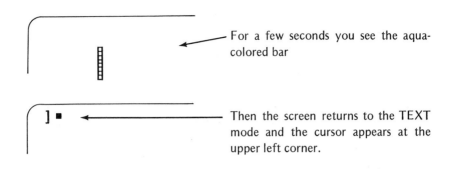

For a few seconds you see the aqua-colored bar

Then the screen returns to the TEXT mode and the cursor appears at the upper left corner.

RELATIONAL STATEMENTS

Two values may be compared by using one of several relational statements. The result of this comparison may be used by the computer to "make a decision" as to what action to perform next.

MATHEMATICAL RELATIONSHIPS

=	is equal to
>	is greater than
<	is less than
>=	is greater than or equal to
<=	is less than or equal to
#	is not equal to

LOGICAL RELATIONSHIPS

AND	true if both conditions are true; otherwise false
OR	true if either or both conditions are true; otherwise false
NOT	Negation of the expression

Examples:

```
200 IF A>5 THEN GOTO 340
300 IF A#B THEN PRINT "A IS NOT EQUAL TO B"
400 IF A=5 AND B>=6 THEN C=A+B
```

PRECEDENCE OF MATHEMATICAL AND LOGICAL RELATIONSHIPS

The computer evaluates expressions by performing operations in a specific order. The order in which it performs these operations is in accordance with the following list. Their order of precedence is from the top downward.

15

Order Operation	Function
1. ( )	Evaluate expression in parentheses
2. NOT	Negate
3. ^	Raise to a power (exponentiate)
4. *, /	Multiply or divide (left to right)
5. +, -	Add or subtract (left to right)
6. =, >, <, >=, <=, #	Compare
7. AND	AND two expressions
8. OR	OR two expressions

STRINGS AND FUNCTIONS

Several statements are used to manipulate strings. We will define only those which will be used in this book. They are ASC, CHR$, and LEFT$. Several intrinsic functions are also available, but we will only use the INTeger function.

ASC — This command returns (or supplies) the decimal ASCII code for the first character in the string which is enclosed in parentheses following the letters ASC.

Example:

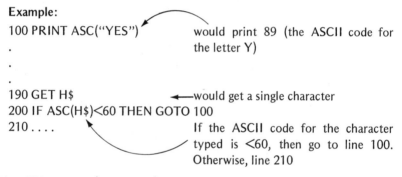

100 PRINT ASC("YES")   would print 89 (the ASCII code for
.   the letter Y)
.
.
.
190 GET H$ ◄—would get a single character
200 IF ASC(H$)<60 THEN GOTO 100
210 . . . .   If the ASCII code for the character
                     typed is <60, then go to line 100.
                     Otherwise, line 210

CHR$ — This returns (or supplies) the ASCII character that corresponds to the value given in parentheses. This value must be between 0 and 255, inclusive.

Example:

300 H = 14   If H = the decimal number 14,
310 PRINT CHR$(H+55)   then H+55 = 69. The character
                     whose ASCII code is 69 is the letter
                     E. The letter E would be printed.

LEFT$ — Returns (or supplies) the specified number of leftmost characters in the string enclosed in parentheses. If no number is specified, it returns only the leftmost character in the string.

16

Examples:

200 PRINT LEFT$("YESTERDAY", 3)

.

.⠀⠀⠀⠀⠀⠀⠀⠀⠀⠀⠀⠀⠀⠀⠀⠀would print: YES (the 3 leftmost

.⠀⠀⠀⠀⠀⠀⠀⠀⠀⠀⠀⠀⠀⠀⠀⠀characters of YESTERDAY)

.

250 INPUT H$

260 IF LEFT$(H$) = "Y" THEN GOTO 100

270 . . .⠀⠀⠀⠀⠀⠀⠀⠀⠀⠀⠀⠀If the leftmost character of the string
⠀⠀⠀⠀⠀⠀⠀⠀⠀⠀⠀⠀⠀⠀⠀⠀input for H$ is a Y, then GOTO line
⠀⠀⠀⠀⠀⠀⠀⠀⠀⠀⠀⠀⠀⠀⠀⠀100. If not, go on to line 270

INT — The INTeger function returns the largest integer less than or equal to the expression in parentheses following the letters INT.

Examples:

100 INT (A/3)

⠀⠀⠀⠀If A = 5, A/3 = 1.66667 and INT(A/3) = 1
⠀⠀⠀⠀If A = 1, A/3 = 0.333333 and INT(A/3) = 0
⠀⠀⠀⠀If A = 15, A/3 = 5 and INT(A/3) = 5
⠀⠀⠀⠀If A = -5, A/3 = -1.66667 and INT(A/3) = -2

BASIC STATEMENTS OF SPECIAL IMPORTANCE

There are three instructions that you will be using over and over again to establish the bridge between BASIC and the machine language programs that you will be creating. These instructions are POKE, PEEK, and CALL.

In BASIC, the line numbers serve as a reference for the computer. Individual statements are found and executed according to the line number associated with a given statement.

Machine language instructions are executed according to their placement in memory. There are no line numbers. Execution begins at a memory location which must be specified. Then the instructions are normally executed in the order that they appear in memory.

The BASIC Operating System (described in Chap. 2) is used to put the machine language instructions and data into the correct memory locations to be used by the machine language program. This is done primarily by the following BASIC instructions.

POKE *address,data*⠀⠀⠀⠀⠀⠀Where address is the decimal address
⠀⠀⠀⠀⠀⠀⠀⠀⠀⠀⠀⠀⠀⠀⠀⠀⠀of the memory location where the
⠀⠀⠀⠀⠀⠀⠀⠀⠀⠀⠀⠀⠀⠀⠀⠀⠀data is to be placed.

Since POKE is a BASIC instruction, the values for address and data must be given as decimal values.

Examples:

100 POKE 768,169   POKE the value 169 into memory
                                    location 768

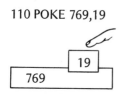

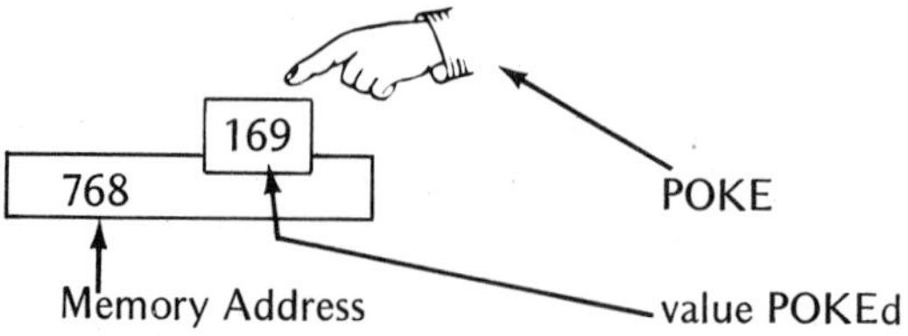

768   169   POKE

↑   �↘ value POKEd
Memory Address

110 POKE 769,19   POKE the value 19 into memory loca-
                                    tion 769

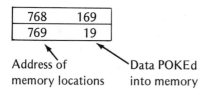

769   19

We now have:

768	169
769	19

Address of   Data POKEd
memory locations   into memory

Each machine language instruction and each data value used in the machine language program will be entered from the BASIC Operating System by a POKE instruction.

Once the machine language program and data have been entered by BASIC POKE statements, control must be passed from BASIC to the machine language program. This is done by the statement:

CALL *address*

CALLs for the execution   The decimal ad-
of a machine language   dress where the
program (or subroutine)   machine language
                                 program begins

Example:

CALL 768   ◀—This would cause the computer
              to execute the machine lan-
              guage program that begins at
              memory location 768.

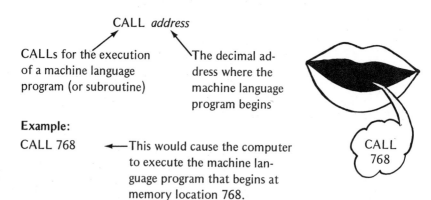

A third BASIC instruction that you will frequently use allows you to examine the content of a specified memory location. You can PEEK at a memory location with the instruction:

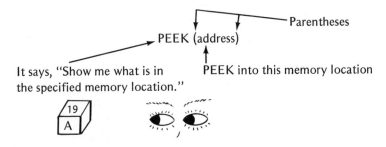

Parentheses

PEEK (address)

It says, "Show me what is in the specified memory location."

PEEK into this memory location

If you want to see what you PEEKed at, use the PRINT statement.

Example:

900 PRINT PEEK (768)

This statement would cause the value contained in memory location 768 to be displayed on the video screen.

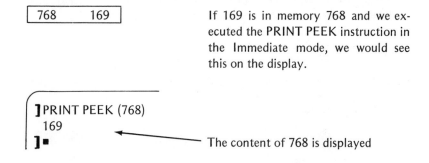

| 768 | 169 |

If 169 is in memory 768 and we executed the PRINT PEEK instruction in the Immediate mode, we would see this on the display.

] PRINT PEEK (768)
  169
] ■

The content of 768 is displayed

The PEEK statement can be used to examine the machine language program itself, or it can be used to display the results of a machine language program that has been placed in a given memory location.

These three statements (POKE, CALL, and PEEK) will be used repeatedly to establish a link between BASIC and machine language. The machine language is POKEd into memory by BASIC. It is then executed by the CALL statement from BASIC. The PEEK statement of BASIC can be used to look at the results of a machine language program or at the program itself.

You can see that you will by relying heavily on these three BASIC statements. If a solid connection is to be made between BASIC and machine language, the three building block statements must be understood. You will see their use again in Chap. 2 when the BASIC Operating System is discussed.

EXERCISES

1. Tell what function each of the following commands performs.

   a. NEW _____

   _____

   b. LIST _____

   _____

   c. GR _____

   _____

2. The TRACE command causes line numbers to be displayed as a program is executed. What command turns off the TRACE feature? _____

3. Name three BASIC statements used to assign values to variables.

   a. _____

   b. _____

   c. _____

4. If you are currently using low resolution graphics and want to return to the Text Display Mode with the cursor in the upper left corner of the screen, what two commands should be entered?

   a. _____

   b. _____

5. Some of the operations shown below are in the wrong order of precedence. Rearrange them correctly according to their precedence.

   ( )   _____

   *, /   _____

   >=   _____

   AND _____

   NOT _____

6. Fill in the values in the correct memory boxes as performed by the following statements.

100 POKE 768,19		768	
110 POKE 770,14		769	
120 POKE 772,18		770	
130 POKE 771,15		771	
140 POKE 769,16		772	

7. What will be displayed on the screen when the instructions of exercise 6 plus the following struction have been executed?

   150 PRINT PEEK (772)

   _____

8. If a machine language program has been POKEd into memory and you desire to execute that program from BASIC, what BASIC statement could you use? 160 _____

ANSWERS TO EXERCISES

1. a. NEW—Erases any old program and clears all variables
   b. LIST — Displays the current program on the video screen
   c. GR — Sets the screen display to the low resolution graphics format

2. NOTRACE

3. a. LET A = 5 (or just plain A=5)
   b. INPUT A
   c. READ A

4. a. TEXT
   b. HOME

5. ( )
   NOT
   *, /
   >=
   AND

6.

768	19
769	16
770	14
771	15
772	18

7.

    ┌─────────
    │   18
    │

8. 160 CALL 768

Chapter 2

Crossing the Bridge

BOS

When you communicate with the computer in BASIC, you are talking through an interpreter. Each program line must be examined in detail by the interpreter and translated into a code which the computer can understand. It is easy for you to write programs in BASIC, but it is a "foreign" language to the computer. The computer cannot understand a single simple BASIC statement. BASIC words and statements must be translated into binary number codes that have a precise meaning to the computer. These number codes are "words" that the computer can understand. They are the language of the computer, called *machine language*. Instructions must be in machine language code before the computer can understand them.

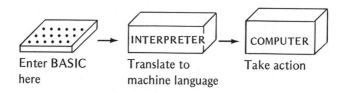

Enter BASIC   Translate to   Take action
here   machine language

Once the BASIC statements have been interpreted, the computer acts on them. Its actions and the results it obtains must be translated once more into a form which BASIC can use and which you will be able to understand easily.

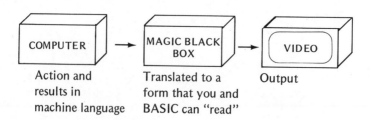

Action and   Translated to a   Output
results in   form that you and
machine language   BASIC can "read"

Translating BASIC is a time-consuming chore for the interpreter, and it is wasteful of computer time. In addition, the BASIC language may not be able to handle everything that you might want the computer to do.

Although machine language programming may be a more time-consuming and detailed task for you than programming in BASIC, it brings you into much closer contact with the computer. When you speak to the computer in machine language, you are talking to it directly. You will get quick responses and will gain a better understanding of your computer's "personality," its full capabilities, and also its shortcomings. You will find that the computer speaks and understands a very limited, formal language. Each word is the same length and follows a rigid format. But its rules of form and syntax are much simpler than those of the English language.

The machine language words can be broken down into eight bits (binary digits) that have only two possible states (or conditions). These tiny bits are much like a light that is either on or off.

OFF   ON

The computer interprets these bits as being one of two numeric symbols, 0 or 1. The pattern of 1's and 0's make a meaningful word, or a complete idea, to the computer. Therefore, we need to learn these words if we are to communicate directly with it.

An example of a pattern of 8 computer bits (a pattern with a size and shape that the computer can understand) is shown.

The computer would recognize this pattern as a unique number code and would respond by taking a specific action or using the number as a specific piece of data.

Since machine language instructions are merely numbers that are placed in the computer's memory, we can use BASIC to perform this operation. The BASIC instruction:

POKE *address, data*

will store the given data into the memory location whose address is given. (See Chap. 1 for a review of this instruction.)

Example:

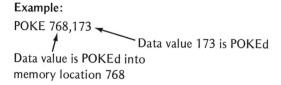

POKE 768,173

Data value is POKEd into
memory location 768

Data value 173 is POKEd

The data given in the POKE statement must be in the range of 0 through 255, due to the nature of the computer's memory locations. Larger numbers will take up more than one memory location. If you try to POKE a number larger than 255 into memory, the computer will not accept the POKE. However, it won't POKE you back. Instead it will merely respond with an ILLEGAL QUANTITY ERROR.

Example:

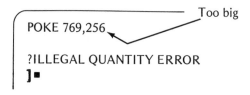

Too big

POKE 769,256

?ILLEGAL QUANTITY ERROR
]■

It is important that you be careful where you POKE values. You may destroy essential values or instructions if you POKE into the wrong memory location.

APPLESOFT II also has an instruction that will let you display the decimal value of the contents of a given memory location. It is:

PEEK (address)

To display the value in a given address, you could use the statement 200 PRINT PEEK(768). The computer would print the decimal value (0 through 255) that was contained in the memory location whose address is 768.

So, you see, the Apple will let you POKE values into its memory, and it will let you PEEK at values that are already in its memory. You should spend some time experimenting with these two instructions in the Immediate Execution mode. Try the following examples and others of your own.

Examples:
First POKE

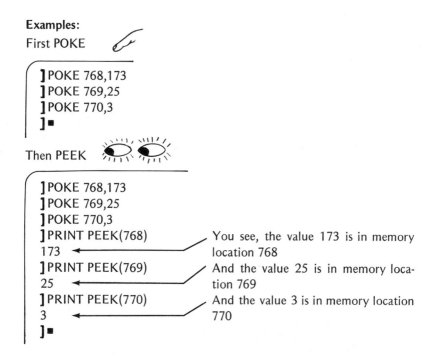

```
]POKE 768,173
]POKE 769,25
]POKE 770,3
]▪
```

Then PEEK

```
]POKE 768,173
]POKE 769,25
]POKE 770,3
]PRINT PEEK(768)          You see, the value 173 is in memory
173  ◄────────────        location 768
]PRINT PEEK(769)          And the value 25 is in memory loca-
25  ◄────────────         tion 769
]PRINT PEEK(770)          And the value 3 is in memory location
3  ◄────────────          770
]▪
```

The decimal values that can be used for the address in the POKE and PEEK statements depend on the memory capacity of your computer.

MEMORY USE

Many memory addresses cannot be used for machine language programs, as they contain information necessary for the Apple's operating system. The operating system might be compared to an airport traffic controller who directs the flow of traffic in and out of the airport. The operating system directs the flow of actions taken by the computer. A POKE into the operating system's memory locations might alter the operation of the system or the operation of your BASIC program.

In addition to the Apple's operating system, you will be using the BASIC Operating System that will be discussed in this chapter. It is written in BASIC, and will be stored in the section of memory that is reserved for BASIC programs (see Memory Map below). It will control the input, revisions, and operation of the machine language programs that you will be using.

Nor can data be successfully stored at addresses that contain Monitor ROMS, APPLESOFT ROMS, or unused Input/Output ports. The ROMs are Read Only Memories from which information can be read, but into which you *cannot* put information. They already contain information that is protected (cannot be changed by a program or immediate mode input).

A memory map follows for the Applesoft firmware version of the Apple computer.

MEMORY MAP
APPLESOFT IN FIRMWARE (ROM)

Address	Function
00000-00511	Program workspace — not for user
00512-00767	Keyboard character buffer
*00768-01023	Free to user for short machine language programs
01024-02047	Screen Display area
02048-XXXXX	User area for BASIC programs and variables. XXXXX is determined by the maximum amount of RAM memory installed in your machine. 16K installed – XXXXX = 16383 32K installed – XXXXX = 32767 64K installed – XXXXX = 49151
08192-16383	Used by high resolution graphics (page 1)
16384-24575	Used by high resolution graphics (page 2)
49152-53247	Hardware I/O addresses
53248-63487	Applesoft Interpreter (if switch set for Applesoft BASIC)
53248-57343	⌈ ROM Area ⌉ (If switch set for Integer
57344-63487	⌊ Apple Integer BASIC and ⌋ BASIC) Mini-Assembler
64488-65535	Apple System Monitor

*This is the area that you will be using for your machine language programs.

Note: If you have Applesoft on diskette, see your Disk Operating System Instructional and Reference Manual (Apple Product #A2L0012) for a memory map.

The area that will be used for your machine language programs has been marked with an asterisk on each memory map. This area, from memory address 768 through address 1023, is the same for both Applesoft versions. It can be used safely for most, if not all, of your machine language programs. If you need more space when your programs get longer, we can place them in the area normally reserved for BASIC programs.

We will use the program below to demonstrate the method of using BASIC to POKE a machine language program into memory. The data in the POKE statements are the elements of the machine language program. We will also PEEK to make sure that the program was correctly POKEd in at the right addresses.

POKE AND PEEK DEMONSTRATION

```
100 REM * CLEAR THE SCREEN *
110 HOME

200 REM * POKE MACHINE LANGUAGE PROGRAM *
210 POKE 768,169
220 POKE 769,19
230 POKE 770,141
240 POKE 771,37
250 POKE 772,3
260 POKE 773,96

300 REM * PEEK AT THE PROGRAM *
310 FOR X = 768 TO 773
320   PRINT PEEK(X)
330 NEXT X
```

Now if you RUN this BASIC program, the values POKEd into memory will be displayed.

```
169
19
141
37
3
96
]■
```

Yes, the machine language program has been POKEd into the correct memory locations by the BASIC program. By using just two BASIC instructions, you have the tools necessary to enter machine language programs (with POKE) and to look at the machine language program (with PEEK). However, we also need a method of executing the machine language program after it has been entered.

The CALL instruction causes the computer to execute the machine language program beginning at a specified address. The address to use with the machine language program that you have just entered is 768. We would execute the program by using the statement:

410 CALL 768

The CALL statement is used to execute a machine language program that is a subroutine of a BASIC program. A GOSUB statement executes a BASIC subroutine from a BASIC program; a CALL statement executes a machine language subroutine from a BASIC program.

We'll add the CALL statement to our program so that we can execute the machine language subroutine. We'll also add a PEEK statement to look at the results of the machine language program to make sure that it executed correctly.

The last instruction executed in the machine language program must be a RETURN FROM SUBROUTINE (RTS). This is a machine language instruction that performs the same function for a machine language subroutine as the RETURN statement in BASIC does for a subroutine in BASIC. It returns control to the BASIC program from which the machine language program was CALLed.

Don't worry now about the machine language instructions being used in the program. Machine language codes will be introduced slowly starting in Chap. 3. For now, an explanation of each section of the program is given to the right of the machine codes. Our completed program looks like this.

POKE and PEEK, THEN PEEK AGAIN

```
100 REM * CLEAR THE SCREEN *
110 HOME
```

```
200 REM * POKE MACHINE LANGUAGE PROGRAM *
210 POKE 768,169          Loads the value 19
220 POKE 769,19
230 POKE 770,141          Store it in memory
240 POKE 771,37
250 POKE 772,3
260 POKE 773,96           Return from subroutine
```

```
300 REM * PEEK AT THE PROGRAM *
310 FOR X = 768 TO 773
320   PRINT PEEK(X)
330 NEXT X
```

```
400 REM * EXECUTE THE PROGRAM *
410 CALL 768
```

```
500 REM * LOOK INTO MEMORY FOR RESULT *
510 PRINT: PRINT PEEK(805)
```

We stored the 19 here.

When the program is run, this is what you'll see:

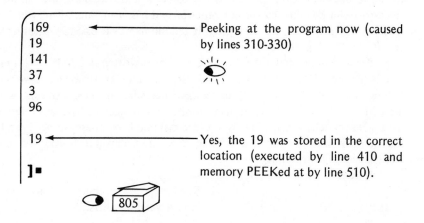

169 ——————→ Peeking at the program now (caused
19   by lines 310-330)
141
37
3
96

19 ——————→ Yes, the 19 was stored in the correct
location (executed by line 410 and
] ■   memory PEEKed at by line 510).

When the program is RUN, you do not see the machine language instructions being POKEd in by statements 210-260. The results of the PEEKs performed by the FOR-NEXT loop (lines 310-330) are seen on the screen:

169   These are machine language codes and data values
19   which were POKEd in by lines 210-260 and
141   PRINTed by the statement at line 320 in the
37   FOR-NEXT loop.
3
96

After the data has been PEEKed at, line 410 causes execution of the machine language program. When the computer returns to the BASIC program (caused by the last instruction in the machine language program), line 510 PRINTs the value 19, thus assuring us that the data has been placed in the memory location that we requested.

A SIMPLE BASIC OPERATING SYSTEM

Based on the BASIC instructions just used, we'll soon build a simple BASIC program that can accept, run, and read the results of a machine language program. It will lack many features that are desirable for more sophisticated programming, but it will be sufficient for our purposes.

It is a BASIC language program, but you may use it to enter each machine language program that you encounter in the rest of this book. You may also use it to examine the machine language programs for errors once they have been entered. You will use it to execute the machine language programs by using the CALL statement at the appropriate time. You can even use the BASIC program to examine the results of the machine language program that it creates.

The BASIC program will be used for so many things that we have decided to call it an Operating System. It is the operator and is in control of all the actions that will be taken by the computer once it has been entered and run. Since it is written in BASIC, we have given it the full name of: BASIC Operating System (Operating System for short).

Keep in mind that the Operating System is written in BASIC, so it understands (or uses) BASIC statements and *decimal* numbers. However, as we stated before, the computer can only understand machine language instructions that are coded as binary numbers. In fact, most standard machine language references list the machine language codes as hexadecimal numbers. These strange hexadecimal numbers will be explained in Chap. 3, where you will be introduced to machine language instructions.

Here is our dilemma:

1. References list machine language codes as *hexadecimal* numbers.

2. The computer only understands the codes as *binary* numbers.

3. The BASIC interpreter must receive *decimal* numbers, which it then converts to *binary* numbers for the computer's use.

We could ask you to convert every hexadecimal machine language code to a decimal value for the BASIC interpreter to use. This conversion is a tedious and time-consuming chore. The computer could do the conversion much faster than a human if it was provided with a program to make the conversion. So, we will include this conversion as part of the BASIC Operating System program.

Come along with us as we design the BASIC Operating System that will form a bridge to take you from BASIC to machine language programming.

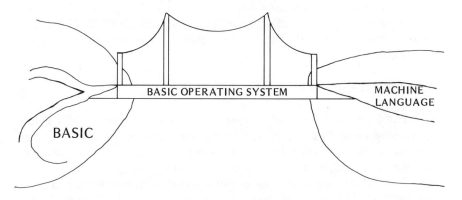

We will now begin the construction of our Operating System. Each functional section will be explained. The short machine language program given previously will be used to show how each section of the Operating System works. Here is a brief description of the Operating System by sections.

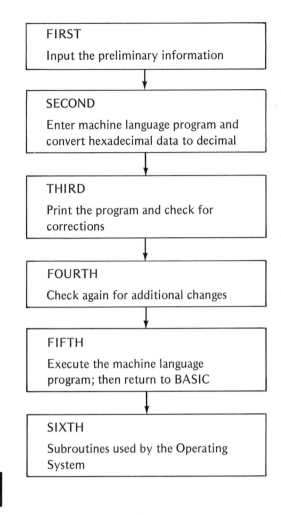

First ☐

We must have some vital information about the machine language program to be used. We need to know its starting address in memory, and we need to know how long the program will be (how many memory locations it will use). In computer terminology, each memory location will hold one *byte* of information. A byte is made up of 8 bits (binary digits). Bits were discussed briefly earlier in this chapter, and both bytes and bits will be discussed more thoroughly in Chap. 3. Here is how we get the information for each memory location.

SECTION 1

```
100 REM * GET MACHINE LANGUAGE INFORMATION *
110 HOME
120 INPUT "STARTING ADDRESS FOR M/L=?"; S     both inputs
130 INPUT "HOW MANY BYTES?"; B                in decimal
140 INPUT "PRESS RETURN TO ENTER PROGRAM"; A$
150 A = S
```

Line 110 clears the screen. You input the starting address at line 120. (We will be using 768 as our starting address.) Line 130 asks for the number of bytes. (The program we will use has 6 bytes.) The starting address is assigned to the variable S in line 120. The number of bytes is assigned to the variable B in line 130. The computer waits at line 140 for you to gather your courage before plunging into the program. After you press the RETURN key, the variable A is assigned the same value that S was assigned. This is done so that the starting address is saved as S. Meanwhile A is used as a working address. It changes to tell the computer which address to POKE successive data into.

Example:

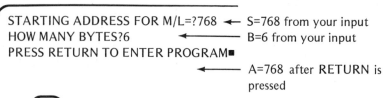

STARTING ADDRESS FOR M/L=?768 ◄— S=768 from your input
HOW MANY BYTES?6   ◄——— B=6 from your input
PRESS RETURN TO ENTER PROGRAM■
                             ◄——— A=768 after RETURN is
                                  pressed

Second

We will next have the Operating System print each address in turn and wait for you to enter a two-digit hexadecimal code for either an instruction code from your machine language reference or a byte of hexadecimal data. Remember, the Operating System will take care of converting the hexadecimal values to decimal values. It does this in a subroutine located at line 1000. After the conversion takes place, the decimal result is POKEd into the specified address. The address is then increased by one at line 290, and the next entry is requested. This continues until you have entered the entire program.

Address + 1 = Next Address

SECTION 2

```
200 REM * ENTER PROGRAM IN HEX – CONVERT TO DECIMAL *
210 FOR E = 1 TO B
220  PRINT A; SPC(2);      ◄——— Address is printed
230  GET H$: PRINT H$;  ⎫ ◄— Hex data follows
240  GET U$: PRINT U$   ⎭
250  IF ASC(H$)<48 OR ASC(H$)>70 OR (ASC(H$)>57 AND
     ASC(H$)<65) THEN PRINT "1ST DIGIT NOT HEX – TRY
     AGAIN": GOTO 220
260  IF ASC(U$)<48 OR ASC(U$)>70 OR (ASC(U$)>57 AND
     ASC(U$)<65) THEN PRINT "2ND DIGIT NOT HEX – TRY
     AGAIN": GOTO 220
270  GOSUB 1000   ◄——————— Convert to decimal
280  POKE A,D     ◄——————— Put data in memory
290  A = A+1      ◄——————— Next address
300 NEXT E
```

Lines 250 and 260 ensure that your data entries are in valid hexadecimal format. They *do not* ensure that a valid machine language instruction has been used. This is up to you, the programmer.

Example:

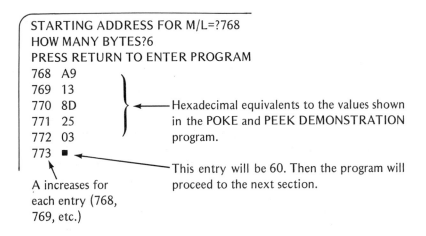

```
STARTING ADDRESS FOR M/L=?768
HOW MANY BYTES?6
PRESS RETURN TO ENTER PROGRAM
768 ■  ←
```
Computer waits for the data entry

After all except the last instruction has been entered.

```
STARTING ADDRESS FOR M/L=?768
HOW MANY BYTES?6
PRESS RETURN TO ENTER PROGRAM
768  A9
769  13
770  8D    ← Hexadecimal equivalents to the values shown
771  25      in the POKE and PEEK DEMONSTRATION
772  03      program.
773  ■  ←
```
This entry will be 60. Then the program will proceed to the next section.

A increases for each entry (768, 769, etc.)

Third

We should now print the program so that you can check it for errors. A subroutine will be written at line 2000 to do this. We'll assume that it has been done for now but come back to it later. We also want to allow provision for making changes in the program in case an error is discovered. Our demonstration program is very short and can be shown in its entirety on the screen by the Section 2 routine. Therefore, this section may seem unnecessary to you. However, your programs will be longer in the future, and some will probably not fit on the screen. The printing subroutine will display your programs 20 lines at a time so that you may see 20-line blocks of your program.

When using this section, look through the entire program and note any changes that you want to make. Changes are made *after* the complete program has been displayed by the subroutine and a RETURN is made to line 420.

```
400 REM *PRINT M/L PROGRAM AND CHECK FOR CHANGES *
410 GOSUB 2000              ◄── Print the program
420 PRINT "IF ANY CHANGES-TYPE ADDRESS"
430 PRINT "IF NOT — TYPE 99"
440 INPUT AD
450 IF AD=99 GOTO 700       ◄── Execute the program
460 PRINT AD;
470 PRINT "DATA=?";         ◄── Get the change
480 GET H$: PRINT H$;
490 GET U$: PRINT U$
500 IF ASC (H$)<48 OR ASC(H$)>70 OR (ASC(H$)>57 AND
    ASC(H$)<65) THEN PRINT "1ST DIGIT NOT HEX — TRY
    AGAIN": GOTO 460
510 IF ASC (U$)<48 OR ASC(U$)>70 OR (ASC(U$)>57 AND
    ASC(U$)<65) THEN PRINT "2ND DIGIT NOT HEX — TRY
    AGAIN": GOTO 460
520 GOSUB 1000
530 POKE AD,D               ◄── Change it
```

If there are some changes, you should type in the address where the change is to be made (line 440). That address is then printed followed by the question DATA=?. You then enter the correct data in hexadecimal format. It is converted to decimal form by the subroutine at line 1000 and entered into memory by line 530.

Example:

No changes to be made after the program is printed.

```
HERE IS YOUR PROGRAM

768   A9
769   13
770   8D
771   25
772   03
773   60
PRESS ANY KEY TO CONTINUE  ◄── We pressed a key here
IF ANY CHANGES—TYPE ADDRESS
IF NOT — TYPE 99
?99   ◄──────────────────  We typed 99 here — no changes. The
                           program would then be executed.
```

If a change is to be made after the program is printed

```
HERE IS YOUR PROGRAM

768  A0        ◄─────────── Error seen here        Oh, Oh!
769  13
770  8D
771  25
772  03
773  60
PRESS ANY KEY TO CONTINUE  ◄── We pressed a key here after
IF ANY CHANGES—TYPE ADDRESS   spotting the error.
IF NOT — TYPE 99
?768        ◄───────────────── We typed the address
768 DATA=?A9   ◄───────────── Then the correct data
```

We must wait for the next section to see what happens now.

Fourth

More than one change may be necessary. So we follow Section 3 with an opportunity for you to make more changes. This section is only executed following a correction to the program.

SECTION 4

```
600 REM * CHECK FOR MORE CHANGES *
610 INPUT "ANY OTHER CHANGES (YES OR NO)?"; C$
620 IF LEFT$(C$,1) = "Y" THEN GOTO 420 ◄── If yes, make changes
630 GOSUB 2000              ◄──────── Then print the program again
640 INPUT "ANY OTHER CHANGES (YES OR NO)?"; C$
650 IF LEFT$(C$,1) = "Y" THEN GOTO 420
```

Line 610 asks if there are any more changes. If the response is NO, the program is printed again to let you examine it one more time. It then returns to give you one last chance for another change at line 640. If your answer is NO again, the program moves on to the execution section.

If your response is YES (or at least begins with Y because of the LEFT$ statement in line 620 and 650), the computer goes back to line 420 for another change. You will stay in this loop until the program has finally changed to your satisfaction.

Let's suppose that you have made two errors in the original entry of your program.

Example:

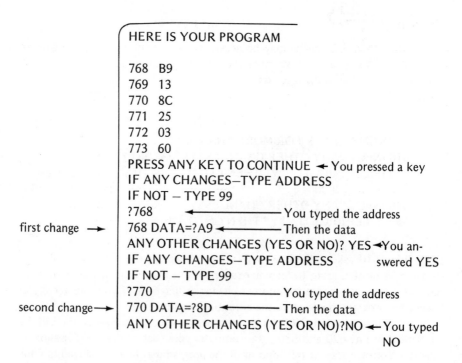

Olde Myth

HERE IS YOUR PROGRAM

768 B9
769 13
770 8C   Do you see the errors?
771 25   New Myth
772 03
773 60
PRESS ANY KEY TO CONTINUE■

To err is human

Computers never err

You spot the errors and want to make changes. Press any key.

HERE IS YOUR PROGRAM

768   B9
769   13
770   8C
771   25
772   03
773   60
PRESS ANY KEY TO CONTINUE ← You pressed a key
IF ANY CHANGES—TYPE ADDRESS
IF NOT — TYPE 99
?768 ←——————————— You typed the address
first change →   768 DATA=?A9 ←——————— Then the data
ANY OTHER CHANGES (YES OR NO)? YES ←You an-
IF ANY CHANGES—TYPE ADDRESS   swered YES
IF NOT — TYPE 99
?770 ←——————————— You typed the address
second change→   770 DATA=?8D ←——————— Then the data
ANY OTHER CHANGES (YES OR NO)?NO ← You typed
                                          NO

The screen then goes blank, and the corrected program is shown.

```
HERE IS YOUR PROGRAM

768   A9
769   13
770   8D
771   25          ←─ It looks ok, so you press a key.
772   03
773   60
PRESS ANY KEY TO CONTINUE          To   this   last   chance,
ANY OTHER CHANGES (YES OR NO)?NO   you type NO
```

The program then goes on to execute the program in the next section.

Fifth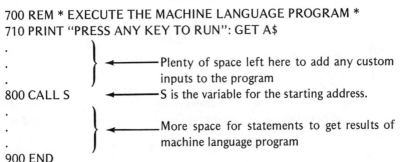

This section executes the machine language program. It stops at line 710 to allow you to gather your courage once more. Will it run correctly or not? You press a key and presto! It's finished, quick as a wink. Boy, that was fast.

SECTION 5

700 REM * EXECUTE THE MACHINE LANGUAGE PROGRAM *
710 PRINT "PRESS ANY KEY TO RUN": GET A$

.
.   ──Plenty of space left here to add any custom
.   inputs to the program
800 CALL S   ──S is the variable for the starting address.
.
.   ──More space for statements to get results of
.   machine language program
900 END

The machine language program is called at line 800. Notice the space left between line 710 and 800. You can enter additional BASIC statements here to provide special inputs to your machine language programs if you desire, i.e., POKE address, DATA. The space between lines 800 and 900 allows BASIC statements to read results from your machine language programs, i.e., PEEK (address).

For example, our demonstration program supposedly loaded the hexadecimal value of 13 and put it into memory location 0325 (also a hexadecimal value). If the program worked correctly, the decimal value 19 (HEX 13) should have been placed into the memory location whose address is 0325 (lines 771 and 772 of the machine language program). This value in decimal form would be 805 ($3 \times 16^2 + 2 \times 16 + 5$). We can find out if it really did this by typing:

PRINT PEEK(805)

after the machine language program has been executed.

37

Example:

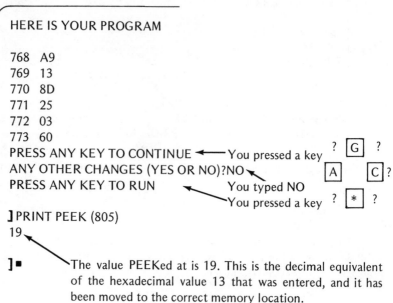

HERE IS YOUR PROGRAM

768   A9
769   13
770   8D
771   25
772   03
773   60
PRESS ANY KEY TO CONTINUE ◄——You pressed a key   ? [G] ?
ANY OTHER CHANGES (YES OR NO)?NO◄
PRESS ANY KEY TO RUN   ◄——   You typed NO   [A]   [C] ?
                                 ◄——You pressed a key   ? [*] ?

] PRINT PEEK (805)
19◄

] ■   The value PEEKed at is 19. This is the decimal equivalent
of the hexadecimal value 13 that was entered, and it has
been moved to the correct memory location.

Sixth

Last of all come the subroutines of the Operating System. The first one converts the hexadecimal data to decimal values for the BASIC interpreter.

SECTION 6A

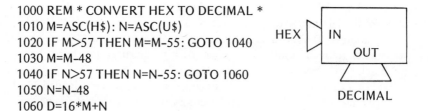

1000 REM * CONVERT HEX TO DECIMAL *
1010 M=ASC(H$): N=ASC(U$)
1020 IF M>57 THEN M=M−55: GOTO 1040
1030 M=M−48
1040 IF N>57 THEN N=N−55: GOTO 1060
1050 N=N−48
1060 D=16*M+N
1070 RETURN

HEX ▷ IN
        OUT
DECIMAL

Line 1020 checks the ASCII code for the first hexadecimal digit. It will be one of the values shown in the following table under the heading ASCII. Lines 1020 and 1030 convert the HEX value to its equivalent decimal value.

Examples:

1. A hexadecimal value of 8 has an ASCII code of 56. Therefore, M is not >57, so line 1030 is executed. The new M $= 56 - 48 = 8$ (the decimal equivalent of 8).

2. A hex value of B has an ASCII code of 66. Therefore, M>57 in line 1020. The New M $= 66 - 55 = 11$ (the decimal equivalent of B).

The same procedure is followed for the second digit at lines 1040 and 1050. Here is a table of conversions between hexadecimal, ASCII, and decimal values.

CONVERSION TABLE

Hexadecimal digit	ASCII code	Converted decimal value
0	48	0
1	49	1
2	50	2
3	51	3
4	52	4
5	53	5
6	54	6
7	55	7
8	56	8
9	57	9
A	65	10
B	66	11
C	67	12
D	68	13
E	69	14
F	70	15

A two-digit hexadecimal number has the following place values:

first digit   M   N   second digit
tells how   tells how
many 16's   many 1's

In hexadecimal form, M and N may be any HEX digit 0 through F. Lines 1020 through 1050 convert these hexadecimal digits (0 through F) to their decimal equivalents (0 through 15).

M is now the decimal number of 16's (0 through 15)
N is now the decimal number of 1's (0 through 15)

The decimal equivalents are then combined into a decimal number by multiplying 16 times the decimal equivalent of M and adding the decimal equivalent of N. Line 1060 performs this final operation.

Example:

Original hexadecimal number = C7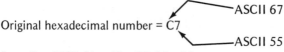

ASCII 67

ASCII 55

from line 1020 New M = 67–55 = 12
from line 1050 New N = 55–48 = 7
from line 1060 D = 16x12 + 7 = 199 (the decimal equivalent of C7 hexadecimal)

The print subroutine displays up to 20 lines of your machine langauge program at one time. The computer waits for you to examine these lines and press a key before displaying the next 20 lines of the program. This subroutine may be entered from the third or fourth section of the program depending on whether changes have been made. It returns to the same section from which the entry was made.

Line 2030 initializes counters J to 0 and I to 19 so that 20 addresses and data values will be displayed on the screen by the FOR-NEXT loop at lines 2200 through 2220.

SECTION 6B

```
2000 REM * SUBROUTINE TO DISPLAY PROGRAM *
2010 HOME: PRINT "HERE IS YOUR PROGRAM"
2020 PRINT
2030 J=0: I=19
2040 ON INT((B-1)/20)+1 GOTO 2090, 2080, 2070, 2060, 2050
2050 GOSUB 2200
2060 GOSUB 2200
2070 GOSUB 2200
2080 GOSUB 2200
2090 I=B-1:GOSUB 2200
2100 RETURN

2200 HOME
2210 FOR E = J TO I
2220   PRINT S+E; SPC(2);: GOSUB 3000
2230 NEXT E
2240 PRINT "PRESS ANY KEY TO CONTINUE": GET A$
2250 J=I+1: I=I+20
2260 RETURN
```

Line 2040 uses the number of program bytes to calculate how many blocks of 20 lines must be displayed. It uses the ON-GOTO statement to select the number of times the block print subroutine will be used (at line 2200). Line 2090 displays the last block of program lines. This block may not be 20 lines long. Therefore, the upper limit of the FOR-NEXT loop is changed to reflect the number of program lines left to be displayed. The screen is cleared at line 2200 each time a new block of lines is to be printed. The program halts at line 2240 so that you can closely examine the lines for errors. When you press any key, the next block of lines is displayed.

Last is the subroutine that converts the data from the decimal values selected by the PEEK (at line 3010) to the hexadecimal values used for data.

SECTION 6C

```
3000 REM * CHANGE TO ASCII AND DISPLAY *
3010 Y = PEEK(S+E)
3020 H = INT(Y/16)
3030 U = Y-16*H
3040 IF H<10 THEN PRINT H;: GOTO 3060
3050 PRINT CHR$(H+55);
3060 IF U<10 THEN PRINT U: GOTO 3080
3070 PRINT CHR$(U+55)
3080 RETURN
```

Line 3010 PEEKs at the content of the address being displayed. Lines 3020 and 3030 separate the decimal value into the number of 16's (H) and the number of 1's (U). Lines 3040 through 3070 convert H and U to their ASCII equivalents for display.

Since we will be using this Operating System quite often in future chapters, it would be to your advantage to enter it in the computer and then save it on cassette or diskette. Then it can be loaded quickly when needed.

Basically the Operating System allows you to:
1. Enter a machine language program

2. Alter any of your entries

3. Run the machine language program

Instruction in the use of the Operating System will be given as needed in the following chapters.

THE COMPLETED BASIC OPERATING SYSTEM

Here is the completed BASIC Operating System. You should enter it into your Apple. When you have tried it out to make sure it works correctly, save it on cassette tape or disk. It will be too tedious to type it in every time you want to use it.

41

```
100 REM * GET MACHINE LANGUAGE INFORMATION *
110 HOME
120 INPUT "STARTING ADDRESS FOR M/L=?"; S
130 INPUT "HOW MANY BYTES?"; B
140 INPUT "PRESS RETURN TO ENTER PROGRAM"; A$
150 A = S


200 REM * ENTER PROGRAM IN HEX — CONVERT TO DECIMAL *
210 FOR E = 1 TO B
220   PRINT A; SPC(2);
230   GET H$: PRINT H$;
240   GET U$: PRINT U$
250   IF ASC(H$)<48 OR ASC(H$)>70 OR (ASC(H$)>57 AND
      ASC(H$)<65) THEN PRINT "1ST DIGIT NOT HEX — TRY
      AGAIN": GOTO 220
260   IF ASC(U$)<48 OR ASC(U$)>70 OR (ASC(U$)>57 AND
      ASC(U$)<65) THEN PRINT "2ND DIGIT NOT HEX — TRY
      AGAIN": GOTO 220
270   GOSUB 1000
280   POKE A,D
290   A = A+1
300 NEXT E


400 REM * PRINT M/L PROGRAM AND CHECK FOR CHANGES *
410 GOSUB 2000
420 PRINT "IF ANY CHANGES—TYPE ADDRESS"
430 PRINT "IF NOT — TYPE 99"
440 INPUT AD
450 IF AD=99 GOTO 700
460 PRINT AD;
470 PRINT "DATA=?";
480 GET H$: PRINT H$;
490 GET U$: PRINT U$
500 IF ASC(H$)<48 OR ASC(H$)>70 OR (ASC(H$)>57 AND
    ASC(H$)<65) THEN PRINT "1ST DIGIT NOT HEX — TRY
    AGAIN": GOTO 460
510 IF ASC(U$)<48 OR ASC(U$)>70 OR (ASC(U$)>57 AND
    ASC(U$)<65) THEN PRINT 2ND DIGIT NOT HEX — TRY
    AGAIN": GOTO 460
520 GOSUB 1000
530 POKE AD,D
```

```
600 REM * CHECK FOR MORE CHANGES *
610 INPUT "ANY OTHER CHANGES (YES OR NO)?"; C$
620 IF LEFT$(C$,1) = "Y" THEN GOTO 420
630 GOSUB 2000
640 INPUT "ANY OTHER CHANGES (YES OR NO)?"; C$
650 IF LEFT$(C$,1) = "Y" THEN GOTO 420

700 REM * EXECUTE THE MACHINE LANGUAGE PROGRAM *
710 PRINT "PRESS ANY KEY TO RUN": GET A$
.
.
.
800 CALL S
.
.
.
900 END

1000 REM *CONVERT HEX TO DECIMAL *
1010 M=ASC(H$): N=ASC(U$)
1020 IF M>57 THEN M=M-55: GOTO 1040
1030 M=M-48
1040 IF N>57 THEN N=N-55: GOTO 1060
1050 N=N-48
1060 D=16*M+N
1070 RETURN

2000 REM * SUBROUTINE TO DISPLAY PROGRAM *
2010 HOME: PRINT "HERE IS YOUR PROGRAM"
2020 PRINT
2030 J=0: I=19
2040 ON INT((B-1)/20)+1 GOTO 2090,2080,2070,2060,2050
2050 GOSUB 2200
2060 GOSUB 2200
2070 GOSUB 2200
2080 GOSUB 2200
2090 I=B-1: GOSUB 2200
2100 RETURN

2200 HOME
2210 FOR E = J TO I
2220   PRINT S+E; SPC(2);: GOSUB 3000
2230 NEXT E
2240 PRINT "PRESS ANY KEY TO CONTINUE": GET A$
2250 J=I+1: I=I+20
2260 RETURN
```

```
3000 REM * CHANGE TO ASCII AND DISPLAY *
3010 Y = PEEK(S+E)
3020 H = INT(Y/16)
3030 U = Y-16*H
3040 IF H<10 THEN PRINT H;: GOTO 3060
3050 PRINT CHR$(H+55);
3060 IF U<10 THEN PRINT U: GOTO 3080
3070 PRINT CHR$(U+55)
3080 RETURN
```

EXERCISES

1. The BASIC language uses _____ numbers.
      (HEX, binary, decimal)

2. When you use the statement:
      POKE   address, data
   both address and data must be _____ numbers.
                  (HEX, binary, decimal)

3. If you executed the following four statements in the Immediate Mode, fill in
   what would be printed on the line following the PRINT PEEK statement.
      POKE 768,169
      POKE 769,19
      POKE 770,141
      PRINT PEEK(769)

   _____

4. Explain the function of the CALL statement. _____
   _____
   _____

5. When using the BASIC Operating System, the addresses for the machine
   language program being entered will be printed on the screen using
   _____ numbers.
         (decimal, HEX, binary)

6. The data and instructions which you enter (by the BASIC Operating System) for the machine language program must be entered using _____
   _____ numbers.
         (decimal, HEX, binary)

ANSWERS TO EXERCISES

1. Decimal

2. Decimal

3. 19

4. The CALL statement causes a machine language subroutine to be executed. The beginning address of the subroutine must be given. (Example: CALL 768 would call a machine language subroutine beginning at the memory location whose address is 768.)

5. Decimal

6. HEX

Chapter 3

Instruction Code Format

The Central Processing Unit (CPU) of the Apple computer was originally manufactured by MOS Technology, Inc. At the present time, two other companies (Synertek and Rockwell) also manufacture the CPU. This unit is named the 6502 microprocessor. It is called a central processing unit because all instructions and numerical values are routed there for processing.

The 6502 microprocessor (and hence, the Apple computer), like many other microprocessors, understands only instructions that are coded in blocks of eight binary digits, called bytes. Therefore, the biggest hurdle to machine language programming is to learn to work with information in binary form.

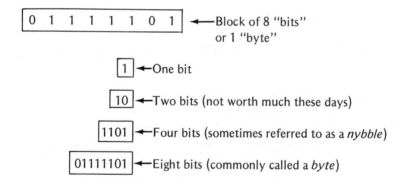

The Apple uses words that are eight bits in length; that is, it can digest words whose size is one byte. All instructions and numerical values must be sent to its *central processing unit* in this byte size. A typical instruction, shown below, loads the computer's *accumulator* with the one byte of data following the instruction in a machine language program.

LOAD ACCUMULATOR IMMEDIATE	
MNEMONIC CODE (abbreviation)	BINARY CODE
LDA	10101001

Don't let the computer terminology throw you. The accumulator is similar to a memory location that is used in special ways we will discuss later on. We are just introducing it here to show the format of an instruction.

The computer is composed of many functional parts that we will introduce as needed to explain the operations taking place. The central processing unit of the Apple is a 6502 microprocessor. The following block diagram shows the "parts" we are presently concerned with.

6502 MICROPROCESSOR
Instruction decoder
Accumulator
Other controls and registers

MEMORY

The instruction decoder of the 6502 "reads" the instruction and decodes it. Most instructions involve the accumulator (discussed later in this chapter) as a center for moving and manipulating data. Memory is separate from the 6502 microprocessor.

NUMBER SYSTEMS

You can see that entering many binary-coded instructions would be tedious. Since there are only two symbols (0 and 1), the binary representation of numbers is quite long. Most computers, including the Apple, have the ability to accept a shorthand representation of binary. This shorthand is the hexadecimal number system (which we will often refer to as HEX). Four binary digits may be represented by one HEX digit. Thus, our 8-bit instruction may be represented by a 2-digit HEX number by breaking the byte (8 bits) into two parts (nybbles).

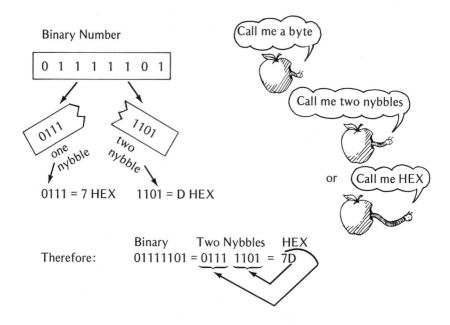

Binary Number

0 1 1 1 1 1 0 1

0111
one nybble

1101
two nybble

0111 = 7 HEX   1101 = D HEX

Call me a byte

Call me two nybbles

or   Call me HEX

Therefore:

Binary	Two Nybbles	HEX
01111101 =	0111 1101	= 7D

The hexadecimal number system has 16 symbols (0,1,2,3,4,5,6,7,8,9,A,B, C,D,E,F). The relationship of decimal, binary, and HEX values is shown in the following table.

Decimal	Binary	HEX
0	0000	0
1	0001	1
2	0010	2
3	0011	3
4	0100	4
5	0101	5
6	0110	6
7	0111	7
8	1000	8
9	1001	9
10	1010	A
11	1011	B
12	1100	C
13	1101	D
14	1110	E
15	1111	F

○
 ○ ○
 ○ ○ ○ ◁⊐CALL me 15, CALL me 1111, or CALL me F — they all
 ○ ○ ○ ○   represent the same thing.
○ ○ ○ ○ ○

To give the table meaning, let's take a look at the binary system. Each place value in the binary system is a power of two, just as each place value in the decimal system is a power of ten. Two is called the *base* of the binary system, and ten is called the base of the decimal system. If we look at the place values of the binary numbers 0000 through 1111, we can attach more meaning to them.

Binary Places				Decimal Equivalent
2^3	2^2	2^1	2^0	
0	0	0	1	0+0+0+1 = 1
0	0	1	0	0+0+2+0 = 2
0	1	0	0	0+4+0+0 = 4
1	0	0	0	8+0+0+0 = 8

Using combinations of these place values, we may obtain any decimal value from 0 through 16 or any HEX value from 0 through F.

Examples:

$0101 = 2^2 + 2^0 = 4 + 1 = 5$ decimal and also 5 HEX
$1010 = 2^3 + 2^1 = 8 + 2 = 10$ decimal which is A HEX
$1100 = 2^3 + 2^2 = 8 + 4 = 12$ decimal which is C HEX
$1101 = 2^3 + 2^2 + 2^0 = 8 + 4 + 1 = 13$ decimal which is D HEX

Let's now take a closer look at how we may express any 8-bit binary number by two HEX digits. We saw earlier that the highest HEX digit (F) corresponds to the four-bit binary value 1111. The next higher binary value is 10000. The one is in the 2^4 place, which equals 16. Therefore, we have one 16 and nothing else. This can be expressed by the HEX value 10, which means one 16 and no 1's. There is a direct relationship between the upper 4 bits of an eight-bit binary number and the sixteen's place digit of a HEX number.

Binary Places				HEX value 16^1
2^7	2^6	2^5	2^4	
0	0	0	1	1
0	0	1	0	2
0	1	0	0	4
1	0	0	0	8

$2^4 = 16$
$2^5 = 2*16 = 32$
$2^6 = 4*16 = 64$
$2^7 = 8*16 = 128$

Next look at the binary place values of the complete 8-bit number.

Binary Places								Decimal Equivalent	HEX Equivalent
2^7	2^6	2^5	2^4	2^3	2^2	2^1	2^0		
0	0	0	0	0	0	0	1	0+0+0+0+0+0+0+1 = 1	1
0	0	0	0	0	0	1	0	0+0+0+0+0+0+2+0 = 2	2
0	0	0	0	0	1	0	0	0+0+0+0+0+4+0+0 = 4	4
0	0	0	0	1	0	0	0	0+0+0+0+8+0+0+0 = 8	8
0	0	0	1	0	0	0	0	0+0+0+16+0+0+0+0 = 16	10
0	0	1	0	0	0	0	0	0+0+32+0+0+0+0+0 = 32	20
0	1	0	0	0	0	0	0	0+64+0+0+0+0+0+0 = 64	40
1	0	0	0	0	0	0	0	128+0+0+0+0+0+0+0 = 128	80

Using combinations of all eight bits, you may obtain any decimal value from 0 through 255, or any HEX value from 0 through FF. If we break an 8-bit binary number into two 4-bit parts, each part may be represented by one HEX digit.

Examples:

Broken (split) into two parts

	BINARY	01111101	64+32+16+8+4+1 = 125 in decimal
	SPLIT-BINARY	0111 1101	
	HEX	7 D	7*16+13 = 125 in decimal
	BINARY	11000011	128+64+2+1 = 195 in decimal
	SPLIT-BINARY	1100 0011	
	HEX	C 3	12*16+3 = 195 in decimal
	BINARY	10101010	128+32+8+2 = 170 in decimal
	SPLIT-BINARY	1010 1010	
	HEX	A A	10*16+10 = 170 in decimal

Instruction manuals for machine language quite often list the instruction codes in both binary and HEX forms. Our BASIC (to machine language) Operating System will use HEX format for entering the instructions of machine language programs. Since BASIC doesn't understand HEX numbers, the operating system will convert them to decimal numbers for BASIC and to binary numbers for the computer. Even though the BASIC Operating System was discussed in Chap. 2, we believe the data-entry section should be repeated here.

Instructions are input in lines 200-300 of the BASIC (to machine language) Operating System as hexadecimal numbers.

SECTION 2

```
200 REM * ENTER PROGRAM IN HEX — CONVERT TO DECIMAL *
210 FOR E = 1 TO B
220  PRINT A; SPC(2);          ◄——————Address is printed
230  GET H$: PRINT H$; |  ◄——HEX data follows
240  GET U$: PRINT U$  |
250  IF ASC(H$)<48 OR ASC(H$)>70 OR (ASC(H$)>57 AND
     ASC(H$)<65) THEN PRINT "1ST DIGIT NOT HEX — TRY
     AGAIN": GOTO 220
260  IF ASC(U$)<48 OR ASC(U$)>70 OR (ASC(U$)>57 AND
     ASC(U$)<65) THEN PRINT "2ND DIGIT NOT HEX — TRY
     AGAIN": GOTO 220
270  GOSUB 1000       ◄——————Convert to decimal
280  POKE A,D         ◄——————Put data in memory
290  A = A+1          ◄——————Next address
300 NEXT E
```

The HEX-to-decimal conversion takes place in the subroutine at lines 1000-1070 of the operating system program. The BASIC interpreter then changes the decimal numbers to binary equivalents for the computer.

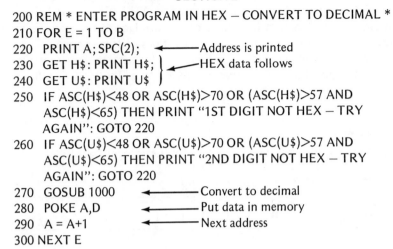

```
                    1000 REM *CONVERT HEX TO DECIMAL*
ASCII codes ——►  1010 M=ASC(H$): N=ASC(U$)
in decimal      /1020 IF M>57 THEN M=M-55: GOTO 1040|
(M,N)           |1030 M=M-48
Conversion ——► <1040 IF N>57 THEN N=N-55: GOTO 1060|
                |1050 N=N-48
                \1060 D=16*M+N
                    1070 RETURN
```

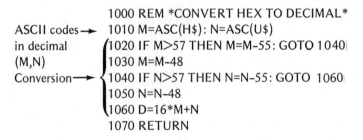

HEX   TO   DECIMAL

BLOCK DIAGRAM OF INPUTS

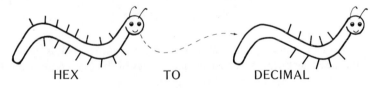

| HEX | ► | HEX TO DECIMAL | ► | DECIMAL TO BINARY | ► | USES THE BINARY |

Keyboard   Operating   BASIC   Computer
Input   System   Interpreter

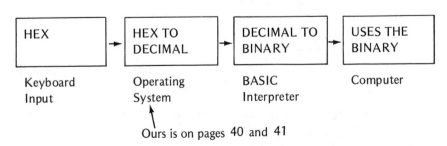

Ours is on pages 40 and 41

The computer handles data in 8-bit blocks called *bytes*. Therefore, one byte of data is limited to the binary value 11111111 (FF hex or 255 decimal). However, by combining two bytes of data, much larger values may be handled. The computer uses this method to access locations in its memory.

When a two-byte number is used, one byte is referred to as the Least Significant Byte (LSB). The other is referred to as the Most Significant Byte (MSB).

Example:

MSB (Most Significant Byte)

2^7	2^6	2^5	2^4	2^3	2^2	2^1	2^0
1	0	0	0	1	0	0	1

LSB (Least Significant Byte)

2^7	2^6	2^5	2^4	2^3	2^2	2^1	2^0
0	1	0	0	0	1	1	1

Don't confuse the Most and Least Significant Bytes with the most and least significant bits. Each byte has an msb (most significant bit) and an lsb (least significant bit)

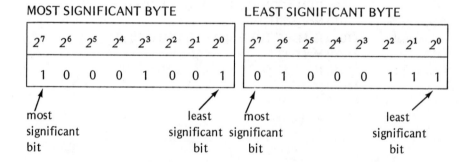

MOST SIGNIFICANT BYTE

2^7	2^6	2^5	2^4	2^3	2^2	2^1	2^0
1	0	0	0	1	0	0	1

most
significant
bit

least
significant
bit

LEAST SIGNIFICANT BYTE

2^7	2^6	2^5	2^4	2^3	2^2	2^1	2^0
0	1	0	0	0	1	1	1

most
significant
bit

least
significant
bit

To use a two-byte number, you consider the Most Significant Byte as an extension of the Least Significant Byte. The place values of the Least Significant Byte were assigned powers of two from 0 through 7.

LSB

2^7	2^6	2^5	2^4	2^3	2^2	2^1	2^0
0	1	0	0	0	1	1	0

= 64 + 4 + 2 = 70 (decimal)

The place values of the Most Significant Byte are assigned the next higher powers of two (8 through 15).

MSB

2^{15}	2^{14}	2^{13}	2^{12}	2^{11}	2^{10}	2^9	2^8
1	0	0	0	1	0	0	1

= 32768 + 2048 + 256 = 35072
(decimal)

The decimal value resulting from the combined bytes (considered as one number) is:

2^{15}	2^{14}	2^{13}	2^{12}	2^{11}	2^{10}	2^9	2^8	2^7	2^6	2^5	2^4	2^3	2^2	2^1	2^0
1	0	0	0	1	0	0	1	0	1	0	0	0	1	1	0

In decimal: 32768 + 2048 + 256 + 64 + 4 + 2 = 35142

Split into 4-bit parts:

```
            1000   1001   0100   0111  ◄──── This binary value
                                             is equivalent to
HEX digits    8      9      4      7   ◄──── this HEX value
```

HEX
format:

MSB	LSB		16^3	16^2	16^1	16^0
89	46	=	8	9	4	6

➞ 8*4096 = 32768
+ 9*256 = 2304
+ 4* 16 =   64
+ 6*1   =   6
               ────
               35142
            (decimal)

ACCUMULATOR

The accumulator is a register (a storage place similar to a memory location) in which data is placed. It is used as a temporary storage area when moving data from one memory location to another. Arithmetic and logical operations on data also take place in the accumulator. Thus it is frequently used, and many of the 6502 instructions involve it. Remember, the Apple computer uses the 6502 central processing unit. The instructions are fixed in the 6502; that is, each instruction has a unique, unchanging machine language code.

The accumulator also holds one byte of data.

1	0	0	1	1	1	0	0
2^7	2^6	2^5	2^4	2^3	2^2	2^1	2^0

The necessity for two-byte values becomes apparent when an instruction is used to acquire data from a memory location. If you want to load data into the accumulator from memory, the following instruction could be used.

One instruction for putting a number into the accumulator was shown previously. It loads the accumulator with a number which immediately follows the instruction.

Example:

Binary Value	HEX Value	
	HEX	◄——This is the value typed in
10101001	A9	◄——Load the accumulator
00001101	13	◄——with HEX value 13

The two bytes (each occupying a separate memory location) provide:

First: the instruction, Load the accumulator (A9)
Second: with the HEX value 13

The next instruction introduced shows a second way to put a number into the accumulator. It obtains the number to be loaded from a specified memory location. Even though the mnemonic code for this instruction is LDA (the same as the one referred to at the beginning of the chapter), the HEX value representing this instruction is different.

When you are loading the accumulator from a specified memory location, the LDA instruction has a HEX code of AD. Even though this means nothing to you, it is a specific instruction to your Apple. The memory location is specified following the instruction. Notice that the *two* bytes necessary for specifying the address of the memory are given in *reverse* order. This may seem ridiculous to you. But to the computer, it is entirely logical. The Least Significant Byte is stored in the lower address of memory, and the Most Significant Byte is stored in the higher memory address.

Memory Address	HEX Value	Mnemonic Code	Operand	Remarks
768	AD	LDA	0325	Load the accumulator from
769	25			memory location 0325
770	03			(HEX)

Instruction · Reversed order for address

54

This is an example of a three-byte instruction.

1. The instruction is given in the first byte.
2. The LSB of the memory appears as the next byte.
3. The MSB of the memory appears as the last byte.

When the computer executes this instruction, the data in memory location 0325 is copied into the accumulator. This one change occurs:

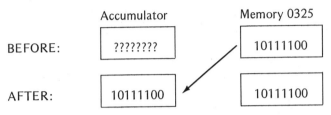

The value in the memory location remains unchanged and is copied into the accumulator. Operations can be performed on the value in the accumulator. The results can then be transferred to another location if desired. The important thing to remember is that most of the computer's action takes place in the accumulator. Therefore, many of the 6502 instructions involve this useful register.

Data from the accumulator can be copied into some memory location with a *store* instruction such as:

	HEX Value	Mnemonic Code	Operand	Remarks
Instruction → Memory Location {	8D 26 03	STA	0326	Store the value contained in the accumulator into memory location 0326 HEX

This is another three-byte instruction. In general, most instructions that refer to a memory location require three bytes. Exceptions will be noted later.

When the computer executes this instruction, the data in the accumulator is copied into the specified memory location. This change occurs:

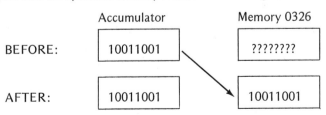

The value in the accumulator stays the same, but that value is copied (or written) into memory location 0326 as well. You can see that with instructions like LDA and STA, the accumulator is going to be a busy place.

It will also be important for you to keep track of what memory locations are being used for different operations. Remember, we are using memory locations 0300 HEX upward (see memory map in Chap. 2). Whenever data is stored in a memory location, the data that was previously there is lost.

Example:

Suppose that the following values are in the memory locations shown.

Memory	Content
0325	19
0326	24
0327	00

This machine language program is then executed.

These machine language instructions work in a similar way to the two consecutive BASIC instructions:

200 LET A=19
210 LET A=24

768	AD	Load accumulator from
769	25	memory location 0325
770	03	

19 now in accumulator

771	8D	Store accumulator in
772	27	memory location 0327
773	03	

Memory locations now
0325   19
0326   24
0327   19 ◄—This has been changed

774	AD	Load accumulator from
775	26	memory location 0326.
776	03	

24 now in accumulator

777	8D	Store accumulator in
778	27	memory location 0327
779	03	

Memory locations now
0325   19
0326   24
0327   24   19 is now gone

Program in these memory locations

Data and instructions

56

INSTRUCTIONS IN MEMORY

Programs must be put into memory before they can be run. Even your BASIC programs occupy memory space. Your BASIC interpreter takes care of BASIC program memory assignments for you, and you are unaware of the exact locations of BASIC instructions. However, you must assign memory locations to your machine language programs. Each instruction byte and each data byte must be assigned specific locations. Each byte occupies one memory location.

Example:

Memory Location	Data or Instruction Byte	Remarks
0300	AD	Load accumulator
0301	25	from memory location
0302	03	0325
.	.	.
.	.	.
.	.	.
0325	2B	Data to be loaded

*{

Some instructions have many forms. This load instruction differs from that used in "Memory Use" in Chap. 2 in that a value is loaded from a memory location rather than from the byte following the instruction.

We will use memory locations 0300 through 03FF (HEX) for our machine language programs. This area of memory is not used by the Apple Operating System nor by the BASIC interpreter. Therefore, it is safe for our use.

We'll use our BASIC Machine Language Operating System to POKE machine language instructions and data into this area of memory.

USE OF THE BASIC-M/L OPERATING SYSTEM

To demonstrate the use of the Operating System, we must first decide on the machine language program that we want to run. Your first effort will be a very short program that places some data into the accumulator and then moves it from there to a memory location.

This program accomplishes the same thing as the BASIC instruction:

LET A = 19 ◄─────────── This stores 19 in location named A

---

*Notice again that the memory location 0325 is entered in the program LSB first, then MSB. This may seem backwards to you, but it is quite normal for the computer. The Most Significant Byte (MSB) is now stored in a higher memory location than the Least Significant Byte (LSB).

The LET statement merely stores the value 19 into a memory location assigned by the BASIC interpreter.

The machine language equivalent takes two instructions:

LDA (load accumulator with data)
STA (store accumulator's contents in memory)

1. We first *load* the accumulator with the data.
   The 6502 instruction for loading the accumulator with data that immediately follows is made up of two bytes.

   A9 ◄———— First byte
   XX ◄———— Second byte

   A9 is the machine language code telling the computer to load the data which follows into the accumulator.

   XX is a two-digit HEX value that is to be loaded.

The mnemonic code for the instruction and the Operand are usually added to give some meaning to the coded instruction. The actual instruction is called the Operation Code (Op Code for short).

Example:

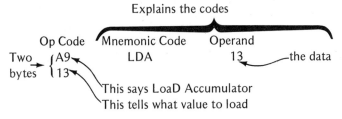

The mnemonic code is just the abbreviation for the instruction. The operand is the data or other item used. The operation code is the HEX code for the instruction to be performed or the data to be used. In this case it is the instruction, Load Accumulator with immediate data.

A list of machine language instructions used in this book is given in Appendix A-2. A complete list of 6502 instructions is given in Appendix D.

The instruction actually consists of two bytes:

A9   (the instruction)
XX   (the HEX data to be loaded)

In our demonstration, we will load the value 19 (HEX=13). Therefore, the two-byte instruction will be:

A9
13

In the different number systems that we have discussed:

Binary	Split-binary	HEX
10101001	1010 1001	A9
00010011	0001 0011	13

These values are entered using the BASIC Operating System.

2. We will then *store* the data in the memory location whose address is 0325 (HEX).

The 6502 instruction necessary to do this is:

STORE ACCUMULATOR ABSOLUTE

OPERATION CODE	MNEMONIC	OPERAND
↓	↓	↓
8D	STA	memory

This instruction takes three bytes:

8D	(The instruction)
25	(The least significant memory byte)
03	(The most significant memory byte)

| 8D |
| 25 | } The instruction is placed in three successive memory locations |
| 03 |

3. We will then return from the machine language program to the operating system.

The 6502 instruction used is:

RETURN FROM SUBROUTINE

OPERATION CODE	MNEMONIC	OPERAND
↓	↓	↓
60	RTS	none

This is a one-byte instruction.

60   (The instruction)

It performs the same function as the BASIC instruction:

RETURN

We noted on the Apple memory maps (Chap. 2) that memory locations 768-1023 (decimal) would be used for machine language programs. That part of the map is shown here for reference.

Decimal Address	HEX Equivalent
768	0300
769	0301
770	0302
771	0303
772	0304
.	.
.	.
.	.
1022	03FE
1023	03FF

Our first program will begin at memory location 0300 HEX. We must tell our Operating System this location as a decimal value. The addresses are POKEd into the computer using decimal numbers that BASIC understands. But the instructions and data must be POKEd in as HEX numbers, which the computer will use in their binary form.

16^3	16^2	16^1	16^0
0	3	0	0

$= 3 \times 16^2 = 3 \times 256 = 768$ decimal

This is the address where the first instruction of the program will be entered. We will also have to supply the Operating System with the operation codes for each address.

Address	OP Code	Remarks
768	A9	LDA with
769	13	data
770	8D	STA
771	25	Memory (LSB)
772	03	Memory (MSB)
773	60	RTS

Notice: The program has 6 bytes (we will have to tell the Operating System this fact).

Here is a step-by-step description of how to use the Operating System to enter and run the above program.

1. Enter the Operating System (see Chap. 2). This can be done from the keyboard, or from cassette or disk if you have previously saved the program.

2. Type: RUN (and press RETURN)

> STARTING ADDRESS FOR M/L=?■

3. Type: 768 (and press RETURN)

> STARTING ADDRESS FOR M/L=?768
> HOW MANY BYTES?■

4. Type: 6 (and press RETURN)

> STARTING ADDRESS FOR M/L=?768
> HOW MANY BYTES?6
> PRESS RETURN TO ENTER PROGRAM■

5. Press the RETURN key

> STARTING ADDRESS FOR M/L=?768
> HOW MANY BYTES?6
> PRESS RETURN TO ENTER PROGRAM
> 768 ■   Computer supplies
>   first address

Now you type in the program. You do not have to press the RETURN key after each entry. The computer will automatically print the next address following your *two-digit* entry. If you make a mistake, go right on to the next entry. You will be able to correct any errors when the program has been entered completely.

6. Type: A

> STARTING ADDRESS FOR M/L=?768
> HOW MANY BYTES?6
> PRESS RETURN TO ENTER PROGRAM
> 768 A■   1st digit of
>   1st address

7. Type: 9

STARTING ADDRESS FOR M/L=?768
HOW MANY BYTES?6
PRESS RETURN TO ENTER PROGRAM
768　A9　◄─────────── 1st entry complete
769　■ ╱ Computer prints next
address

Since you don't have to press RETURN after each keystroke, we will include both keystrokes for each address in each step from now on.

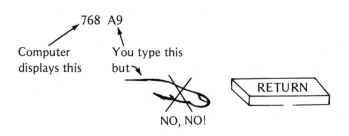

768　A9

Computer　　　You type this
displays this　　but

RETURN

NO, NO!

The GET instruction does not require you to press RETURN. If you do press RETURN, the GET instruction interprets it as one of your characters, and the Operating System will display:

768
1ST DIGIT NOT HEX – TRY AGAIN
768　■

Getting back to the program,

8. Type: 13

STARTING ADDRESS FOR M/L=?768
HOW MANY BYTES?6
PRESS RETURN TO ENTER PROGRAM
768　A9
769　13
770　■

9. Type: 8D

```
STARTING ADDRESS FOR M/L=?768
HOW MANY BYTES?6
PRESS RETURN TO ENTER PROGRAM
768  A9
769  13
770  8D
771  ■
```

10. Type: 25

```
STARTING ADDRESS FOR M/L=?768
HOW MANY BYTES?6
PRESS RETURN TO ENTER PROGRAM
768  A9
769  13
770  8D
771  25
772  ■
```

11. Type: 03

```
STARTING ADDRESS FOR M/L=?768
HOW MANY BYTES?6
PRESS RETURN TO ENTER PROGRAM
768  A9
769  13
770  8D
771  25
772  03
773  ■
```

12. Type: 60

```
HERE IS YOUR PROGRAM

768  A9
769  13
770  8D
771  25
772  03
773  60
IF ANY CHANGES—TYPE ADDRESS
IF NOT — TYPE 99
?■
```

Before going on, let's compare this machine language program with its equivalent in BASIC. These six machine language instructions perform a function very similar to two BASIC instructions:

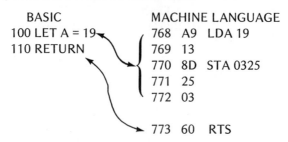

BASIC	MACHINE LANGUAGE
100 LET A = 19	768 A9 LDA 19
110 RETURN	769 13
	770 8D STA 0325
	771 25
	772 03
	773 60 RTS

The machine language program loaded the accumulator with the HEX number 13 (19 decimal). It then stored it in a memory location. The BASIC statement LET A = 19 does the same thing. It stores the value named by the letter A into memory. The machine language instruction RTS (ReTurn from Subroutine) performs the same function as the RETURN instruction in BASIC.

Study the program to make sure all entries are correct. If you made an error in your entries, you would type in the address where the error was made. The computer would then display:

```
IF ANY CHANGES—TYPE ADDRESS
IF NOT — TYPE 99                    Suppose:
?771 DATA=?■    ◄─────────────── Error seen at
                                   address 771
```

You would then type in the correct data (two digits).

```
IF ANY CHANGES—TYPE ADDRESS
IF NOT — TYPE 99
?771 DATA=?25           ◄──── Correct data entered
ANY OTHER CHANGES (YES OR NO)?
```

You would then type YES or NO. If you type YES, the computer would again ask for the address and data. The process is repeated until you give a negative reply (NO more changes). The computer then prints the corrected program and asks if there are any more changes. On the last negative reply to changes, the computer displays:

```
PRESS ANY KEY TO RUN■
```

You press any key, and the machine language program is run. You will immediately see the prompt and blinking cursor. My, that machine language is fast!

PRESS ANY KEY TO RUN
]■

Did our machine language program really run? How can we find out?

BASIC has an instruction named PEEK which will let you see what is in a specified memory location. If you tell it:

PRINT PEEK (805)

325 HEX (the location where the program stored the value, 19

it will print the value that is stored in memory location 805 (decimal).

Since the M/L program was supposed to put the HEX number 13 (decimal 19) into memory location 0325 HEX, we can PEEK at that location to see what's there.

0325 HEX = (3 X 256)+(2 X 16)+(5 X 1) = 768 + 32 + 5 = 805 decimal

Type: PRINT PEEK(805) and press RETURN

Presto! There it is!

]PRINT PEEK(805)
19   ←————————————— It really worked!

]■

You can add a line to the Operating System between lines 800 and 900 to print the value in memory using the PEEK statement.

810 PRINT PEEK(805)

This part of the operating system (lines 800-900) can be changed to custom fit each program you run. Add line 810 to the Operating System for your next program.

The first program loads data into the accumulator and then stores it in memory. Practically all programs use this type of operation to move data from place to place within the computer.

The accumulator is also used in performing operations on numbers. One such operation shifts each bit in the accumulator left one place. This operation is abbreviated ASL (Arithmetic Shift Left). Its OPeration CODE (OP CODE) is OA.

Example:

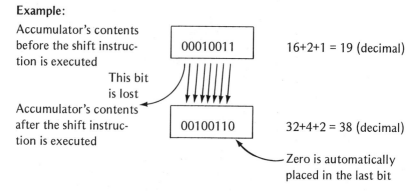

Accumulator's contents before the shift instruction is executed

00010011   16+2+1 = 19 (decimal)

This bit is lost

Accumulator's contents after the shift instruction is executed

00100110   32+4+2 = 38 (decimal)

Zero is automatically placed in the last bit

You can see that an ASL instruction is one way to multiply a number by two, since the value of each bit is doubled.

You can now load a number into the accumulator and shift each bit one place to the left (or multiply it by two). You can then store the result in a memory location. The PEEK statement, which you have added at line 810 in the Operating System program, will then print the result stored in memory.

Use the Operating System to load this program. After all 7 bytes have been entered, the display should show:

HERE IS YOUR PROGRAM

768 A9   ◄— Load Accumulator with HEX value 13
769 13   (19 decimal)
770 0A   ◄— Shift bits left 1 place
771 8D   ◄— Store results in memory (0325)
772 25
773 03
774 60   ◄— Return to Operating System
IF ANY CHANGES—TYPE ADDRESS
IF NOT — TYPE 99
?■

When you type in 99, the program will immediately show the value that has been stored in memory 0325 HEX (805 decimal). Remember that the value will be displayed as a decimal number. It should be 38. Here is the display when the program has been run:

```
HERE IS YOUR PROGRAM

768  A9
769  13  ◄─────── (13 HEX = 19 decimal)
770  0A
771  8D
772  25
773  03
774  60
IF ANY CHANGES—TYPE ADDRESS
IF NOT — TYPE 99
?99
PRESS ANY KEY TO RUN
38  ◄────────────── Answer comes back in decimal form from
                      the BASIC instruction: PRINT PEEK(805)
]■
```

Since the value in the accumulator is doubled each time the ASL instruction is executed, you can imagine what would happen if we executed ASL twice. The value would be doubled and then redoubled (or multiplied by four). Try it by adding a second ASL instruction to the program above. After you have entered the revised program and executed it, your display should look like this (remember, the program will now be 8 bytes long).

```
HERE IS YOUR PROGRAM

768  A9
769  13
770  0A  }
771  0A  }  ◄──── Two ASL instructions
772  8D
773  25
774  03
775  60
IF ANY CHANGES—TYPE ADDRESS
IF NOT — TYPE 99
?99
PRESS ANY KEY TO RUN
76  ◄────────────── (19 times 4 = 76)
]■
```

Here is what happened:

```
            00010011      ◄—— Original value in accumulator
ASL executed:
            00100110      ◄—— Shifted left once
ASL executed again:
            01001100      ◄—— Shifted left twice, which is 4 times 19
              ↑ ↑ ↖
Result: 64 + 8 + 4 = 76
```

We will cover the arithmetic capabilities in more detail later in the book. Remember that the accumulator can hold only eight bits of data. Memory locations also hold only eight bits. If we shift left too many times, the number will be shifted right out of the accumulator. We will have to find new techniques to take care of big numbers.

Arithmetic and logic functions are performed by the Arithmetic Logic Unit of the 6502 microprocessor.

6502 MICROPROCESSOR
Instruction decoder
Accumulator
Arithmetic Logic Unit

You have discovered that you can load numbers into the computer, change the values that you put in, move the values within the computer, and print out the results. In the next chapter, you'll discover something far more fascinating. You'll find out how to display graphics on the video display.

SUMMARY

You're off to a good start. In this chapter, you have learned:

1. That the computer only understands binary instructions and data

2. How to convert between decimal, binary, and HEX values

3. That memory locations hold one byte or eight bits of data

4. That the accumulator (a special register similar to a memory location) is used to conduct most computer operations

5. To use machine language instructions:

  a. LDA (LoaD Accumulator) used to load the accumulator with an immediate value. Its OP CODE (A9) is followed by one byte of data which is loaded into the accumulator.

  Example: A9 ◄—— OP CODE
                    13 ◄—— data to be used

  b. STA (STore Accumulator) used to store the value in the accumulator in an absolute memory location. Its OP CODE (8D) is followed by the two-byte address.

  Example: 8D ◄—— OP CODE
                    25 ◄—— least significant byte of address
                    03 ◄—— most significant byte of address

  c. RTS (ReTurn from Subroutine) used to cause a return from a machine language program (or subroutine).

  Example: 60 ◄—— OP CODE

  d. ASL (Arithmetic Shift Left) used to shift each bit in the accumulator one place to the left. It doubles the value in the accumulator.

  Example: 0A ◄—— OP CODE

6. To put all these instructions into a machine language program, entered and controlled by the BASIC Operating System

Although you have only touched on a few machine language instructions, you were able to understand and use a machine language program.

Most of the instructions that you will be using have several forms (or modes). They are shown in Appendix A. The ones that you will be using most are Immediate, Absolute, Implied, and Zero Page.

You have used LDA in the Immediate Mode. In this mode, the data to be used *immediately* follows the OP CODE. You have also used the STA instruction in the Absolute Mode. In this mode, the complete (or *absolute*) address follows the OP CODE of the instruction. This address is given with the Least Significant Byte first, followed by the Most Significant Byte. The Implied Mode was used for the RTS instruction. Its function is *implied* by the instruction. Therefore, no address or data is needed.

These modes will become more familiar to you as they are used in future chapters.

EXERCISES

Fill in the blanks in the following exercises.

1. BASIC uses _____ numbers, but the computer only
   (decimal, binary)
   understands _____ numbers.
   (decimal, binary)

2. One HEX digit can be used to represent how many binary digits? _____

3. Give the HEX and decimal equivalents of these binary numbers.

Binary	HEX	Decimal
1001	_____	_____
1101	_____	_____
01010111	_____	_____

4. Data is copied into the accumulator from memory with a _____
   instruction.   (load, store)

5. Data is copied into memory from the accumulator with a _____
   instruction.   (load, store)

6. Explain what the execution of the following instruction would do.

Address	Op Code	Remarks
771	8D	STA
772	40	memory
773	03	

   _____

   _____

7. The BASIC Operating System displays _____ values for
   (decimal, HEX)
   program addresses and _____ values for Op Codes and data.
   (decimal, HEX)

8. Fill in the results that would be placed in memory location 0333 by this
   program.

768	A9	LDA 2C
769	2C	
770	0A	ASL
771	BD	STA 0333
772	33	
773	03	
774	60	RTS

   _____ hex (in memory)   _____ decimal equivalent

9. Tell what each of the following instructions accomplishes when executed.
   a. A9   LDA 15
      15

   _____

   _____

b. 8D   STA 0310
   10
   03

_____
_____

c. 0A   ASL

_____
_____

d. 60   RTS

_____
_____

ANSWERS TO EXERCISES

1. Decimal; binary

2. 4

3.
Binary	HEX	Decimal
1001	9	9
1101	D	13
01010111	57	87

4. Load

5. Store

6. Store the value contained in the accumulator in memory location 0340.

7. Decimal; HEX

8. 58 HEX (in memory); 88 decimal equivalent
   (0010 1100 shifted left = 0101 1000 = 58 HEX
   58 HEX = 5 X 16 + 8 = 88 decimal)

9. a. LDA 15 loads the accumulator with the value 15 (HEX).
   b. STA 0310 stores the accumulator's content into memory location 0310.
   c. ASL shifts each bit in the accumulator one place to the left.
   d. RTS causes a return from the subroutine where it is used.

Chapter 4

Simple Graphics

BOS

In Chap. 3, you found out how to load a number into the accumulator, perform an operation on it (shift the bits left), and store it into memory. In this chapter, you'll learn how to plot points and draw lines on the screen. You'll use some of the built-in capabilities of the Apple machine language monitor. You'll take advantage of some subroutines that are permanently stored in Read Only Memory (ROM). This will save you a lot of work, since these routines will be used over and over again in future programs.

You have no doubt used subroutines in BASIC many times. A machine language subroutine works the same way, but the instructions are different, of course. In BASIC, you used GOSUB 2000 to tell the computer to go to the subroutine located at line 2000. Then the last line of the BASIC subroutine RETURNed the computer to the main program.

In machine language, the instruction used is:

JSR XXXX

Jump to ——————————↑   ↑—————— HEX memory address
SubRoutine   where subroutine is
                                                      located

The machine language OPeration CODE for JSR is 20.

Example of JSR as used in a program:

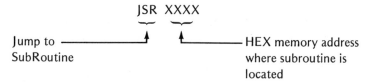

779 20 ◀——— JSR F800   Jump to subroutine
780 00 ◀————————   at memory location
781 F8   F800 (hex)

The last instruction used in the subroutine must be a return to the main program. In machine language, this would be:

RTS   (ReTurn from Subroutine)

If you are using one of Apple's built-in subroutines, the RTS instruction is already there, and you don't have to worry about it.

PLOTTING A POINT ON THE SCREEN

We will use three subroutines in our program to plot a point, the beginning step in learning to use graphics. If you have used Applesoft BASIC, you know that several program steps are necessary to do this. In planning our machine language program, we know that we must:

BASIC Equivalent Statements

1. Clear the screen	HOME
2. Set the Graphics mode	GR
3. Select the color to be used	COLOR = 15
4. Select the screen position of the point to be plotted	C=5 R=32
5. Plot the point	PLOT C,R
6. Return to BASIC Operating System	RETURN

Here is a sample program to plot a point. Each function of the program is presented in a block that is numbered according to the above plan. The computer prints the first column. You type in the second column.

1. REMARK ** CLEAR THE SCREEN **
   768 20 ← JSR FC58   Jump to the subroutine
   769 58   at FC58. A built-in sub-
   770 FC   routine

2. REMARK ** SET GRAPHICS MODE **
   771 20 ← JSR FB40   Jump to the subroutine
   772 40   at FB40. Another built-
   773 FB   in subroutine

3. REMARK ** SELECT COLOR **
   774 A9 ← LDA FF   Load accumulator with
   775 FF   color value = 15 or F in
                             HEX (both bytes).
   776 85 ← STA 0030   Store in memory at lo-
   777 30   cation 0030

4. REMARK ** SCREEN POSITION **
   778 A0 ← LDY 05   Load the Y register
   779 05   with column number, 5

   780 A9 ← LDA 20   Load the accumulator
   781 20   with row, 32 (20 HEX)

5. REMARK ** PLOT THE POINT **
   782 20 ← JSR F800   Jump to the subroutine
   783 00   at F800. Another built-
   784 F8   in subroutine.

6. REMARK ** RETURN TO BASIC **
   785 60 ← RTS   Return to BASIC Oper-
                             ating System

Notice the store instruction (85 HEX) at memory location 776. Ordinarily, a load from or store to a memory location requires two additional bytes to give the full memory address. The 6502 central processor unit recognizes the code 85 as a special instruction that will supply only the Least Significant Byte of the address. The computer "understands" that the Most Significant Byte of these special Zero Page instructions is zero. Hence, they are called Zero Page instructions. They can be executed faster than those where a two-byte address is needed.

The operation of this program is dependent upon the correct performance of the subroutine at location F800 that plots the point. Steps 3 and 4 of the program supply values that must be used by the point-plotting subroutine.

STEP 3 — Puts the color value (0-15) into memory location 0030. Note that this store instruction STA uses only the last part of the address (the first part 00 is not needed). The color value is given at program location 775. The color values are entered as HEX numbers 0 through F (0 through 15 in decimal numbers). The correct HEX digit must be entered in both bytes.

Example:

Orange: A9 LDA 99
          99
          85 STA 30   9 in both
          30   HEX digits

The color values are given in the following table.

COLOR TABLE

Color Value	HEX Value	Color
0	0	Black
1	1	Magenta
2	2	Dark blue
3	3	Light purple
4	4	Dark green
5	5	Grey
6	6	Medium blue
7	7	Light blue
8	8	Brown
9	9	Orange
10	A	Grey
11	B	Pink
12	C	Green
13	D	Yellow
14	E	Blue/green
15	F	White

When the PLOT-THE-POINT subroutine is executed, it looks for the color value in memory location 0030. Therefore, the machine language program must store the color value there (which it does at program locations 776 and 777).

The subroutine must also be told where to plot the point on the video screen. This information is supplied in Step 4 of the program.

STEP 4 — Provides the column and row where you desire the point to be plotted. In low resolution graphics, these values may range from 0 through 39 inclusive. The column is loaded into the Y register (a special storage location used by several machine instructions — 8 bits long). The row is loaded into the accumulator. Remember that these are machine language instructions; hence the values must be in HEX format.

STEP 5 — The PLOT-THE-POINT subroutine looks at the Y register and the accumulator to find the row and column where the point is to be plotted. The subroutine then plots the point.

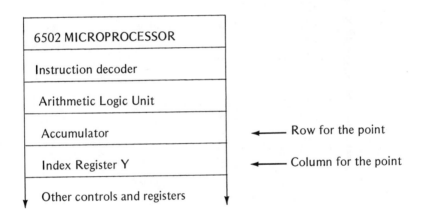

STEP 6 — After the point has been plotted, the Return from Subroutine instruction returns the program to the BASIC Operating System at the point following the CALL S instruction at line 800 (see Operating System, Chap. 2).

The subroutines at Steps 1 and 2 merely clear the screen and set the low resolution Graphics mode so that the points may be plotted.

For this program, it would be convenient to be able to change the color value, the column of the plot, and the row of the plot. To do this easily, add these lines to the BASIC Operating System Program.

810 INPUT "WANT TO CHANGE DATA (YES OR NO)?"; A$
820 IF A$="YES" GOTO 300

Then, when you want to change values after a run, you can change the COLOR value at 775, the Column at 779, or the Row at 781. This change saves you the trouble of typing the complete program again.

Here is a sample display just after entry.

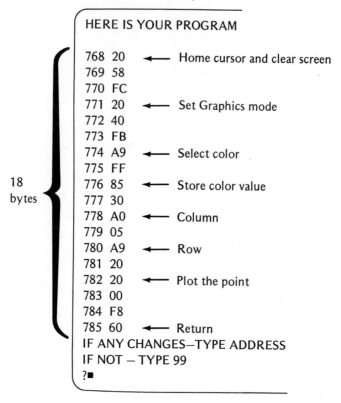

```
HERE IS YOUR PROGRAM

768  20  ◄──── Home cursor and clear screen
769  58
770  FC
771  20  ◄──── Set Graphics mode
772  40
773  FB
774  A9  ◄──── Select color
775  FF
776  85  ◄──── Store color value
777  30
778  A0  ◄──── Column
779  05
780  A9  ◄──── Row
781  20
782  20  ◄──── Plot the point
783  00
784  F8
785  60  ◄──── Return
IF ANY CHANGES—TYPE ADDRESS
IF NOT — TYPE 99
?■
```

18 bytes

Here is the display after the run.

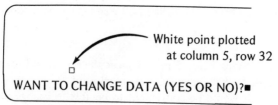

White point plotted
at column 5, row 32

WANT TO CHANGE DATA (YES OR NO)?■

76

Now change the color to 3 (light purple), the column to 14 (HEX), and the row to 14 (HEX). This would put a light purple point at the center of the screen. After typing YES to the question for data, the display shows:

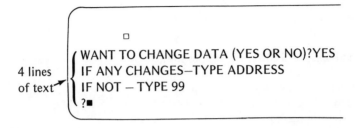

4 lines
of text

□

WANT TO CHANGE DATA (YES OR NO)?YES
IF ANY CHANGES—TYPE ADDRESS
IF NOT — TYPE 99
?■

Type: 775 and press RETURN. The bottom 4 lines of text now show:

IF ANY CHANGES—TYPE ADDRESS
IF NOT — TYPE 99
?775
775 DATA=?■

Type: 33 and press RETURN. The bottom 4 lines now show:

IF NOT — TYPE 99
?775
775 DATA=?33
ANY OTHER CHANGES (YES OR NO)?■

Type: YES and press RETURN. The 4 lines now show:

ANY OTHER CHANGES (YES OR NO)?YES
IF ANY CHANGES—TYPE ADDRESS
IF NOT — TYPE 99
?■

Type: 779 and press RETURN. The 4 lines show:

```
IF ANY CHANGES—TYPE ADDRESS
IF NOT — TYPE 99
?779
779  DATA=?■
```

Type: 14 and press RETURN. The 4 lines show:

```
IF NOT — TYPE 99
?779
779  DATA=?14
ANY OTHER CHANGES (YES OR NO)?■
```

Type: YES and press RETURN. The 4 lines show:

```
ANY OTHER CHANGES (YES OR NO)?YES
IF ANY CHANGES—TYPE ADDRESS
IF NOT — TYPE 99
?■
```

Type: 781 and press RETURN. The 4 lines show:

```
IF ANY CHANGES—TYPE ADDRESS
IF NOT — TYPE 99
?781
781  DATA=?■
```

Type: 14 and press RETURN. The 4 lines show:

```
IF NOT — TYPE 99
?781
781  DATA=?14
ANY OTHER CHANGES (YES OR NO)?■
```

Type: NO and press RETURN. Your program spins by on the four lines at the bottom of the screen and ends up at:

```
783  00
784  F8
785  60
ANY OTHER CHANGES (YES OR NO)?■
```

Type: NO and press RETURN. The 4 lines show:

```
785  60
ANY OTHER CHANGES (YES OR NO)?NO
PRESS ANY KEY TO RUN■
```

Type: Any key that you desire to see your newly plotted point.

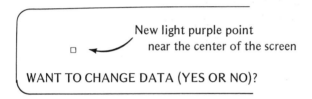

New light purple point
near the center of the screen

WANT TO CHANGE DATA (YES OR NO)?

Now it's up to you. If you want to plot some points in other colors and in other places, type YES and repeat the process. If you have had enough, type NO and the computer will return to the BASIC Operating System. You will then be ready to enter the next program.

FOUR-CORNER PLOT

Before we leave the point plotting technique, let's write a program to put a point at each corner of the graphics area. The points would be:

Column		Row		
Dec.	HEX	Dec.	HEX	
0	0	0	0	Upper left
0	0	39	27	Lower left
39	27	0	0	Upper right
39	27	39	27	Lower right

79

The program will be similar to the last one. The exception will be that sections 4 and 5 will be repeated, once for each additional point.

FOUR-CORNER PLOT PROGRAM

1. $\left\{\begin{array}{ll} 768 & 20 \\ 769 & 58 \\ 770 & FC \end{array}\right.$ Clear the screen

2. $\left\{\begin{array}{ll} 771 & 20 \\ 772 & 40 \\ 773 & FB \end{array}\right.$ Set Graphics mode

3. $\left\{\begin{array}{lll} 774 & A9 & \text{Select color} \\ 775 & FF & \text{WHITE} \\ \\ 776 & 85 & \text{Store it in 0030} \\ 777 & 30 & \end{array}\right.$

4. $\left\{\begin{array}{lll} 778 & A0 & \text{Column 0} \\ 779 & 00 & \\ \\ 780 & A9 & \text{Row 0} \\ 781 & 00 & \end{array}\right.$

5. $\left\{\begin{array}{ll} 782 & 20 \\ 783 & 00 \\ 784 & F8 \end{array}\right.$ Plot upper left corner

4. $\left\{\begin{array}{ll} 785 & A9 \\ 786 & 27 \end{array}\right.$ Change row, leave column the same

5. $\left\{\begin{array}{ll} 787 & 20 \\ 788 & 00 \\ 789 & F8 \end{array}\right.$ Plot lower left corner

4. $\left\{\begin{array}{lll} 790 & A0 & \text{Change column, leave row the same} \\ 791 & 27 & \\ \\ 792 & A9 & \text{Reload row in accumulator} \\ 793 & 27 & \end{array}\right.$

5. $\left\{\begin{array}{ll} 794 & 20 \\ 795 & 00 \\ 796 & F8 \end{array}\right.$ Plot lower right corner

4. $\left\{\begin{array}{ll} 797 & A9 \\ 798 & 00 \end{array}\right.$ Change row, leave column the same

5. $\left\{\begin{array}{ll} 799 & 20 \\ 800 & 00 \\ 801 & F8 \\ 802 & 60 \end{array}\right.$

799 20 — Plot upper right corner

802 60 — Return to BASIC Operating System

This is the longest machine language program that you have had so far. There are 35 bytes. When the program has been completely entered, the computer will display the first 20 lines as follows:

```
HERE IS YOUR PROGRAM

768  20
769  58
770  FC
771  20
772  40
773  FB
774  A9
775  FF
776  85
777  30
778  A0
779  00
780  A9
781  00
782  20
783  00
784  F8
785  A9
786  27
787  20
PRESS ANY KEY TO CONTINUE
■
```

Do not make any changes yet, but make a note of any errors in the first 20 lines. You will have your chance for corrections after the entire program has been displayed.

To look at the rest of the program, press any key. The computer will clear the screen and display the next 20 lines if there are that many. This is what you will see this time:

```
788  00
789  F8
790  A0
791  27
792  A9
793  27
794  20
795  00
796  F8
797  A9
798  00
799  20
800  00
801  F8
802  60
PRESS ANY KEY TO CONTINUE
■
```

You can see now that the complete program has been displayed. When you press any key on the keyboard, you will see your chance for corrections. The lines following PRESS ANY KEY TO CONTINUE are:

IF ANY CHANGES—TYPE ADDRESS
IF NOT — TYPE 99
?■

Type: 99 if there are no changes.
The program then says: PRESS ANY KEY TO RUN
Type: Any key and you will see:

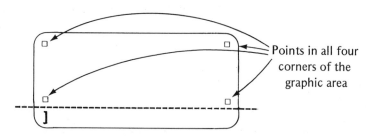

Points in all four
corners of the
graphic area

Once again you can add temporary lines to the BASIC Operating System program to let you change values.

DRAWING A HORIZONTAL LINE

If you can plot a point, you can draw a line by plotting a series of points. In the last program, it took quite a long program just to draw four points. Fortunately, the Apple Machine Language Monitor contains a built-in subroutine that will draw a horizontal line. All we have to do is store the row of the last point of the line in memory location 002C where the line-drawing subroutine can find it.

The subroutine used in Step 6 below is equivalent to the Applesoft BASIC statement:

HLIN 16,32 AT 20

Here is the entire program laid out in functional sections.

HORIZONTAL LINE PROGRAM

1. REMARK ** CLEAR THE SCREEN **

768 20	JSR FC58	Built-in subroutine
769 58		
770 FC		

2. REMARK ** SET GRAPHICS MODE **

771 20	JSR FB40	Built-in subroutine
772 40		
773 FB		

3. REMARK ** SET COLOR **

774 A9	LDA FF	Load white color
775 FF		
776 85	STA 30	Store in 0030
777 30		

4. REMARK ** GIVE END POINT **

778 A9	LDA 20	End point at 20 (32 decimal)
779 20		
780 85	STA 2C	Store in 002C
781 2C		

5. REMARK ** GIVE START POINT **

782 A0	LDY 10	Start point at 10 (16 decimal)
783 10		

784 A9	LDA 14	Load accumulator with
785 14		row 14 (20 decimal)

6. REMARK ** PLOT THE LINE **

786 20	JSR F819	Built-in subroutine
787 19		
788 F8		

7. REMARK ** RETURN TO BASIC **

789 60	RTS	Return to Operating System

If you compare this program with the original PLOT-THE-POINT program shown earlier in this chapter, you will find that they are very similar. In our new program, we must give the end value (column) before plotting the line. The subroutine to plot the line is located at a different memory location than the one that plotted a point in the old program.

After you have entered the program by means of the BASIC Operating System, the program is displayed as usual. There are 22 bytes starting at memory location 768.

```
HERE IS YOUR PROGRAM

768  20
769  58
770  FC
771  20
772  40
773  FB
774  A9
775  FF
776  85
777  30
778  A9
779  20
780  85
781  2C
782  A0
783  10
784  A9
785  14
786  20
787  19
PRESS ANY KEY TO CONTINUE
■
```

Check for correctness. Then press any key.

```
788  F8
789  60
PRESS ANY KEY TO CONTINUE
■
```

After pressing a key:

```
788  F8
789  60
PRESS ANY KEY TO CONTINUE
IF ANY CHANGES—TYPE ADDRESS
IF NOT — TYPE 99
?■
```

If all is correct, you type 99.

```
788  F8
789  60
PRESS ANY KEY TO CONTINUE
IF ANY CHANGES—TYPE ADDRESS
IF NOT — TYPE 99
?99
PRESS ANY KEY TO RUN
■
```

Now when you press a key, you see:

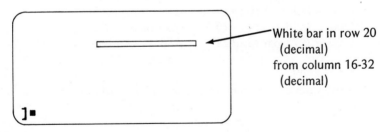

White bar in row 20
(decimal)
from column 16-32
(decimal)

Once again, you may want to make some changes. The lines you used before would work well in the Operating System.

810 INPUT "WANT TO CHANGE DATA (YES OR NO)?"; A$
820 IF A$="YES" GOTO 300

If these lines are used, the program will display the line and then let you change the data in any address that you want. If lines 810 and 820 are in the Operating System, it will be easy to change from the HORIZONTAL LINE PROGRAM to the next program that draws vertical lines.

DRAWING VERTICAL LINES

The Clear Screen, Set Graphics, and Set Color sections of the Horizontal Line Program will also work for the Vertical Line Program, so we will leave them as they are.

Section 4, the Give-End-Point routine, requires that we change only the storage location of the vertical end point. This will now be stored in location 002D instead of 002C as in the Horizontal Line Program. The subroutine that draws vertical lines looks for its end point at 002D. This will require that we change the value stored in program memory location 781.

Section 5 of the Horizontal Line Program gave the beginning point of the line (the column where the line started). It also gave the row in which the horizontal line was to be drawn. You must change the beginning point of the horizontal line to the column at which the vertical line will begin. To do this, change the value stored in program memory location 783. You must also change program memory location 785, which did contain the row in which the horizontal line was drawn. This must now be changed to the starting row at which the vertical line will be drawn.

Section 6 must also be changed. Instead of jumping to the subroutine that draws a horizontal line, you must jump to the subroutine that draws a vertical line. You need only to change program memory location 787.

Here is a summary of the four changes:

Change 781 from 2C to 2D	Storage for End Point
Change 783 from 10 to 14	Column for the line
Change 785 from 14 to 10	Start point of line
Change 787 from 19 to 28	Address of subroutine F828 instead of F819

The subroutine at memory location F828 is equivalent to the BASIC statement:

VLIN 16,32 AT 20

If lines 810 and 820 have been added to the Operating System and the Horizontal Line Program has been run, the computer will end with the question that asks for changes.

```
┌─────────────────────────────────────────────┐
│            ▭▭▭▭▭▭▭▭▭▭▭▭▭                      │
│                                              │
│                                              │
│   WANT TO CHANGE DATA (YES OR NO)?■          │
│                                              │
└─────────────────────────────────────────────┘
```

Type: YES and press RETURN. The four bottom lines show:

    WANT TO CHANGE DATA (YES OR NO)?YES
    IF ANY CHANGES—TYPE ADDRESS
    IF NOT — TYPE 99
    ?■

Type: 781 and press RETURN.

    IF ANY CHANGES—TYPE ADDRESS
    IF NOT — TYPE 99
    ?781
    781   DATA=?■

Type: 2D   ◄─────── Memory location where end point is stored

    IF NOT — TYPE 99
    ?781
    781   DATA=?2D
    ANY OTHER CHANGES (YES OR NO)?■

Type: YES and press RETURN.

    ANY OTHER CHANGES (YES OR NO)?YES
    IF ANY CHANGES—TYPE ADDRESS
    IF NOT — TYPE 99
    ?■

Type: 783 and press RETURN.

    IF ANY CHANGES—TYPE ADDRESS
    IF NOT — TYPE 99
    ?783
    783   DATA=?■

Type: 14   ◄─────── Column of line

    IF NOT — TYPE 99
    ?783
    783   DATA=?14
    ANY OTHER CHANGES (YES OR NO)?■

Type: YES and press RETURN

```
ANY OTHER CHANGES (YES OR NO)?YES
IF ANY CHANGES—TYPE ADDRESS
IF NOT — TYPE 99
?■
```

Type: 785 and press RETURN

```
IF ANY CHANGES—TYPE ADDRESS
IF NOT — TYPE 99
?785
785  DATA=?■
```

Type: 10 ⟵─────── Start point of line

```
IF NOT — TYPE 99
?785
785  DATA=?10
ANY OTHER CHANGES (YES OR NO)?■
```

Type: YES and press RETURN

```
ANY OTHER CHANGES (YES OR NO)?YES
IF ANY CHANGES—TYPE ADDRESS
IF NOT — TYPE 99
?■
```

Type: 787 and press RETURN

```
IF ANY CHANGES—TYPE ADDRESS
IF NOT — TYPE 99
?787
787  DATA=?■
```

Type: 28 ⟵─────── Address of new subroutine
(Least Significant Byte of F828)

```
IF NOT — TYPE 99
?787
787  DATA=?28
ANY OTHER CHANGES (YES OR NO)?
```

Type: NO

Your program is then listed for you in two sections, as was done for the Horizontal Line Program.

When you RUN the program, you will see:

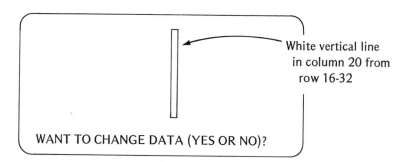

White vertical line
in column 20 from
row 16-32

WANT TO CHANGE DATA (YES OR NO)?

If you want to experiment with the Vertical Line Program, make your changes at this time and try the program again. You will soon be an expert in plotting points and drawing lines at any place you wish on the screen. Practice so you will be ready for a program that will join lines together to form a rectangle.

DRAWING A RECTANGLE

Since you know how to draw horizontal and vertical lines, you will be able to draw a rectangle by joining pairs of lines together. The program that follows will draw the rectangle shown.

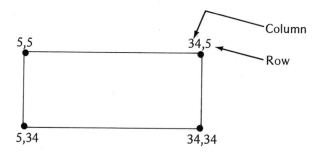

Column

5,5   34,5

Row

5,34   34,34

No new instructions are used, but the program is longer (45 bytes this time). We'll once again show the program in sections with the mnemonic codes as well as the OP CODES.

RECTANGLE PROGRAM

1. REMARK ** CLEAR THE SCREEN **

```
768 20      JSR FC58      Jump to subroutine FC58
769 58
770 FC
```

2. REMARK ** SET GRAPHICS MODE **

771 20	JSR FB40	Jump to subroutine FB40
772 40		
773 FB		

3. REMARK ** SET COLOR **

774 A9	LDA FF	Load accumulator with color
775 FF		

776 85	STA 0030	Store value in memory 0030
777 30		

4. REMARK ** END POINT FOR BOTH LINES **

778 A9	LDA 22	End at column and at row 34
779 22		(decimal)

780 85	STA 2C	End column stored at 002C
781 2C		

782 85	STA 2D	End row stored at 002D
783 2D		

5. REMARK ** START HORIZONTAL AND ROW **

784 A0	LDY 05	Start of horiz. lines
785 05		

786 A9	LDA 05	Row 5
787 05		

6. REMARK ** DRAW TOP OF RECTANGLE **

788 20	JSR F819	Jump to subroutine F819
789 19		
790 F8		

7. REMARK ** RESET START AND ROW **

791 A0	LDY 05	Reset start point
792 05		

793 A9	LDA 22	Move to row 34 (dec.)
794 22		

8. REMARK ** DRAW BOTTOM OF RECTANGLE **

    795 20   JSR F819   Jump to subroutine F819
    796 19
    797 F8

9. REMARK ** START VERTICAL AND COLUMN **

    798 A0   LDY 05   Column 5
    799 05

    800 A9   LDA 05   Start of vert. lines
    801 05

10. REMARK ** DRAW LEFT SIDE **

    802 20   JSR F828   Jump to subroutine F828
    803 28
    804 F8

11. REMARK ** RESET START AND COLUMN **

    805 A0   LDY 22   Move to column 34 (dec.)
    806 22

    807 A9   LDA 05   Reset start point
    808 05

12. REMARK ** DRAW RIGHT SIDE **

    809 20   JSR F828   Jump to subroutine F828
    810 28
    811 F8

13. REMARK ** RETURN TO BASIC **

    812 60   RTS

This program has 45 bytes. After you have entered it, the computer will display it in 3 sections (20 lines at a time). If there are mistakes, correct them. If not, RUN it. Here is what you will see:

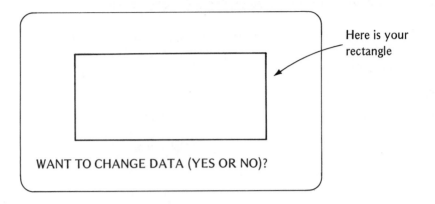

Here is your rectangle

WANT TO CHANGE DATA (YES OR NO)?

SUMMARY

Machine language subroutines were used heavily in this chapter. The Apple Machine Language Monitor has several built-in programs for this purpose. You used the subroutines to clear the screen, to set the Graphics mode, to plot points, and to draw horizontal and vertical lines.

You again used the load and store instructions to move data to locations where they could be found by the appropriate subroutine.

You learned to use these instructions:

1. JSR Jump to SubRoutine) — used in the Absolute Mode to take advantage of built-in subroutines to supplement your programs.

    Example: 20 OP CODE
    19 least significant address byte
    FB most significant address byte

2. LDY (LoaD Y register) — used as a special place to store a value in the Immediate Mode. This value was used by a subroutine.

    Example: A0 OP CODE
    22 data loaded in Y register

3. STA (STore Accumulator) — used this time in the Zero Page Mode. This mode is only used when data is to be transferred to or from low memory (where the most significant byte of the memory address is zero). Memory from 0000 through 00FF is called *zero page memory*.

    Example: 85 OP CODE
    30 least significant address byte

The machine language instructions that you have used so far in this book are:

Mnemonic Code	Addressing Mode	OP CODE	Bytes Used	Function
LDA	Immediate	A9	2	Load accumulator
LDY	Immediate	A0	2	Load Y register
STA	Absolute	8D	3	Store accumulator in
STA	Zero Page	85	2	memory
JSR	Absolute	20	3	Jump to subroutine
RTS	Implied	60	1	Return from sub- routine
ASL	Accumulator	0A	1	Shift bits left in accumulator

The accumulator and Y register and certain memory locations were used to store values to be used by the built-in subroutines. Here is a summary of these uses.

Subroutine	Y reg.	Accum.	0030	002C	002D
Clear Screen	—	—	—	—	—
Set Graphics Mode	—	—	—	—	—
Plot a Point	Column	Row	Color	—	—
Horizontal Line	Start column	Row	Color	End column	—
Vertical Line	Column	Start row	Color	—	End row

You are well on your way to machine language programming. In the next chapter we'll look at how to put alphanumeric characters on the video screen.

EXERCISES

Fill in the blanks.
1. The mnemonic code JSR is an abbreviation of _____
   _____

2. The color values used in a machine language program are two-digit HEX numbers. Which of the following are within the recommended range?
   a. CC   b. 0H   c. FG   d. 33

3. To plot a point on the screen using the built-in subroutine, these things must be done first.
   a. set the graphics mode
   b. select a color value
   c. load the Y register with _____
   d. load the accumulator with _____

4. What range of values may be used to plot a point in the low resolution graphics that we have used in Chap. 3?
   a. Column _____ to _____ inclusive
   b. Row _____ to _____ inclusive

5. The built-in program that draws a vertical line and the one that draws a horizontal line use _____ subroutine(s).
   (the same, different)

6. Explain when the Zero Page Mode instruction STA (Op Code 85) may be used.

_____

ANSWERS TO EXERCISES

1. Jump to SubRoutine

2. a and d

3. c. column number (0-27 HEX)
   d. row number (0-27 HEX)

4. a. column 0 to 39 decimal (or 0 to 27 HEX)
   b. row 0 to 39 decimal (or 0 to 27 HEX)

5. Different (horizontal line at F819, vertical line at F828)

6. When data from the accumulator is to be stored in zero page memory (0000 through 00FF). The most significant byte is 00 and is unneccessary for a Zero Page Mode instruction.

Chapter 5

Displaying Text

BOS

The video display is a window through which you may see what the computer is doing. The screen can display the contents of certain memory locations. In Chap. 4, you displayed graphics on the screen by using the computer's subroutines. In this chapter, you will learn how to place text directly into the video display's memory area so that messages can be seen on the screen.

You will be introduced to some new instructions that will be used to form a loop similar to IF-THEN and FOR-NEXT loops that you have used in BASIC.

The computer has two registers that can be used as "counters." These counters (the X register and the Y register) can be used to *index*, or count, the number of times the computer executes a loop. They can also be used to index the memory locations from which data is loaded or to which data is stored. This operation leads to the use of a new addressing mode called Absolute Indexed Addressing.

DISPLAYING A CHARACTER

We'll start with a simple program that will display the letter A in the upper left corner of the screen. You have used all the instructions that appear in this program. The only new item is the use of ASCII codes. Since the computer can understand only numerical instructions and data, all alphabetic and punctuation characters (as well as certain other special characters) must be given in numerical form. ASCII codes are used for this purpose. (A complete list of codes is given later in this chapter.)

DISPLAY ONE LETTER PROGRAM

1. REMARK ** CLEAR SCREEN **

```
768  20    JSR FC58    Jump to subroutine
769  58
770  FC
```

2. REMARK ** SELECT LETTER 'A' ** ⟋ C1 is the HEX code for
an "A"

771 A9   LDA C1 ◄   Load accumulator with ASCII code
772 C1   for A

3. REMARK ** DISPLAY IT **

773 8D   STA 0400   Store it in display's memory area
774 00
775 04

4. REMARK ** RETURN TO BASIC **

776 60   RTS   Return to Operating System

You have seen Section 1 before. It is the built-in subroutine that clears the screen.

In Section 2, the ASCII code for the letter A (HEX value C1) is loaded into the accumulator. Other values would give other characters.

Section 3 uses the Absolute Addressing Mode for the STA instruction. The location of this memory element (0400 HEX) is the upper left corner of the display.

Section 4 returns to the BASIC Operating System.

Enter the program using the BASIC Operating System. Then, RUN the short machine language program. You will see the letter A appear in the upper left corner of the screen. The blinking cursor will indicate that the program has returned to the Operating System.

The display:

```
 A
]■
```

Next comes a program that will display an alphabetic character several times across the top of the screen. You may want to experiment with this program. Add these lines to the BASIC Operating System:

810 PRINT: PRINT
820 INPUT "WANT TO CHANGE DATA (YES OR NO)?"; A$
830 IF A$="YES" THEN 420

Then, use the Operating System to enter this program. Do not enter the RE-MARKS, Mnemonic Codes, or Operands.

Example:

1. REMARK ** CLEAR SCREEN **

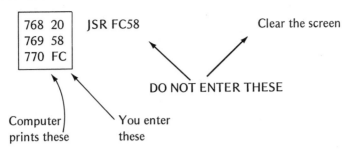

768 20	JSR FC58
769 58	
770 FC	

Clear the screen

DO NOT ENTER THESE

Computer prints these

You enter these

Only the address and data are entered. The rest of the notes and comments are just to help you understand the function of each program section. The program contains 16 bytes.

CHARACTER DISPLAY PROGRAM

1. REMARK ** CLEAR SCREEN **

768 20	JSR FC58	Clear the screen again
769 58		
770 FC		

2. REMARK ** SET INDEX TO ZERO **

771 A0	LDY 0	Used to index display memory and to
772 00		exit loop

3. REMARK ** SELECT CHARACTER **

773 A9	LDA C1	Load an A, just like the last program
774 C1		

4. REMARK ** HERE IS THE LOOP **

775 99	STA 0400, Y	Store in memory location 0400+con-
776 00		tents of Y register
777 04		
778 C8	INY	Increment Y register for next location
779 C0	CPY 28	Compare Y with 40 (decimal)
780 28		
781 D0	BNE F8	Branch (if the two values are *not* equal)
782 F8		to location 0775

Loop

97

5. REMARK ** RETURN TO BASIC **

  783 60   RTS

Let's now go through the program section by section. We will discuss the instructions used and what each does when the program is run.

The screen is cleared in Section 1. This subroutine will be used in most, if not all, of our programs.

In Section 2, the Y register is loaded with the value zero. The LDY instruction was discussed in Chap. 4. For this program, the Y register is used to keep track of how many times the loop in Section 4 is performed. We set it to zero in preparation for the counting process.

Y register | 0 0 0 0 0 0 0 0 | (in binary)

In Section 3, the LDA instruction is used in the Immediate Mode to load the HEX value C1 into the accumulator. This value will be used to display the letter A in Section 4 of the program.

Accumulator | 1 1 0 0 0 0 0 1 | (in binary)

A complete set of ASCII codes is given in the Appendix. C1, the code for the letter A, is the only ASCII code used in this program.

Section 4 forms the loop that prints the letter A at each position along the top line of the video display. The loop works this way:

First time through the loop: Y register = 0

1. The STA instruction stores the code for A in memory location 0400+0 (1st position, top line). Notice that the value stored in Y (0 at this time) is added to the value 0400 to determine the memory location used for storage.
2. The INY instruction (Operation Code = C8) increments the value held in the Y register by one. Therefore, the Y register now holds a value of 1.
3. The CPY instruction (Operation Code = C0) compares the value in the Y register (now 1) with the HEX value 28 (the second byte of the instruction).
4. The BNE instruction (Operation Code = D0) will cause a branch back to the beginning of the loop if the two values compared in Step 3 are *not* equal. Since 1 and 28 are not equal, the computer returns to the beginning of the loop this time. If the values were equal, the computer would go on to Section 5 of the program.

Second time through the loop: Y register = 1

1. The STA instruction stores the A in the memory location 0400+1 (0401 is the 2nd position, top line).
2. The Y register is incremented by the INY instruction and now holds a value of 2.
3. The value of 2 in the Y register is compared to the value 28.

4. Since 2 does not equal 28, the BNE instruction once again sends the computer back to the beginning of the loop.

Third time through the loop: Y register = 2

.
.
.
.

etc.

.
.
.
.

Each time through the loop, the character A is printed one place to the right of the preceding position.

Fortieth time through the loop, Y = 27 HEX

1. The STA instruction stores A in the last position on the top line (0400+27).

2. The Y register is incremented to 28.

3. The content of the Y register is compared to 28 HEX.

4. Since Y = 28, do *not* branch back. Go on to the next instruction, which is in Section 5.

Section 5 returns the computer to the BASIC Operating System, where you are asked if you want to change data.

Since the Apple computer displays 40 characters on each line, you will see 40 A's on the screen.

AAAAAAAAAAAAAAAAAAAAAAAAAAAAAAAAAAAAAAAA
WANT TO CHANGE DATA(YES OR NO)?■

DISCUSSION OF THE NEW INSTRUCTIONS

The first new instruction encountered in the program was:

99 STA 0400,Y

OP CODE   Operator   Index

This instruction is an Absolute Indexed Address instruction and is similar to the Absolute Address store instruction. However, this new instruction adds the content of the Y register to the absolute value of the address used.

Example:

Absolute address

STA 0400, Y   Index

If Y=0, STA 0400+0 is equivalent to STA 0400
If Y=1, STA 0400+1 is equivalent to STA 0401
If Y=27, STA 0400+27 is equivalent to STA 0427

Thus we have a way to make the store instruction store in different locations each time the loop is executed.

In the previous program you have discovered that the top line of the display screen is assigned consecutive memory locations, 0400 through 0427, inclusive.

Top line memory locations: AAAAAAAAAAAAAAAAAAAAAAAAAAAAAAAAAAAAAAAAA

0400 0401 0402 . . . . etc. to 0427

The INY instruction at program memory location 778 is an Implied Addressing instruction that increases the value of the Y register. It is similar to the BASIC instruction Y = Y + 1, and is used to increment the memory location for storing the character A on the display each time through the loop.

The CPY 28 instruction is used here in the Immediate Addressing Mode. The current value of the Y register is compared to the HEX value 28. This comparison enables the computer to make a decision in the next step as to whether or not to return to the start of the loop. Together with the BNE instruction, CPY performs a similar function to the BASIC statement:

IF N< >28 THEN GOTO XX   (where XX is the line that will be branched to)

The final new instruction, BNE F8, requires some explanation. It is a Relative Addressing instruction that completes the loop.

BNE F8   Branch if Not Equal –8 locations

If the result of the preceding instruction (CPY 28) is *not* zero, a branch is taken back to the beginning of the loop. The branch is made to a memory location *relative* to the position of the program counter. The value F8 HEX is equivalent to the negative number –8, and will cause a branch *backwards* 8 steps from the current position of the program counter.

When used as the operand in a branch instruction such as BNE, all HEX values from 01 through 7F inclusive cause a branch *forward* from the current position of the program counter. The following instruction would cause a branch *forward* from memory location 783 (where the program counter points as the BNE instruction is executed) to memory location 78B (783+8).

781 D0   BNE 08
782 08

An example of the above as used in a section of a program follows.

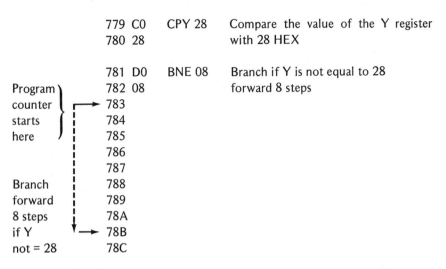

	779 C0	CPY 28	Compare the value of the Y register
	780 28		with 28 HEX
	781 D0	BNE 08	Branch if Y is not equal to 28
Program	782 08		forward 8 steps
counter	783		
starts	784		
here	785		
	786		
	787		
Branch	788		
forward	789		
8 steps	78A		
if Y	78B		
not = 28	78C		

All HEX values from 80 through FF are used by branch instructions as backward (or negative) branches. In the Character Display Program, the instruction used is:

| 781 D0 | BNE F8 | Branch if Y is not equal to 28 back- |
| 782 F8 | | ward 8 steps |

The branch is made backwards (or in the negative direction) since F8 is between 80 and FF. Counting back 8 steps from location 783 puts the branch destination at 775, the start of the loop.

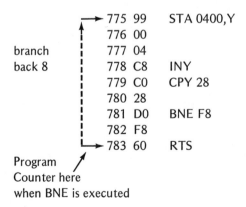

	775 99	STA 0400,Y
	776 00	
branch	777 04	
back 8	778 C8	INY
	779 C0	CPY 28
	780 28	
	781 D0	BNE F8
	782 F8	
	783 60	RTS

Program
Counter here
when BNE is executed

We will not go into the method used by the computer to determine the values of negative numbers. Instead, we will provide tables to determine the operand used with branch instructions.

TABLE TO DETERMINE FORWARD BRANCHES

Steps Forward (Decimal)	Branch Operand (HEX)	Steps Forward (Decimal)	Branch Operand (HEX)	Steps Forward (Decimal)	Branch Operand (HEX)
1	01	49	31	97	61
2	02	50	32	98	62
3	03	51	33	99	63
4	04	52	34	100	64
5	05	53	35	101	65
6	06	54	36	102	66
7	07	55	37	103	67
8	08	56	38	104	68
9	09	57	39	105	69
10	0A	58	3A	106	6A
11	0B	59	3B	107	6B
12	0C	60	3C	108	6C
13	0D	61	3D	109	6D
14	0E	62	3E	110	6E
15	0F	63	3F	111	6F
16	10	64	40	112	70
17	11	65	41	113	71
18	12	66	42	114	72
19	13	67	43	115	73
20	14	68	44	116	74
21	15	69	45	117	75
22	16	70	46	118	76
23	17	71	47	119	77
24	18	72	48	120	78
25	19	73	49	121	79
26	1A	74	4A	122	7A
27	1B	75	4B	123	7B
28	1C	76	4C	124	7C
29	1D	77	4D	125	7D
30	1E	78	4E	126	7E
31	1F	79	4F	127	7F
32	20	80	50		
33	21	81	51		
34	22	82	52		
35	23	83	53		
36	24	84	54		
37	25	85	55		
38	26	86	56		
39	27	87	57		
40	28	88	58		
41	29	89	59		
42	2A	90	5A		
43	2B	91	5B		
44	2C	92	5C		
45	2D	93	5D		
46	2E	94	5E		
47	2F	95	5F		
48	30	96	60		

Examples Using Forward Branches:

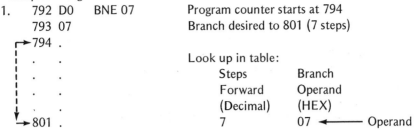

1. 792 D0   BNE 07   Program counter starts at 794
    793 07   Branch desired to 801 (7 steps)
    →794 .
    │   .   .   Look up in table:
    │   .   .   Steps   Branch
    │   .   .   Forward   Operand
    │   .   .   (Decimal)   (HEX)
    →801 .   7   07 ◄——— Operand

If condition tested is not equal to zero, branch forward to 801
(794+7 steps).

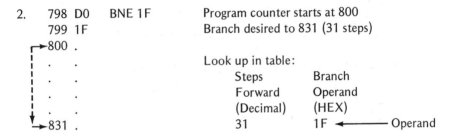

2. 798 D0   BNE 1F   Program counter starts at 800
    799 1F   Branch desired to 831 (31 steps)
    →800 .
    │   .   .   Look up in table:
    │   .   .   Steps   Branch
    │   .   .   Forward   Operand
    │   .   .   (Decimal)   (HEX)
    →831 .   31   1F ◄——— Operand

If condition tested is not equal to zero, branch forward to 831
(800+31 steps).

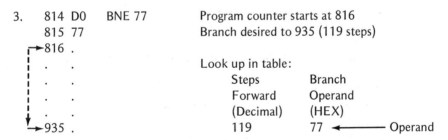

3. 814 D0   BNE 77   Program counter starts at 816
    815 77   Branch desired to 935 (119 steps)
    →816 .
    │   .   .   Look up in table:
    │   .   .   Steps   Branch
    │   .   .   Forward   Operand
    │   .   .   (Decimal)   (HEX)
    →935 .   119   77 ◄——— Operand

If condition tested is not equal to zero, branch forward to 935
(816+119 steps).

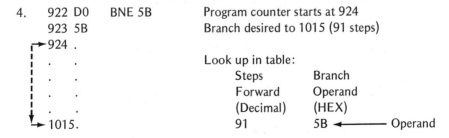

4. 922 D0   BNE 5B   Program counter starts at 924
    923 5B   Branch desired to 1015 (91 steps)
    →924 .
    │   .   .   Look up in table:
    │   .   .   Steps   Branch
    │   .   .   Forward   Operand
    │   .   .   (Decimal)   (HEX)
    → 1015.   91   5B ◄——— Operand

If condition tested is not equal to zero, branch forward to 1015
(924+91 steps).

TABLE TO DETERMINE BACKWARD BRANCHES

Steps Backward (Decimal)	Branch Operand (HEX)	Steps Backward (Decimal)	Branch Operand (HEX)	Steps Backward (Decimal)	Branch Operand (HEX)
1	FF	49	CF	97	9F
2	FE	50	CE	98	9E
3	FD	51	CD	99	9D
4	FC	52	CC	100	9C
5	FB	53	CB	101	9B
6	FA	54	CA	102	9A
7	F9	55	C9	103	99
8	F8	56	C8	104	98
9	F7	57	C7	105	97
10	F6	58	C6	106	96
11	F5	59	C5	107	95
12	F4	60	C4	108	94
13	F3	61	C3	109	93
14	F2	62	C2	110	92
15	F1	63	C1	111	91
16	F0	64	C0	112	90
17	EF	65	BF	113	8F
18	EE	66	BE	114	8E
19	ED	67	BD	115	8D
20	EC	68	BC	116	8C
21	EB	69	BB	117	8B
22	EA	70	BA	118	8A
23	E9	71	B9	119	89
24	E8	72	B8	120	88
25	E7	73	B7	121	87
26	E6	74	B6	122	86
27	E5	75	B5	123	85
28	E4	76	B4	124	84
29	E3	77	B3	125	83
30	E2	78	B2	126	82
31	E1	79	B1	127	81
32	E0	80	B0	128	80
33	DF	81	AF		
34	DE	82	AE		
35	DD	83	AD		
36	DC	84	AC		
37	DB	85	AB		
38	DA	86	AA		
39	D9	87	A9		
40	D8	88	A8		
41	D7	89	A7		
42	D6	90	A6		
43	D5	91	A5		
44	D4	92	A4		
45	D3	93	A3		
46	D2	94	A2		
47	D1	95	A1		
48	D0	96	A0		

Examples of Backward Branches:

1.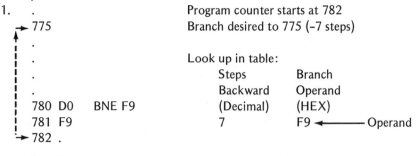

Program counter starts at 782
Branch desired to 775 (−7 steps)

Look up in table:

Steps Backward (Decimal)	Branch Operand (HEX)
7	F9 ◄——————— Operand

If condition tested is not equal to zero, branch backward to 775 (782-7 steps).

2.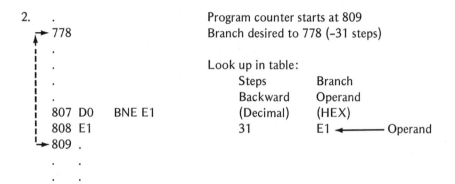

Program counter starts at 809
Branch desired to 778 (−31 steps)

Look up in table:

Steps Backward (Decimal)	Branch Operand (HEX)
31	E1 ◄——————— Operand

If condition tested is not equal to zero, branch backward to 778 (809-31 steps).

3.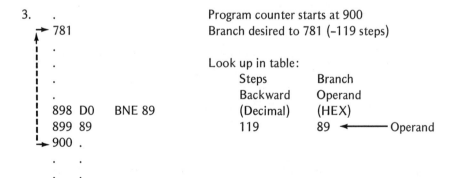

Program counter starts at 900
Branch desired to 781 (−119 steps)

Look up in table:

Steps Backward (Decimal)	Branch Operand (HEX)
119	89 ◄——————— Operand

If condition tested is not equal to zero, branch backward to 781 (900-119 steps).

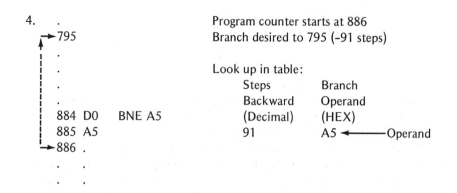

4.

```
       ┌─►795        Program counter starts at 886
       ▲  .          Branch desired to 795 (-91 steps)
       ┊  .
       ┊  .          Look up in table:
       ┊  .                    Steps         Branch
       ┊  .                    Backward      Operand
       ┊  884  D0    BNE A5    (Decimal)     (HEX)
       ┊  885  A5              91            A5 ◄────────Operand
       └─►886  .
          .    .
          .    .
```

While you have the program in the computer, experiment by changing the ASCII values used at memory address 774. Use the values C1 through DA to see different letters of the alphabet. When you have finished experimenting, the next program displays all the 26 alphabetic characters on one line.

We have now talked about these parts of the 6502 microprocessor.

```
┌──────────────────────────┐
│ 6502                     │
│                          │
│ Instruction decoder      │
│                          │
│ Accumulator              │
│                          │
│ X register               │
│                          │
│ Y register               │
│                          │
│ Program counter          │  ◄─ Keeps track of where
│                          │     the computer is in a
│ Other controls and       │     program
│ registers                │
└──────────────────────────┘
```

RUNNING THROUGH THE ALPHABET

In the previous program STA 0400, Y was used to place a letter in consecutive positions on the top line of the video display. The Y register was used to *index* the position.

The X register can be used in the same way. If the ASCII codes for the letters of the alphabet are stored in consecutive memory locations, they can be loaded into the accumulator by the instruction:

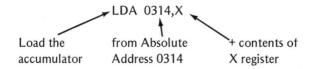

LDA 0314,X

Load the
accumulator

from Absolute
Address 0314

+ contents of
X register

Either of the two registers (X or Y) may be used with the STA instruction or the LDA instruction. They may also be used with other instructions, as we will see later.

After each ASCII code is accessed in the program, the X register can be incremented to provide the correct code for the next pass through the loop. By adding a new section to the previous program, you can access each alphabetic character in order while displaying it in a new position on the screen.

RUNNING ALPHABET PROGRAM

1. REMARK ** INITIALIZATION **

768 20	JSR FC58	Clear the screen
769 58		
770 FC		
771 A0	LDY 0	
772 00		
773 A2	LDX 0	New instruction – load X register with
774 00		zero

2. REMARK ** LOAD AND DISPLAY LOOP **

775 BD	LDA 0314,X	New instruction – load accumulator
776 14		from 0314+X
777 03		
778 99	STA 0400,Y	
779 00		
780 04		
781 E8	INX	New instruction – increment the X
		register
782 C8	INY	
783 C0	CPY 1A	1A hex = 26 (the number of letters in
784 1A		alphabet)
785 D0	BNE F4	Branch if not =, back 12 locations (F4
786 F4		from table)

Loop

107

3. REMARK ** BACK TO BASIC **

    787 60   RTS

4. REMARK ** DATA LIST **

788 C1	Letter A	ASCII codes
789 C2	Letter B	
790 C3	Letter C	
791 C4	.	
792 C5	.	
793 C6	.	
794 C7	.	
795 C8	.	
796 C9	.	
797 CA	.	
798 CB	.	
799 CC	.	
800 CD	.	
801 CE	.	
802 CF	.	
803 D0	.	
804 D1	.	
805 D2	.	
806 D3	.	
807 D4	.	
808 D5	.	
809 D6	.	
810 D7	.	
811 D8	.	
812 D9	Letter Y	
813 DA	Letter Z	

Section 1 initializes the X and Y registers to zero.

Section 2 loads an ASCII character from memory and displays it on the top line.

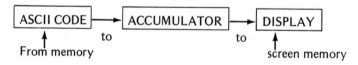

The LDA 0311,X instruction is similar to the BASIC READ statement. The ASCII code is READ from the DATA stored in memory. Section 2 is a loop that is executed 26 times (one for each letter of the alphabet).

Section 3 returns control to the BASIC Operating System after the RUN is completed.

Section 4 provides the DATA to be READ by the LDA 0314,X instruction. This section is used like the DATA statement in BASIC.

Use your BASIC Operating System to load and run the program. The program begins at memory location 768 and is 46 bytes long. Here is how the display looks after the program is run.

ABCDEFGHIJKLMNOPQRSTUVWXYZ

WANT TO CHANGE DATA (YES OR NO)?■

You have learned how to display information on the top line of the screen. In the next program, you will use a built-in subroutine that will let you type in characters from the keyboard. It will display the ASCII codes that are used to represent the letters of the alphabet.

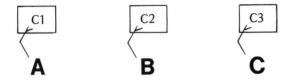

DISPLAYING ASCII CODES

This program uses a built-in subroutine (JSR FD35) that reads a character you have typed on the keyboard. It puts the ASCII code for that character in the accumulator.

Another subroutine (JSR FDDA) is used to print the ASCII code for the character you have typed. The program is designed to let you input all 26 alphabetic characters from the keyboard before returning to the BASIC Operating System. Spaces and carriage returns are provided in the program so that the typed characters and the ASCII codes will be clearly shown in columns along the left side of the screen. There are 41 bytes.

DISPLAY ASCII CODES PROGRAM

1. REMARK ** CLEAR SCREEN AND INITIALIZE **

| 768 A2 | LDX 0 | Set counter |
| 769 00 | | |

770 20	JSR FC58	Clear screen
771 58		
772 FC		

X register = ☐ 00000000 ☐

```
┌─────────────┐
│             │              Clear
└─────────────┘
```

2. REMARK ** GET KEYSTROKE AND PRINT **

Start

```
    ┌──→  773  20    JSR FD35      Get keystroke
    │     774  35
    │     775  FD
    │
    │     776  8D    STA 0340      Save it in memory
    │     777  40
    │     778  03
    │
    │     779  20    JSR FDED      Print it
    │     780  ED
    │     781  FD
```

3. REMARK ** SPACE DISPLAY **

```
    │     782  A9    LDA E0        Load ASCII code for a space
    │     783  E0
    │
    │     784  20    JSR FDED      Display the space. The subroutine uses
    │     785  ED                  the accumulator for other things so if
    │     786  FD                  we want another space we must:
    │
    │     787  A9    LDA E0        Load another space
    │     788  E0
    │
    │     789  20    JSR FDED      Display it
    │     790  ED
    │     791  FD
```

4. REMARK ** PRINT ASCII CODE **

```
    │     792  AD    LDA 0340      Load accumulator from memory
    │     793  40                  where character was saved
    │     794  03
    │
    │     795  20    JSR FDDA      Print the code as two hex digits
    │     796  DA
    │     797  FD
```

5. REMARK ** MOVE TO NEW LINE **

798	A9	LDA 8D	Load an ASCII code for a carriage re-
799	8D		turn
800	20	JSR FDED	Do a carriage return
801	ED		
802	FD		

6. REMARK ** BRANCH BACK IF NOT DONE **

803	E8	INX	Increase counter (X register)
804	E0	CPX 1A	Compare X register with 26 (dec)
805	1A		
806	D0	BNE DD	If not equal, branch back 35 steps (DD
807	DD		from Table to Determine Backward Branches)

Loop to 773 for new keystroke

7. REMARK ** RETURN TO BASIC **

808	60	RTS	Return from this subroutine to the Operating System

Section 1 sets the X register (counter for the number of keystrokes) to zero and clears the screen.

Section 2 uses the subroutine at FD35 to read the character that is typed. The character is then saved in memory 0340 for future use in section 4. The subroutine at FDED then prints the character on the screen.

Section 3 provides two spaces between the character that was typed and the ASCII code that will be printed in section 4. The ASCII code for space is E0.

Section 4 loads the accumulator with the character that was saved in memory 0340 in section 2. It then uses the subroutine at FDDA to print the character as two HEX digits (the ASCII code for the character).

Section 5 provides a carriage return (ASCII code 8D) so that the next keystroke and code will appear on a new line.

Section 6 increases the counter (register X), compares its value with 26 (since there are 26 letters in the alphabet), and branches back to get a new keystroke if its value is not equal to 26. If it does equal 26, it moves on to section 7.

Section 7 returns control to the BASIC Operating System.

A suggested addition to the BASIC Operating System for this program is:

```
810 PRINT
820 INPUT "DO YOU WANT TO RUN AGAIN (YES OR NO)?"; A$
830 IF A$="YES" THEN 700
```

This would allow you to repeat the program with new inputs from the keyboard.

RUNNING THE PROGRAM

When the program is run, you will see the blinking cursor in the upper left corner of the screen. This means that the computer is ready for your first entry.

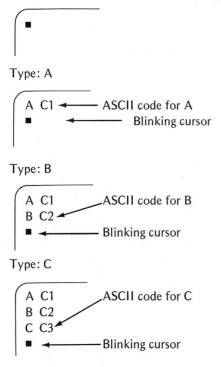

Type: A

```
A  C1 ◄──── ASCII code for A
■      ◄──────── Blinking cursor
```

Type: B

```
A  C1        ASCII code for B
B  C2 ◄
■ ◄──────── Blinking cursor
```

Type: C

```
A  C1        ASCII code for C
B  C2
C  C3 ◄
■ ◄──────── Blinking cursor
```

Continue in this manner until you have seen all 26 character codes.

```
Y  D9
Z  DA

DO YOU WANT TO RUN AGAIN (YES OR NO)?■
```

If you are curious, you will type in YES and try some characters that are not alphabetic. Remember that the program is only fixed to let you input 26 keystrokes before returning to the Operating System.

You may want to try the decimal numerals 0 through 9, punctuation marks, spaces, etc.

Here are the results that we saw when we typed in decimal symbols.

```
0  B0
1  B1
2  B2
3  B3
4  B4
5  B5
6  B6
7  B7
8  B8
9  B9
■
```

You may want to make a table of ASCII codes for all the keys that you try. Compare them with the ASCII code table in Appendix A.

Would you like to see the letters printed on an inverted background (black-on-white)? Or even blinking back and forth from black-on-white to white-on-black? The next program will demonstrate how to do just that. Move on when you are ready.

DISPLAYING MORE THAN ONE LINE

The last program and the next one make use of one of the Apple Monitor's built-in subroutines that places a character (whose ASCII code is contained in the accumulator) on the screen. It then moves over automatically to the next printing position on that line. The ASCII code for a carriage return (8D) is used to move to the beginning of the next line when desired.

You will want to experiment with this program, so be sure to include lines in the BASIC Operating System that will allow you to change data. We will be using:

810 PRINT
820 INPUT "WANT TO CHANGE DATA (YES OR NO)?"; A$
830 IF A$="YES" THEN 420

You will want to change data because we will show you how to PRINT white on black, black on white, and letters blinking on and off.

MULTI-LINE DISPLAY PROGRAM

1. REMARK ** CLEAR SCREEN AND INITIALIZE **

```
768  20    JSR FC58
769  58
770  FC

771  A2    LDX 0
772  00
```

2. REMARK ** GET CHARACTER AND PRINT **

```
773 BD    LDA 0311,X
774 11
775 03

776 20    JSR FDED
777 ED              Put character in accumulator on the
778 FD              screen

779 E8    INX

780 E0    CPX 16    New instruction – compares value in
781 16              X register with 16

782 D0    BNE F5    Branch back if not equal (–11 loca-
783 F5              tions)
```

3. REMARK ** BACK TO BASIC **

```
784 60    RTS       Return to BASIC
```

4. REMARK ** DATA LIST OF ASCII CODES **

```
785 C1              Letter A
786 D0              Letter P
787 D0              Letter P
788 CC              Letter L
789 C5              Letter E
790 8D              A carriage return (new line)
791 C3              Letter C
792 CF              Letter O
793 CD              Letter M
794 D0              Letter P
795 D5              Letter U
796 D4              Letter T
797 C5              Letter E
798 D2              Letter R
799 8D              A carriage return (new line)
800 C4              Letter D
801 C9              Letter I
802 D3              Letter S
803 D0              Letter P
804 CC              Letter L
805 C1              Letter A
806 D9              Letter Y
```

Section 1 initializes the X register to zero and clears the screen.

Section 2 loads an ASCII code from memory (indexed by X) and uses the built-in subroutine to display it on the screen. This section is a loop. Each time through, the X register is incremented so that the next ASCII code in memory can be loaded. The value in the X register is compared to 16 HEX (22 decimal) since there are 22 characters in the data list. If X is not equal to 22, a branch is taken back to the beginning of the loop (location 773).

Section 4 is the data list used by the loop.

Once again, use the BASIC Operating System to load and run the program. Everything begins at location 768 and is 39 bytes long. We saved a few lines by using the built-in subroutine to display the data. When the run is completed, the display will show:

```
APPLE
COMPUTER
DISPLAY

WANT TO CHANGE DATA (YES OR NO)?■
```

This program is similar to the Running Alphabet Program. However, the carriage returns in the data list allowed the use of more than one line on the screen.

Up to now, the book has shown the video display as black letters on a white background. Actually, your computer displays light-colored letters on a dark background. However, books are traditionally printed in black letters on white pages. Oh well, we can't all be perfect. The versatility of computers is amazing. Read on and you will see.

The Apple computer has the ability to reverse the color of text material so that the background for an individual letter is white and the letter is black. This is called an *inverse display*. To accomplish this inverse effect, you change the normal ASCII code as in the following examples:

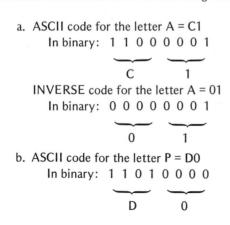

a. ASCII code for the letter A = C1
   In binary: 1 1 0 0 0 0 0 1
                  C   1
   INVERSE code for the letter A = 01
   In binary: 0 0 0 0 0 0 0 1
                  0   1
b. ASCII code for the letter P = D0
   In binary: 1 1 0 1 0 0 0 0
                  D   0

INVERSE code for the letter P = 10

In binary: 0 0 0 1 0 0 0 0

$$\underbrace{}_{1}\quad\underbrace{}_{0}$$

To cause the character to be inverted, the two most significant bits (those in the two far left positions) are removed.

1 1 0 0 0 0 0 1 C1	or	1 1 0 1 0 0 0 0 D0
to		to
0 0 0 0 0 0 0 1 01		0 0 0 1 0 0 0 0 10

To demonstrate this feature, make the following changes to the MULTI-LINE DISPLAY PROGRAM.

785	01	Inverted A
786	10	Inverted P
787	10	Inverted P
788	0C	Inverted L
789	05	Inverted E

Now, when you run the changed program, you will see this difference in the display.

Original Program   Changed Program

Another change to the ASCII code of the character to be displayed will make the character blink on and off. To demonstrate, change the codes of the word DISPLAY.

800	44	blinking D
801	49	blinking I
802	53	blinking S
803	50	blinking P
804	4C	blinking L
805	41	blinking A
806	59	blinking Y

Once again, notice the changes for the three possibilities for the letter A.

Normal A = C1	1100 0001 in binary	
Inverse A = 01	0000 0001 in binary	(left 2 digits = 0)
Blink A = 41	0100 0001 in binary	(left digit = 0)

Use the BASIC Operating System to make the changes in memory at locations 800 through 806. Now when you run the program, the word DISPLAY will blink — first inverse, then normal, then inverse, then normal, etc.

Black on white

White on black

Blinking

You can change the message displayed by this program by using any letters in the following table at the data locations beginning at 800. You may make the message longer or shorter by changing the value in location 781 to match the number of characters used.

CODE TABLE FOR ALPHABET

NORMAL	INVERSE	BLINK	LETTER
C1	01	41	A
C2	02	42	B
C3	03	43	C
C4	04	44	D
C5	05	45	E
C6	06	46	F
C7	07	47	G
C8	08	48	H
C9	09	49	I
CA	0A	4A	J
CB	0B	4B	K
CC	0C	4C	L
CD	0D	4D	M
CE	0E	4E	N
CF	0F	4F	O
D0	10	50	P
D1	11	51	Q
D2	12	52	R
D3	13	53	S
D4	14	54	T
D5	15	55	U
D6	16	56	V
D7	17	57	W
D8	18	58	X
D9	19	59	Y
DA	1A	5A	Z

Other codes that you might want to try are:

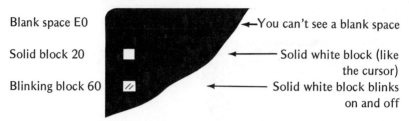

Blank space E0 ————————————→ ←—You can't see a blank space

Solid block 20 ■ ←——————— Solid white block (like
the cursor)

Blinking block 60 ▨ ←——————— Solid white block blinks
on and off

Have some fun experimenting with this program before moving on to a program that will let you print information on the screen as you type from the keyboard. I bet you always wanted to see your name in flashing lights. Now's your chance!

The last program of this chapter is one of the simplest that you have had so far, but it is one of the most powerful. It will allow you to fill the screen with text as you type it in from the keyboard. You may use spaces, punctuation, the return key, numbers, letters, etc. Three new instructions are used.

After a key is read from the keyboard, the CMP (Compare) instruction is used to compare the value taken from the keyboard (whose ASCII code is in the accumulator after the key is pressed) with the value AF (the ASCII code for a backslash, /). If the keystroke has been a backslash, the next instruction BEQ (branch if equal) will cause a branch to the end of the subroutine. Therefore, you type a backslash when you are through using the keyboard. This would be similar to the BASIC statement:

776 IF X = 175 THEN GOTO 784

784 RETURN   (AF HEX=175 decimal)

or
776 IF X$ = "/" THEN GOTO 784

784 RETURN

A JMP (Jump Absolute) instruction follows the print subroutine. JMP sends the computer back to look for another keystroke, and is similar to the BASIC statement:

781 GOTO 771

DISPLAY ANY MESSAGE PROGRAM
1. REMARK ** CLEAR SCREEN **

768 20   JSR FC58
769 58
770 FC

2. REMARK ** LOOP TO GET AND PRINT KEY **

►771	20	JSR FD35	Get a key
772	35		
773	FD		
774	C9	CMP AF	Compare accumulator to AF
775	AF		
776	F0	BEQ 06	Branch if equal 6 steps
777	06		EXIT from loop
778	20	JSR FDED	Print the character
779	ED		
780	FD		
781	4C	JMP 0303	Go back for another keystroke
782	03		(0303 HEX=771 decimal)
783	03		

3. REMARK ** BACK TO BASIC **

784	60	RTS	Return to Operating System

In Section 2 of the program we used three new instructions. The CMP instruction is similar to CPX and CPY. The Immediate mode is used to compare the value in the accumulator with the value that follows the instruction. The BEQ instruction that follows CMP causes a branch to take place if the two values are equal. If the branch is taken, it is to the RTS instruction 6 steps forward (from the program counters present position 778). If the branch is not taken, the JSR FDED instruction prints the character and steps the cursor forward one place.

At the end of Section 2 is the third new instruction — JMP. This is an Absolute Jump. The program will always perform the jump if this instruction is executed. It works like the GOTO statement in BASIC.

The program is only 17 bytes long, but it will let you type all day on the screen. When the screen is filled, it merely scrolls up to make room for more entries. When you want the program to stop, type the backslash mark. That will get you out of the loop to return to the BASIC Operating System. Of course, if you want to use the backslash while you are typing, you are out of luck. This program uses the backslash to end its operation.

We can't show you how the screen looks, as you are in complete command. It will display whatever you type.

SUMMARY

You found additional useful built-in subroutines in this chapter for displaying characters and reading characters from the keyboard. Thus you are now able to use machine language programs to display both graphics and text. You learned the memory locations that are assigned to the video display, and you learned to use ASCII codes.

You used all the instructions that were introduced in previous chapters as well as several new instructions. Here is a summary of the instructions introduced in this chapter:

1. LDX (Load X register) — used in the Immediate mode as a counter in the same way that LDY was used with the Y register.

   Example: A2 OP CODE
   00 data loaded into the X register

2. INY (Increment register Y) — used to increase the value held in the Y register by one. Implied mode.

   Example: C8 OP CODE

3. INX (Increment register X) — used to increase the value held in the X register by one. Implied mode.

   Example: E8 OP CODE

4. CPY (Compare Y register) — used to compare the value held in the Y register to the given number. It was used in the Immediate mode.

   Example: C0 OP CODE
   1A data to which the value held in the Y register is compared

5. CPX (Compare X register) — used to compare the value held in the X register to the given number. It was used in the Immediate mode.

   Example: E0 OP CODE
   06 data to which the value held in the X register is compared

6. BNE (Branch if Not Equal) — used after a compare instruction to tell where the next instruction to be executed will be found if the result of the comparison is not equal to zero. It is a Relative Mode instruction that includes data telling the computer where to move the program counter relative to its present position.

   Example: D0 OP CODE
   F5 data telling how
   far to move the
   program counter
   (−11 in this
   example)

7. STA (Store Accumulator) — used this time in the Absolute Indexed mode. Stores whatever value the accumulator holds in memory assigned by the Absolute location given plus the value held in the Y register.

Example: 99   OP CODE
            00   Least Significant Byte of Absolute location
            04   Most Significant Byte of Absolute location

8. LDA (Load Accumulator) — used in the Absolute Indexed Mode this time. Loads the accumulator with data from the Absolute memory location given plus the value held in the X register.

Example: BD   OP CODE
            14   Least Significant Byte of Absolute location
            03   Most Significant Byte of Absolute location

9. CMP (Compare Accumulator) — used in the Immediate mode to compare the value held in the accumulator with the given number.

Example: C0   OP CODE
            AF   data to which the value held in the accumulator is compared

10. BEQ (Branch if equal) — used in the Relative mode after a compare instruction. Causes a branch if the values compared are equal. The data following the instruction tells how far and in what direction the branch will be taken.

Example: F0   OP CODE
            06   data telling where to branch (6 locations forward in this example)

11. JMP (Jump) — used in the Absolute mode to cause an unconditional jump to the specified memory location.

Example: 4C   OP CODE
            03   Least Significant Byte of destination address
            03   Most Significant Byte of destination address

TABLE OF SUBROUTINES USED SO FAR

Function	Location in Memory
Clear the screen	FC58
Set Graphics Mode	FB40
Plot a point	F800
Draw a horizontal line	F819
Draw a vertical line	F828
Get a keystroke	FD35
Print character in accumulator	FDED
Print value in accumulator as two hex digits	FDDA

TABLE OF MACHINE LANGUAGE INSTRUCTIONS USED SO FAR

Mnemonic Code	Addressing Mode	OP CODE	Bytes Used	Function
ASL	Accumulator	0A	1	Shift bits left
BEQ	Relative	F0	2	Branch if equal
BNE	Relative	D0	2	Branch if not = 0
CMP	Immediate	C9	2	Compare accumulator
CPX	Immediate	E0	2	Compare X reg. to value
CPY	Immediate	C0	2	Compare Y reg. to value
INX	Implied	E8	1	Increment X register
INY	Implied	C8	1	Increment Y register
JMP	Absolute	4C	3	Jump
JSR	Absolute	20	3	Jump to subroutine
LDA	Immediate	A9	2	Load Accumulator
LDA	Absolute Indexed	BD	3	Load Accumulator
LDX	Immediate	A2	2	Load X register
LDY	Immediate	A0	2	Load Y register
RTS	Implied	60	1	Return from subroutine
STA	Zero Page	85	2	Store Accumulator
STA	Absolute	8D	3	Store Accumulator
STA	Absolute Indexed	99	3	Store Accumulator

You covered a lot of ground in this chapter. You can now display both graphics and text on the screen. In the next chapter, we'll see if you can bring the Apple to life with some living sounds.

EXERCISES

1. The Absolute mode instruction STA 0400 would store the value contained in the accumulator into memory location 0400. Describe what the Absolute Indexed mode instruction STA 0400,Y would do. _____

2. How many characters can the Apple computer display on each line? _____
_____ (decimal value)

3. If the value in the Y register is currently 26(HEX) as the following portion of
a machine language program is executed, tell which instruction will be executed following the BNE instruction.

```
778 C8    INY
779 C0    CPY 28
780 28
781 D0    BNE FB
782 FB
783 60    RTS
```

4. If the value in Y is 27(HEX) and that portion of the program shown in Exercise 3 is executed again, which instruction would be executed following the
BNE instruction?_____

5. If the ASCII code for the letter A is C1, what is the ASCII code for the
letter G? _____

6. Given that the accumulator holds the ASCII code for the letter A. If the
built-in subroutine at FDED is executed, an A is displayed on the screen.
If the built-in subroutine at FDDA is executed while the same value is in the
accumulator what will be displayed on the screen?_____

7. The ASCII code for the normal display of white on black for the letter C is
C3 HEX (11000011 binary). The code for an inverted (black on white)
letter C would be:
a. _____ HEX or _____ binary.
The code for a blinking C would be:
b. _____ HEX or _____ binary.

8. Explain what the following instructions cause when executed.
a. E0   CPX 06
   06

_____
_____

b. C0   CPY 1A
   1A

_____
_____

c. C9   CMP AF
   AF

_____
_____

ANSWERS TO EXERCISES

1. Store the value contained in the accumulator into memory location 0400 + the content of the Y register. (If Y=5, the location where stored would be 0400+5 or 0405.)

2. 40

3. 778 C8 INY (FB = -5 counting *from* 783)

4. 783 60 RTS (Y= 27+1 = 28. Therefore BNE is not taken)

5. C7

6. C1 (the ASCII code for A)

7. a. 03 HEX or 00000011 binary
   b. 43 HEX or 01000011 binary

8. a. The value in the X register is compared to 06.
   b. The value in the Y register is compared to 1A HEX.
   c. The value in the accumulator is compared to AF HEX.

Chapter 6

Apple Sounds

BOS

You learned how to plot points and draw lines in Chap. 4. In this chapter, we'll explore an Apple feature that will appeal to another of your senses.

Inside the Apple computer is a speaker that you can "tweak" or "strum" to your heart's content. A program can control the speaker so that it will make various sounds. The paper cone of the speaker can be in either of two positions, in or out.

Cone in   Cone out

Exaggerated Side View of the Speaker Cone

Each time a program references memory address C030 (HEX), the speaker changes from in to out or vice versa. This change causes the speaker to emit an audible click. By referencing address C030 frequently (which we call "tweaking" the speaker) a tone is produced. If you tweak it at different rates, different tones will be produced. You can also control the duration of the tweaking to produce tones of various lengths.

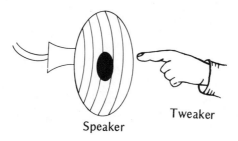

Tweaker

Speaker

With a little patience, you can produce a musical scale that you can use to play tunes. If you desire, you can draw graphics on the screen and accompany them with music of your own creation.

But, first let's take a look at the sound capabilities of the Apple with a simple tone-producing program. An addition is made to the BASIC Operating System to allow you to choose the pitch for each sound you wish to play. After the pitch is selected, the machine language program is called to play the note. Then control is returned to the Operating System so that you can select a new pitch. This process is continued until you decide to quit.

TONE EXPERIMENT PROGRAM

1. REMARK ** INITIALIZE AND CLEAR SCREEN **

768 A9 769 C8	LDA C8	Set the duration of the note
770 85 771 01	STA 0001	Store it in a special memory location
772 20 773 58 774 FC	JSR FC58	Clear the screen

2. REMARK ** SPEAKER TWEAKER **

* 775 AD 776 30 777 C0	LDA C030	Load accumulator from memory C030; this reference to C030 tweaks the speaker
* 778 88	DEY	Decrement the Y register
779 D0 780 04	BNE 04	Branch +4 (if not equal to zero) to 785
* 781 C6 782 01	DEC 0001	Decrement memory location 0001
783 F0 784 08	BEQ 08	Branch +8 (if equal to zero) to 793
* 785 CA	DEX	Decrement the X register
786 D0 787 F6	BNE F6	Branch -10 (if not equal to zero) to 778
* 788 A6 789 00	LDX 0000	Load X register from memory 0000

```
790 4C    JMP 0307        Jump back to 0307 hex (775 decimal)
791 07
792 03
```

3. REMARK ** BACK TO BASIC **

```
793 60    RTS             Return to Operating System
```

---

*New instructions or subroutines

MODIFICATION TO THE BASIC OPERATING SYSTEM

The Tone Experiment Program requires that we add some lines to the BASIC Operating System (Chap. 2) to choose the pitch of the notes to be played. We will also include a statement that will let us decide when to terminate the program. The added lines are:

720 INPUT "PITCH (1-255 OR 0 TO QUIT)?"; P

730 IF P=0 THEN 900   Input 1-255 for pitch or
                             a zero (0) to quit

740 POKE 0,P

810 GOTO 720

These new lines are inserted in the Operating System in the section that executes the machine language program as shown. Notice that the lines 720, 730, and 740 are inserted *before* subroutine S is called in line 800 of the Operating System. Line 810 is executed after the return from the subroutine so that a new pitch may be selected.

```
          700 REM * EXECUTE THE MACHINE LANGUAGE PROGRAM *
          710 PRINT "PRESS ANY KEY TO RUN": GET A$
added   ( 720 INPUT "PITCH (1-255 OR 0 TO QUIT)?"; P
        { 730 IF P=0 THEN 900
          ( 740 POKE 0,P
              .
              .
              .

              .
          800 CALL S
added   ( 810 GOTO 720
        (   .

              .
          900 END
```

127

Line 720 allows you to input the desired pitch. The value that you input should be in the range of 1 through 255 as indicated by the INPUT prompt in line 720. If you input a zero (0), line 730 will cause a branch to line 900, where the program will END.

DESCRIPTION OF THE TONE EXPERIMENT PROGRAM

Section 1 loads the value C8 HEX (200 decimal) into memory location 0001 using the zero page store instruction. This value is used to control the duration of the notes. The video screen is also cleared in this section to avoid visual distractions.

Section 2 is a loop that tweaks the speaker. It uses the X and Y registers to control the number of times the speaker is tweaked within the duration of the note.

Several new instructions appear in this section.

at 775:   AD LDA C030   Loads the accumulator from memory
           30   location C030, causing the speaker to
           C0   be tweaked. An Absolute Mode in-
                                         struction.

at 778   88   DEY   An Implied mode instruction that de-
                                           creases the value in the Y register by 1.

$$\boxed{Y = Y-1 \text{ in BASIC}}$$

at 781   C6   DEC 0001   A zero page instruction that decreases
           01   the value in memory location 0001 by
                                         1.

$$\boxed{MEM = MEM-1 \text{ in BASIC}}$$

at 785   CA   DEX   An Implied mode instruction that de-
                                           creases the value in the X register by 1.

$$\boxed{X = X-1 \text{ in BASIC}}$$

at 788   A6   LDX 0000   A zero page instruction that loads the
           00   X register from memory location 0000
                                         (pitch).

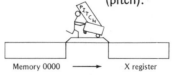

Memory 0000   ⟶   X register

Section 2 is composed of several values used as counting functions to determine how often and for how long the speaker is to be tweaked. If this section is not completely clear to you, don't worry about it — it works.

Here is a flowchart showing the operation of Section 2.

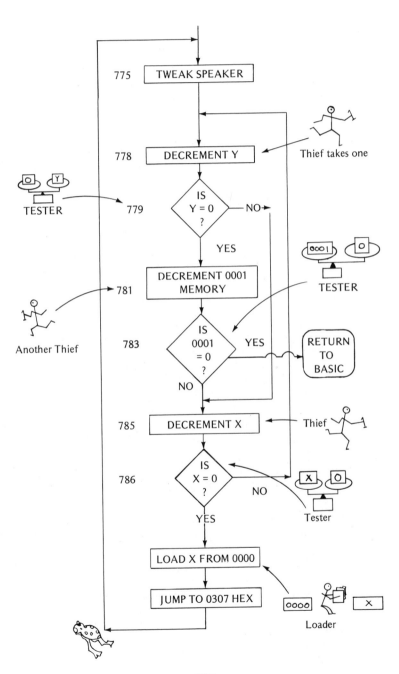

Section 3 returns control to the BASIC Operating System to allow a new note to be selected.

Thus we have created a loop from the operating system to the machine language program and back to the operating system.

Flow Diagram

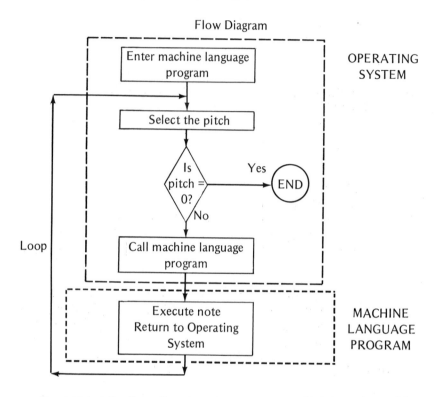

By studying the flow diagram, you can get some idea as to the usefulness of a machine language program used as a subroutine to a BASIC program. Although BASIC may be easier for you to program, there are times when some part of a program may require great speed. The computer can execute a machine language program much faster than it can BASIC (since BASIC must be interpreted). Therefore, a machine language subroutine can be used to execute that part of the program which must be done quickly. A return to BASIC is then used to perform the rest of the program, which does not require such quickness.

EXECUTING THE PROGRAM

After you have modified the operating system by adding lines 720, 730, 740, and 810 as suggested, enter the machine language program. It begins at memory location 768 and is 26 bytes long. When it has been entered and checked for errors, you will see the usual message:

```
IF ANY CHANGES—TYPE ADDRESS
IF NOT — TYPE 99
?■
```

After you type: 99 it will request the pitch.

```
IF ANY CHANGES—TYPE ADDRESS
IF NOT — TYPE 99
?99
PITCH (1-255 OR 0 TO QUIT)?■
```

Type in a value that is in the requested range (1-255) and press the return key. The screen will go blank, the note will be played, and you will get a request for another pitch.

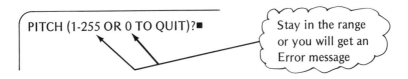

PITCH (1-255 OR 0 TO QUIT)?■   Stay in the range or you will get an Error message

Try the complete range of tones from very low (255) to very high (1). Don't try 0 unless you want to stop experimenting.

You will probably want to see if you can construct a musical scale. If you have a piano or other musical instrument handy, this should be fairly easy. If your musical ear is not too good, don't let it bother you. Experiment anyway. We do not profess to be experts in the field of music, but we couldn't resist trying to build a musical scale.

Our piano is upstairs in the living room, and our Apple is downstairs in the den. Therefore, we used a tape recorder to copy the notes of one octave from the piano. We than took the tape recorder downstairs to the computer and played back the results to construct the scale.

PIANO-TO-COMPUTER CONVERSION

Piano →	C	D	E	F	G	A	B	C
Pitch value →	133	127	121	116	111	107	103	100

Middle C ⎯⎯

Try keying in these values in quick succession to see how it sounds to you. We will be using these values (and others) in future programs. If some notes don't sound quite right to you, make the necessary changes to the offending values. Then play the scale up and down. Get in lots of practice so that you will be ready for the music of the future.

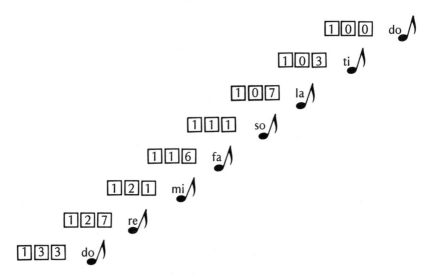

After practicing the scale, you can relax with the next program. It plays the scale for you. A loop is used to play all eight notes in an octave. Then control is returned to the operating system. Several useful new instructions are introduced.

Two of these new instructions are used to transfer data back and forth between the X register and the accumulator.

TXA is used to transfer the value in the X register to the accumulator. It is a single-byte instruction in the Implied mode. Its operation code is 8A.

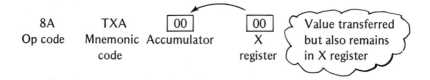

TAX is used to transfer data in the opposite direction, from the accumulator to the X register. It, too, is a single-byte instruction. Its operation code is AA.

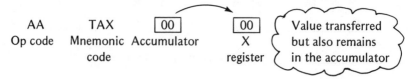

The other two new instructions involve the use of a special section of memory called a *stack*. You might think of the stack as a pile of papers. You add to the pile by placing a paper on the top of the pile. You remove papers from the pile, one at a time, from the top.

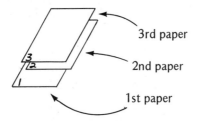

3rd paper

2nd paper

1st paper

In the sketch above, the third paper must be removed before the second. The second must be removed before the first. For you business-oriented people, it's like a Last In — First Out (LIFO) file.

To push a value on the stack, the PHA (PusH Accumulator on stack) instruction is used. Its operation code is 48.

The Call instruction of the BASIC Operating System automatically causes the correct address for the return from the machine language subroutine to be pushed on the stack.

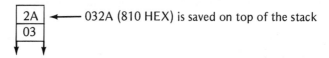

032A (810 HEX) is saved on top of the stack

If the accumulator holds a value of zero and the PHA instruction is executed, the value of zero is pushed on top of the stack, and the other two values are pushed down one spot.

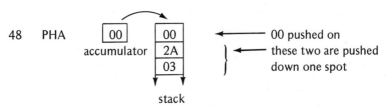

48   PHA   accumulator   stack

00 pushed on

these two are pushed down one spot

To pull a value off the stack, the PLA (PulL off stack to Accumulator) is used. Its operation code is 68.

Suppose the stack holds the previous values.

| 00 |
| 2A |
| 03 |

The PLA instruction is then executed:

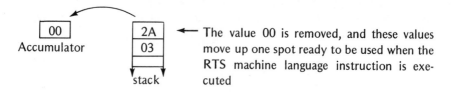

00
Accumulator

2A
03
stack

← The value 00 is removed, and these values move up one spot ready to be used when the RTS machine language instruction is executed

AUTOMATED SCALE PROGRAM
1. REMARK ** CLEAR SCREEN AND INITIALIZE **

768 20	JSR FC58	Clear screen
769 58		
770 FC		

| 771 A9 | LDA C8 | Set duration |
| 772 C8 | | |

| 773 85 | STA 0001 | |
| 774 01 | | |

| 775 A2 | LDX 00 | Set counter to zero |
| 776 00 | | |

Section 1 of the program clears the screen.

Screen cleared

The duration of C8 (190 decimal) is loaded into the accumulator and stored from there into memory location 0001. It will be used in the note-playing loop in Section 3.

0001 | C8 |

The X register, which is used to index the LDA instruction in Section 2, is set to zero.

X | 00 |

All instructions used in this section are familiar friends to you.

134

2. REMARK ** LOAD PITCH **

777	BD	LDA 032E,X	Indexed Absolute load,
778	2E		X register used to index
779	03		
780	85	STA 0000	Put in memory 0000
781	00		
782	E8	INX	Get ready for next note
*783	8A	TXA	Transfer value in X register to accumulator
*784	48	PHA	Save on the stack
785	E0	CPX 08	See if all notes have been played
786	08		
787	F0	BEQ 17	Branch (if they have) to end
788	17		

3. REMARK ** PLAY THE NOTE **

789	AD	LDA C030	Tweak speaker
790	30		
791	C0		Same loop as in the last program. This loop is nested inside the loop that gets
792	88	DEY	a new note.
793	D0	BNE 04	
794	04		
795	C6	DEC 0001	
796	01		
797	F0	BEQ 08	
798	08		
799	CA	DEX	
800	D0	BNE F6	
801	F6		
802	A6	LDX 0000	
803	00		
804	4C	JMP 0315	
805	15		
806	03		
*807	68	PLA	Pull saved value off stack
*808	AA	TAX	Transfer to X register
809	4C	JMP 0309	Go back for new note
810	09		
811	03		

Get new note loop Note loop

HOW SECTIONS 2 AND 3 WORK

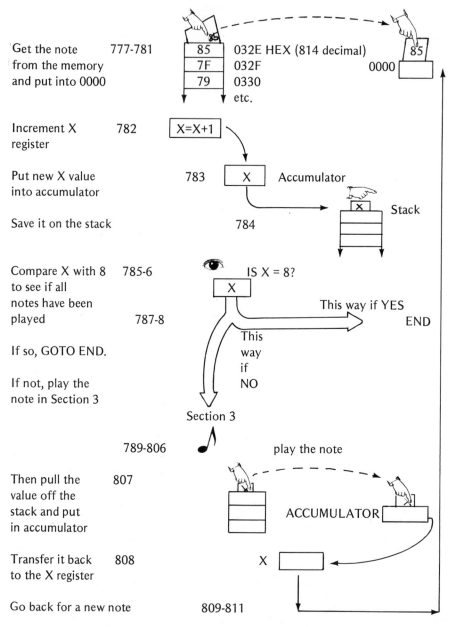

Get the note
from the memory
and put into 0000

777-781

85	032E HEX (814 decimal)
7F	032F
79	0330
	etc.

0000

Increment X
register

782

X=X+1

Put new X value
into accumulator

783

X   Accumulator

Save it on the stack

784

X   Stack

Compare X with 8
to see if all
notes have been
played

785-6

IS X = 8?

X

787-8

This way if YES

END

If so, GOTO END.

This
way
if
NO

If not, play the
note in Section 3

Section 3

789-806

play the note

Then pull the
value off the
stack and put
in accumulator

807

ACCUMULATOR

Transfer it back
to the X register

808

X

Go back for a new note

809-811

When the last note has been played, a branch is made to Section 4. The old value of X is pulled off the stack so that the correct return address will be available at the top of the stack. If we didn't remove the old X register value from the stack, the computer would think *that number* was part of the address to which it was to return.

The RTS instruction at 813 returns the computer to the BASIC Operating System.

Section 5 holds the data used for the notes.

4. REMARK ** BACK TO BASIC **

812 68   PLA   Pull value off stack

813 60   RTS

5. REMARK ** DATA LIST **

814 85
815 7F   ←—— Music scale in HEX
816 79
817 74
818 6F
819 6B
820 67
821 64

Just as a DATA list in BASIC is not executed, so the data list in the machine language program is not executed. It is there to provide the values accessed in Section 2 by the LDA instruction at location 777.

Enter the program as usual by means of the Operating System. The program begins at memory location 768 and is 54 bytes long. Check for any errors. When all is ready, run the program. Although you will see nothing on the screen, an octave of notes is played from low note to high note. The computer then obediently returns to the Operating System. If you want to repeat the scale, type:

GOTO 700 and press the RETURN key.

The display will show:

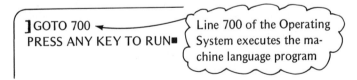

```
]GOTO 700 ←——————      Line 700 of the Operating
PRESS ANY KEY TO RUN■    System executes the ma-
                         chine language program
```

When you press a key, the octave will be repeated.

You could add more data to Section 5 so that the notes would go up and then back down the scale. You would also have to change the value at 786 in the program to give the total number of notes in the new data list.

That wraps up this chapter. In the next chapter, we'll add graphics to our sounds and learn to play some notes directly from the keyboard.

SUMMARY

One new built-in subroutine and seven new machine language instructions were added to your programming capabilities in this chapter. The use of sound has added a new dimension to your programming power. You can now use the speaker to go along with the keyboard and video display.

You learned to move data back and forth between the accumulator and the X register. You also learned to use the stack to save information for later retrieval.

Here is a summary of the new subroutine and the new instructions introduced in this chapter.

New Subroutine

1. LDA C030 was used to toggle the speaker. When this is done rapidly, the speaker produces a tone. The pitch of the tone as well as its duration can be controlled by the program.

   Example: AD   OP code for Load Accumulator
   30   least significant byte of address
   C0   most significant byte of address

New Instructions

1. DEC (DECrement memory) — used in the Zero Page mode to decrement (decrease by one) the value held in the specified memory location of zero page memory.

   Example: C6   OP code for DEC
   01   least significant byte of memory location 0001 (the most significant byte is implied to be 00)

2. DEX (DEcrement X register) — used in the Implied mode to decrease the value held in the X register by one.

   Example: CA   OP code for DEX

3. LDX (LoaD the X register) — used in the Zero Page mode to load the X register with the value held in the specified memory location of zero page memory

   Example: A6   OP code for LDX
   00   least significant byte of memory location 0000 (most significant byte is implied as 00)

4. PHA (PusH Accumulator on stack) — used to push the value held in the accumulator on the top of the stack. This value is later retrieved for further use. Implied mode.

   Example: 48   OP code for PHA

5. PLA (PulL from stack to Accumulator) — used to retrieve a value previously pushed on the stack. The value is placed in the accumulator for use. Implied mode.

   Example: 68   OP code for PLA

6. TAX (Transfer data from Accumulator to X register) — used to transfer (or copy) data from the accumulator to the X register. Implied mode.

   Example: AA   OP code for TAX

7. TXA (Transfer data from the X register to the Accumulator) — used to transfer (or copy) data from the X register to the accumulator. Implied mode.

   Example: 8A   OP code for TXA

TABLE OF SUBROUTINES USED SO FAR

Function	Location in Memory
Toggle the speaker	C030
Clear the screen	FC58
Set graphics mode	FB40
Plot a point	F800
Draw a horizontal line	F819
Draw a vertical line	F828
Get a keystroke	FD35
Print character in accumulator	FDED
Print accumulator content as hex digits	FDDA

TABLE OF MACHINE LANGUAGE INSTRUCTIONS

Mnemonic Code	Addressing Mode	Op Code	Bytes Used	Function
ASL	Accumulator	0A	1	Shift bits left
BEQ	Relative	F0	2	Branch if equal
BNE	Relative	D0	2	Branch if not equal
CMP	Immediate	C9	2	Compare accumulator
CPX	Immediate	E0	2	Compare X register
CPY	Immediate	C0	2	Compare Y register
*DEC	Zero Page	C6	2	Decrement memory
*DEX	Implied	CA	1	Decrement X register
INX	Implied	E8	1	Increment X register
INY	Implied	C8	1	Increment Y register

139

Mnemonic Code	Addressing Mode	Op Code	Bytes Used	Function
JMP	Absolute	4C	3	Jump to memory
JSR	Absolute	20	3	Jump to subroutine
LDA	Immediate	A9	2	Load accumulator
LDA	Abs. Indexed	BD	3	Load accumulator
LDX	Immediate	A2	2	Load X register
*LDX	Zero Page	A6	2	Load X register
LDY	Immediate	A0	2	Load Y register
NOP	Implied	EA	1	No operation
*PHA	Implied	48	1	Push accumulator on stack
*PLA	Implied	68	1	Pull stack to accumulator
RST	Implied	60	1	Return from subroutine
STA	Zero Page	85	2	Store accumulator
STA	Absolute	8D	3	Store accumulator
STA	Abs. Indexed	99	3	Store accumulator
*TAX	Implied	AA	1	Transfer Acc. to X register
*TXA	Implied	8A	1	Transfer X register to Acc.

*Instructions introduced in this chapter

EXERCISES

1. Explain the result of executing each of the following machine language instructions.

   a. CA   DEX

   _____

   b. C6   DEC 0001
      01

   _____

   c. A6   LDX 0000
      00

   _____

2. What happens if you input a 0 (zero) for the pitch in the Tone Experiment Program?

   _____

3. A low value for pitch in the Tone Experiment Program produces a _____
                                                                    (low, high)

   tone. A high value produces a _____ tone.
                                 (low, high)

4. Describe the operation caused by these instructions:

   a. 8A   TAX

   _____

   b. AA   TXA

   _____

5. The stack looks like this ⟶

32
43

   The accumulator holds the value [C1].
   The instruction PHA is then executed. Show how the stack looks following
   that execution.

6. If the stack looks like this ⟶

17
BD
03

   and the instruction PLA is executed, show the value in the accumulator and
   the contents of the top of the stack.

   Accumulator

   Stack

ANSWERS TO EXERCISES

1. a. Decrease the value in the X register by 1.
   b. Decrease the value in memory location 0001 by 1.
   c. Load the X register from memory location 0000.

2. Execution of the machine language program is stopped. Control is returned
   to the Operating System.

3. high, low

4. a. TXA copies data from the X register into the accumulator.
   b. TAX copies data from the accumulator into the X register.

5.
   | C1 | ◄C1 on top
   |----|
   | 32 |
   | 43 | Everything else pushed down one

   Stack

6. | 17 | | BD | 17 has been pulled off.
     |----| |----| Everything else moves up one.
     Accumulator | 03 |

                   Stack

141

Chapter 7

More Sounds and Graphics

$$\boxed{\text{BOS}}$$

You learned how to tweak the Apple's speaker in Chap. 6 in order to produce sounds. Sound is fine, but it is not very satisfying by itself. In this chapter, we'll combine some sounds with graphics to stimulate two of our senses at the same time.

COMBINING THE SPEAKER AND VIDEO DISPLAY

We'll build a new program using the graphics techniques learned in Chap. 4 with the Automated Scale Program used in Chap. 6. The length of the program will increase, and some modification will be made to make the sound and graphics fit together in a smooth, coordinated manner.

Only one new instruction will be necessary. That instruction, LDY, loads the Y register from a memory location program indexed by the X register. Remember, the point-plotting program uses the Y register to hold the column for plotting a point. These values are held in a data list starting at memory location 0834.

Before looking at the program, study the flow diagram that follows. The diagram is laid out in blocks that correspond to individual sections of the program.

You have seen every instruction in Section 1 before. The duration of the notes is loaded in the accumulator (by the LDA instruction at 768). The screen is cleared (by the subroutine at FC58). The X register, which is used as a counter, is set to zero (by the LDX instruction at 775). The low resolution Graphics mode is set (by the subroutine at FB40). The color to be used for plotting the notes is set to white (by the LDA instruction at 780 and the STA instruction at 782).

Flow Diagram for Scale with Notes Program

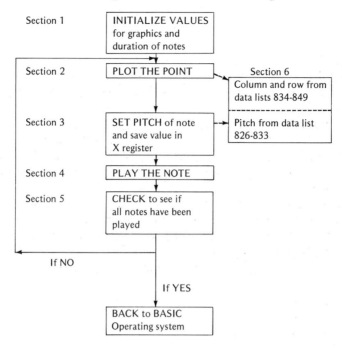

Section 1 — INITIALIZE VALUES for graphics and duration of notes

Section 2 — PLOT THE POINT

Section 6 — Column and row from data lists 834-849

Section 3 — SET PITCH of note and save value in X register

Pitch from data list 826-833

Section 4 — PLAY THE NOTE

Section 5 — CHECK to see if all notes have been played

If NO

If YES

BACK to BASIC Operating system

SCALE WITH NOTES PROGRAM

1. REMARK ** INITIALIZE **

768 A9	LDA C8	Set duration
769 C8		
770 20	JSR FC58	Clear screen
771 58		
772 FC		
775 A2	LDX 00	Set counter to zero
776 00		
777 20	JSR FB40	Set Graphics mode
778 40		
779 FB		
780 A9	LDA 0F	Set color to white
781 0F		
782 85	STA 0030	Store it in memory
783 30		

Section 2 loads the column where the point is to be plotted into the Y register and the row where the point is to be plotted into the accumulator. A subroutine is then called to plot the point. The column and row values are stored in data tables at the end of the program. The X register is used as a pointer to access this data.

2. REMARK ** PLOT THE POINT **

784 BC	LDY 0342,X	Load Y register from 0342 indexed by
785 42		value in X register
786 03		

787 BD	LDA 034A,X	Load accumulator for 034A indexed
788 4A		by value in X register
789 03		

790 20	JSR F800	Call the point-plotting subroutine
791 00		built-in
792 F8		

In Section 3, the value for the pitch of the note is loaded into the accumulator from the data table and is then placed in memory location 0000, where it will be needed when the note is played. The value in the X register is placed in the accumulator and then pushed onto the stack for safekeeping. This has to be done, as the X register is used in Section 4 for another purpose. The value (saved on the stack) will be retrieved later when needed.

3. REMARK ** GET READY FOR NOTE **

793 BD	LDA 033A,X	Load the pitch value from 033A in-
794 3A		dexed by the value in X register
795 03		

| 796 85 | STA 0000 | Store in memory 0000 |
| 797 00 | | |

798 8A	TXA	Put the value in the X register into
		accumulator
799 48	PHA	Push on the stack to save it

Section 4 plays the note. It is the same as that used in Section 3 of the Automated Scale Program in Chap. 6.

4. REMARK ** PLAY THE NOTE **

800 AD	LDA C030	Tweak the speaker
801 30		
802 C0		

803	88	DEY	Same as previous sound programs
804	D0	BNE 04	
805	04		
806	C6	DEC 0001	
807	01		
808	F0	BEQ 08	
809	08		
810	CA	DEX	
811	D0	BNE F6 (-10)	
812	F6		
813	A6	LDX 0000	
814	00		
815	4C	JUMP 0320	
816	20		
817	03		

In Section 5, the computer checks to see if all of the notes of the scale have been played. If they have not, the program returns to Section 2 where a new note is plotted and played. If all notes have been played, control is returned to the BASIC Operating System. The old value of the X register is pulled off the stack and placed back in the X register. This value is then increased by one. Then the new value is compared to 8 (the number of notes desired).

5. REMARK ** CHECK FOR ALL NOTES PLAYED **

818	68	PLA	Pull old X value from stack
819	AA	TAX	Transfer it into X register
820	E8	INX	Increase count by one
821	E0	CPX 08	Compare notes played with 8
822	08		
823	D0	BNE D7	If not, go back to get values for a new
824	D7		note to plot and play at 784
825	60	RTS	If done, go back to monitor

The data tables for the column and row used for plotting the notes and the pitch values of the notes make up Section 6.

6. REMARK ** DATA LIST **

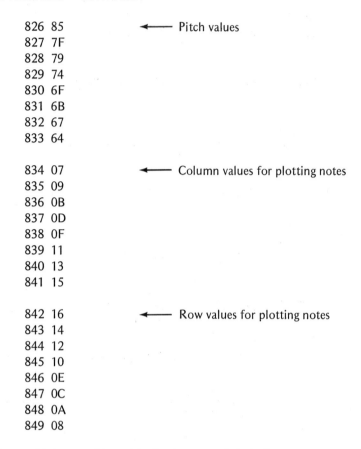

826	85	←——— Pitch values
827	7F	
828	79	
829	74	
830	6F	
831	6B	
832	67	
833	64	
834	07	←——— Column values for plotting notes
835	09	
836	0B	
837	0D	
838	0F	
839	11	
840	13	
841	15	
842	16	←——— Row values for plotting notes
843	14	
844	12	
845	10	
846	0E	
847	0C	
848	0A	
849	08	

By combining graphics with the Automated Scale Program, you are able to display each note as it is played.

Section 1 sets the note duration, clears the screen, and sets the X register to zero so that data may be accessed from various memory locations. The Graphics mode is then set, and the color is selected (you may change this if you like at location 781).

Section 2 loads the Y register with the column and the accumulator with the row at which the note will be plotted. Both instructions use the X register as an index to select the correct values from a table located in memory beginning at the specified locations. The point-plotting routine at F800 is then "called" to plot the point.

Section 3 selects the pitch by the LDA and STA instructions at 793 and 796. It also performs some housekeeping chores at 798-799 to save the index value on the stack.

Section 4 is an old friend that plays the note.

Section 5 restores the index value and compares it to 8 to see whether all the notes have been played. If they have not, the branch instruction at 823 causes a return to 784 to plot and play a new note. If all eight notes have been played, a return is made to the BASIC Operating System.

Section 6 provides the data in three blocks. The first block (826-833) provides pitch values for playing the 8 notes. The second block (834-841) provides values for the column in which each of the 8 notes is to be plotted. The third block (842-849) provides values for the row in which the notes are to be plotted.

ENTERING AND RUNNING THE PROGRAM

It's now time to enter the program. Once again, it begins at memory location 768. It is a long program, 82 bytes.

After you have entered it, be sure to check for errors. When it is error free, run the program.

First one note appears, and middle C is heard from the speaker.

Then a second note appears, and the second tone is heard.

This continues until all 8 notes have been displayed and played.

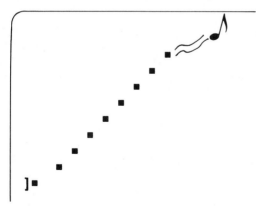

The program then returns to the BASIC Operating System. If you want to see and hear the results again, type: GOTO 700 and press RETURN. The display shows:

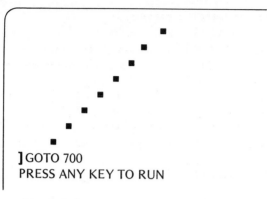

```
]GOTO 700
PRESS ANY KEY TO RUN
```

Press any key, and the process will repeat.

By now, you are thinking of many variations that could be made. You could plot each note in a different color. You could put in a short melody instead of the scale. You could make each note disappear after it has been played. There are many variations you can try. We encourage you to try all of these and any others that you may think of. You now have the basis for a color organ that can play music as well as displaying colors on the screen. You don't have to stick to plotting a single point. You may want to fill the screen with color or project random color patterns as the notes are played.

When you have experimented with the above program for some time, you may desire a change of pace. Wouldn't it be nice to be able to play notes that you select from the keyboard? Then you would be able to compose and play your own music. Read on, and we will show you a program that allows you to "tickle the ebonies" on the keyboard to play your own music.

USING THE KEYBOARD TO PLAY THE NOTES

You have used a program where you input the note that you wanted played. You also had a program where the computer played the musical scale for you. The next program combines the two techniques so that you can key in continuous notes. It restricts you to one octave to keep things simple. The values for each note are stored in a data list, and by striking one of the numeric keys 1, 2, 3, 4, 5, 6, 7, or 8, the computer will select the corresponding note. You do not even have to press the RETURN key. Remember, our crude scale is supposed to contain the octave starting with middle C. The keystrokes and corresponding notes are shown below.

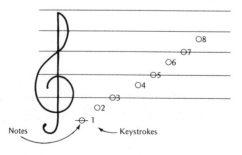

PLAY YOUR OWN TUNE PROGRAM

1. REMARK ** CLEAR THE SCREEN **

768	20	JSR FC58	Built-in routine to clear screen
769	58		
770	FC		

2. REMARK ** GET A KEYSTROKE **

771	20	JSR FD35	Built-in routine to read keyboard
772	35		
773	FD		

774	C9	CMP B0	Is key too low?
775	B0		

*776	30	BMI F9	If so, go back and look again
777	F9		(−7 steps)

778	F0	BEQ 25	If it is a zero, go back to BASIC
779	25		

780	C9	CMP B9	Is key too high?
781	B9		

*782	10	BPL F3	If so, go back and look again
783	F3		(−13 steps)

3. REMARK ** CONVERT ASCII KEYSTROKE — USE TO INDEX **

*784	29	AND OF	Strip off upper 4 bits of ASCII code
785	0F		

786	AA	TAX	Transfer result to X register to use as an index

4. REMARK ** GET DURATION AND PITCH **

787	A9	LDA 60	Load duration
788	60		

789	85	STA 0001	Store it
790	01		

791	BD	LDA 0332,X	Load accumulator from data list
792	32		
793	03		

794	85	STA 0000	Store it
795	00		

5. REMARK ** PLAY THE NOTE **

```
796 AD    LDA C030       Tweak speaker
797 30
798 C0

799 88    DEY

800 D0    BNE 04
801 04

802 C6    DEC 0001
803 01

804 F0    BEQ 08
805 08

806 CA    DEX

807 D0    BNE F6
808 F6

809 A6    LDX 0000
810 00

811 4C    JMP 031C
812 1C
813 03
```

6. REMARK ** GET A NEW NOTE OR END **

```
814 4C    JMP 0303       Get a new note
815 03
816 03

817 60    RTS            Back to BASIC Operating System
```

7. REMARK ** DATA LIST **

```
*818 EA   NOP
 819 85                  ←— Lowest note in octave
 820 7F
 821 79
 822 74
 823 6F
 824 6B
 825 67
 826 64                  ←— Highest note in octave
```

*New instruction

150

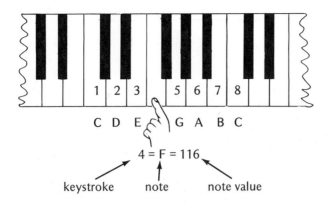

keystroke   note   note value

DESCRIPTION OF THE PROGRAM

Section 1 clears the screen. Section 2 uses the Apple machine language monitor's built-in subroutine to look for a keystroke. When found, the ASCII code for the character of that key is placed in the accumulator. The ASCII codes for the ten symbols used are:

Digits	ASCII Codes (in HEX)
0	B0
1	B1
2	B2
3	B3
4	B4
5	B5
6	B6
7	B7
8	B8
9	B9

After a keystroke has been made, the value in the accumulator is compared to B0 and B9 (the correct range for the digits). If the ASCII code is below B0 or above B9, the keystroke will not be accepted. The program will not play a note, but will return to read another keystroke. This is accomplished by the BMI (Branch if MInus) and the BPL (Branch if PLus) instructions. These two new instructions are similar to the BNE (Branch if Not Equal) and BEQ (Branch if EQual) instructions that you have used before.

BMI (BRANCH ON RESULT MINUS)

Addressing Mode	Mnemonic Code	OP Code
Relative	BMI	30

As used in the Program:

774 C9   Compare ASCII code for keystroke to B0
775 B0

776 30   Branch on result minus back 7 steps (F9=-7)
777 F9

If the ASCII code of the keystroke is less than B0, the Branch on Minus instruction sends the program execution back to 771 to read the keyboard again. Thus, any keystroke whose ASCII code is less than B0 *will not be accepted.*

BPL (BRANCH ON RESULT PLUS)

Addressing Mode	Mnemonic Code	OP Code
Relative	BPL	10

As used in the program:

780 C9   Compare ASCII code for keystroke to B9
781 B9

782 10   Branch on result plus back 13 steps (F3=-13)
783 F3

If the ASCII code of the keystroke is greater than B8 (zero is considered positive by this instruction), the Branch on Plus instruction sends the program execution back to 771 to read the keystroke again. Thus, any keystroke whose ASCII code is greater than B8 *will not be accepted.*

If the zero key is struck, a branch is taken to the RTS instruction which returns you to the Operating System. It is used to stop the program after you have decided to discontinue playing notes.

Section 3 converts the ASCII value to a decimal digit so that it can be used in the X register as an index to access the correct note from the data list. By looking at the above ASCII code table for the decimal digits, you can see a similarity between the digit and its ASCII code. A new instruction, AND, is used to "strip" the upper four bits from the ASCII code. In other words, the B is removed from the values B0 through B9, leaving only the decimal digit on the right side of the two-digit HEX value.

AND (AND WITH ACCUMULATOR)

Addressing Mode	Mnemonic Code	OP Code
Immediate	AND	29

152

As used in this program:

ASCII code for the keystroke is in the accumulator.

784 29   AND the value in the accumulator
785 0F   with the HEX value 0F

To show an example, we will look at the ASCII code in its binary form. The AND instruction operates on the ASCII code in the accumulator and the value immediately following the AND instruction. It compares corresponding bits of the two values. If a particular bit is a one (1) for both values, the corresponding bit of the result will be a one. If the bit of either value (or both) is a zero, the corresponding bit of the result will be a zero.

Examples:

AND accumulator with the value 0F

The keystroke is a 5.

ASCII code is B5 =   1 0 1 1 0 1 0 1 in binary

AND with value 0F = 0 0 0 0 1 1 1 1 in binary
_____

Result left in   0 0 0 0 0 1 0 1 Ones only in the bits that
accumulator   have a 1 in B5 AND 0F

Result = 05 (the keystroke)

AND accumulator with the value 0F

The keystroke is a 9.

ASCII code is B9 = 1 0 1 1 1 0 0 1 in binary

AND with 0F   = 0 0 0 0 1 1 1 1 in binary
_____

Result left in   0 0 0 0 1 0 0 1 Ones only if B9 AND 0F both
accumulator   contain ones

Reslut = 09 (the keystroke)

Because of the way the AND is used in this program (AND 0F), the result will always throw away the left four bits (Most Significant Bits) of the value in the accumulator and keep the right four bits (Least Significant Bits) the same. The program then places this result in the X register (instruction TAX at 786) so that it can be used to index the LDA command in Section 4 to load the correct pitch for a given keystroke from memory.

The sequence resulting from a keystroke is shown below:

If you
type this,   this note will be played.

Key Stroke	ASCII Code	After AND	Memory accessed by LDA 0332,X	Memory HEX	Address Decimal	Memory Content (Note Value)
1	B1	01	0332+1 ➤	0333	819	85
2	B2	02	0332+2 ➤	0334	820	7F
3	B3	03	0332+3 ➤	0335	821	79
4	B4	04	0332+4 ➤	0336	822	74
5	B5	05	0332+5 ➤	0337	823	6F
6	B6	06	0332+6 ➤	0338	824	6B
7	B7	07	0332+7 ➤	0339	825	67
8	B8	08	0332+8 ➤	033A	826	64

This value put in X register
for this index

Once again, we see that the action takes place in the accumulator (caused by the AND instruction), and the result is then transferred to the location (X register in this case) where it will be used.

Section 4 loads the note duration (60 HEX) into memory location 0001. Then the pitch value is loaded from memory location 0332 + the value in the X register. This is stored in memory location 0000. Because of the AND instruction used in Section 3, the note will be loaded from 0332 + whatever key was struck (1, 2, 3, 4, 5, 6, 7, or 8).

Section 5 should be very familiar to you by now. It plays the note using the values for pitch and duration that were stored in Section 4.

Section 6 provides a jump instruction to return for another note. It also has an RTS instruction following the jump. The RTS instruction will only be reached from the branch in Section 2 (778 BEQ) resulting from the keystroke of zero (0). RTS, of course, returns you to the Operating System as in previous programs.

Section 7 is the data list from which the note selections are made. A new instruction (NOP) that does nothing is used at the beginning of the data list. This instruction (No OPeration) is used as a buffer to separate the program from the data list. The instruction that loads from the data list (BD at location 791) points to the value EA (No OPeration), but it is indexed by the X register which is always equal to or greater than one. Therefore, the NOP instruction (EA) is never executed. NOP instructions are quite often used to "save a place" for instructions that may be added later to modify a program. If we wanted to insert a note lower than middle C, we could use the memory occupied by the NOP instruction. The program could then be modified to use the keystroke zero to access this new note.

The data list pointer works like this:

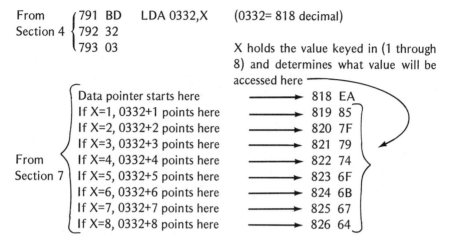

From
Section 4 { 791 BD   LDA 0332,X   (0332= 818 decimal)
792 32
793 03

X holds the value keyed in (1 through 8) and determines what value will be accessed here

Data pointer starts here   ⟶ 818 EA
If X=1, 0332+1 points here   ⟶ 819 85
If X=2, 0332+2 points here   ⟶ 820 7F
If X=3, 0332+3 points here   ⟶ 821 79
From   If X=4, 0332+4 points here ⟶ 822 74
Section 7 If X=5, 0332+5 points here ⟶ 823 6F
If X=6, 0332+6 points here   ⟶ 824 6B
If X=7, 0332+7 points here   ⟶ 825 67
If X=8, 0332+8 points here   ⟶ 826 64

ENTERING AND RUNNING THE PROGRAM

Enter the program that begins at memory location 768 decimal. It is 59 bytes long. Check your entries for errors, correct any errors, and run the program.

The screen will go blank. Then the blinking cursor will appear in the upper left corner.

It's time now for you to enter notes. Pressing any of the number keys 1 through 8 will cause a note to be played. After each note, the blinking cursor flashes in the upper left corner. The computer is waiting for your next entry. Play around with the scale until you have a good feel for the computer "organ." Then call in your friends and show off your musical talent.

There are many modifications that you can make to this program. By increasing the size of the data list, you can increase the number of notes available to you. You might want to add some color graphics to this program in order to have a color organ.

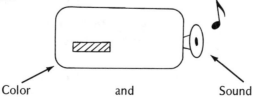

Color   and   Sound

SUMMARY

Two long programs were used in this chapter to demonstrate the use of color and sound. You learned to coordinate the use of the speaker, the video display, and the keyboard. Five additional instructions were introduced. The list of instructions that you have used has grown large enough to construct more complex and useful programs.

You learned more about the capabilities of the Y register through two new instructions. Two new branch instructions were introduced, and you used the logic instruction (AND) to convert an ASCII code into its equivalent decimal digit.

Here is a summary of the new instructions introduced in this chapter.

1. AND (AND with accumulator) — used in the Immediate mode to logically AND the value following the instruction with the value in the accumulator. The result contains 1's in the bits where both values have ones. Otherwise, zeros.

   Example: 29   OP code for AND
                  0F   HEX value to be ANDed

2. BMI (Branch on MInus) — used in the Immediate mode to branch when a given condition is negative. The data following the instruction tells which direction and how far to branch from the existing position of the program counter.

   Example: 30   OP code for BMI
                  F9   data says to go back 7 steps (F9 = -7)

3. BPL (Branch on PLus) — used in the Immediate mode to branch when a given condition is positive or zero. The data following the instruction tells which direction and how far to branch from the existing position of the program counter.

   Example: 10   OP code for BPL
                  F3   data says go back 13 steps (F3 = -13)

4. DEY (DEcrement Y register) — used in the Implied mode to decrease the value held in the Y register by one.

   Example: 88   OP code for DEY

5. LDY (LoaD Y register) — used in the Absolute Indexed mode to load the Y register from a memory location indexed by the value in the X register.

   Example: BC   OP code for LDY (Absolute Indexed)
                  42   least significant byte of memory location
                  03   most significant byte of memory location

   The value in the X register is added on to this "base" address to get the true address

TABLE OF MACHINE LANGUAGE INSTRUCTIONS USED

Mnemonic Code	Addressing Mode	Op Code	Bytes Used	Function
*AND	Immediate	29	2	AND bits with accumulator
ASL	Accumulator	0A	1	Shift bits left
BEQ	Relative	F0	2	Branch if equal
*BMI	Relative	30	2	Branch if minus
BNE	Relative	D0	2	Branch if not equal
*BPL	Relative	10	2	Branch if plus
CMP	Immediate	C9	2	Compare accumulator
CPX	Immediate	E0	2	Compare X register
CPY	Immediate	C0	2	Compare Y register
DEC	Zero Page	C6	2	Decrement memory
DEX	Implied	CA	1	Decrement X register
*DEY	Implied	88	1	Decrement Y register
INX	Implied	E8	1	Increment X register
INY	Implied	C8	1	Increment Y register
JMP	Absolute	4C	3	Jump to memory
JSR	Absolute	20	3	Jump to subroutine
LDA	Immediate	A9	2	Load accumulator
LDA	Abs. Indexed	BD	3	Load accumulator
LDX	Immediate	A2	2	Load X register
LDX	Zero Page	A6	2	Load X register
LDY	Immediate	A0	2	Load Y register
*LDY	Abs. Indexed	BC	3	Load Y register
NOP	Implied	EA	1	No operation
PHA	Implied	48	1	Push accumulator on stack
PLA	Implied	68	1	Pull from stack to accumulator
RST	Implied	60	1	Return from subroutine
STA	Zero Page	85	2	Store accumulator
STA	Absolute	8D	3	Store accumulator
STA	Abs. Indexed	99	3	Store accumulator
TAX	Implied	AA	1	Transfer accumulator to X register
TXA	Implied	8A	1	Transfer X register to accumulator

*Instructions introduced in this chapter

TABLE OF SUBROUTINES USED SO FAR

Function	Location in Memory
Toggle the speaker	C030
Clear the screen	FC58
Set graphics mode	FB40
Plot a point	F800
Draw a horizontal line	F819
Draw a vertical line	F828
Get a keystroke	FD35
Print character in accumulator	FDED
Print accumulator content as hex digits	FDDA

EXERCISES

1. Explain the result of executing the following machine language instructions.
   a. BC   LDY 0342,X
      42
      03

   _____

   _____

   b. 88   DEY

   _____

2. A Compare X with 08 (CPX 08) instruction is used at 821 and 822 of the Scale with Notes Program. Which of the following operations does it perform?
   a. 08 − value in X register
   b. value in X register − 08

   _____

3. A subroutine at memory address FD35 is used to read the keyboard in the Play Your Own Tune Program. When you press a key in this program to play a note, is it necessary to press the RETURN key following the keystroke?

   _____

4. If the following HEX values are ANDed with 0F, what are the results?
   a. B7 _____ b. B4 _____ c. E5 _____

5. What would be the result of 3F (HEX) ANDed with 63 (HEX)?

   _____

6. In the Play Your Own Tune Program, which of the following ASCII values will cause a note to be played?
   a. A9   b. B3   c. BA   d. B0

   _____

158

ANSWERS TO EXERCISES

1. a. The Y register is loaded from the memory location whose address is 0342 + the value in the X register.

   b. The value in the Y register is decreased (decremented) by one.

2. b. Value in X register — 08

3. No

4. a. 07 (or 7)

   b. 04 (or 4)

   c. 05 (or 5)

5. 23   3F = 0011 1111
            63 = 0110 0011
            ─────────────
         AND = 0010 0011
                   ⌣   ⌣
                   2   3

6. b. (B3 only) (A9 is too low—not accepted, BA is too high—not accepted, B0 will return the machine language program to the BASIC Operating System)

Chapter 8

The Apple System Monitor

SM

In the previous chapters you have been using BASIC to write and execute machine language programs. This convention has allowed you to make use of your knowledge of BASIC as you became acquainted with the language of the computer. It's time now to discard the BASIC Operating System as a tool. You've outgrown your need for it.

The Apple computer has a System Monitor way up high in its memory (see memory maps in Chap. 2).

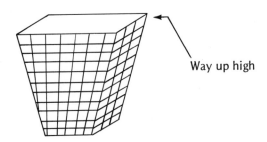

Way up high

The monitor controls *all* programs, and *all* programs use it. Maybe you didn't realize it, but you have been using it all through this book. From here on, you'll communicate with it directly.

You can use the monitor to look directly into memory locations, change the contents of memory, and even write machine language programs to be executed directly by the 6502 microprocessor.

Remember, the computer understands only binary-coded instructions. The System Monitor will accept these instructions in hexadecimal form from the keyboard. You may want to return to Chap. 3 for a brief review of instruction code format.

Let's go back to one of your first machine language programs described in Chap. 3. It loaded the accumulator with the HEX value 13 and stored the value in memory location 0325 (HEX). The program was stored in memory as:

| Address | | Op | |
Decimal	HEX	Code	Remarks
768	0300	A9	LDA with
769	0301	13	data
770	0302	8D	STA in memory
771	0303	25	
772	0304	03	0325
773	0305	60	RTS

That program was called from our BASIC Operating System, so the last instruction was RTS (ReTurn from Subroutine). The Apple System Monitor treats machine language programs as subroutines. Therefore, RTS can also be used as the last instruction in its machine language programs. The program above can be entered directly using the System Monitor.

We'll now show you how to use the monitor so that you can see how easy it is to load, examine, and execute a machine language program directly.

Look at your User's Manual to see how to enter the System Monitor for your Apple version. For ours, all we have to do is press the RESET key. Another way would be to turn the computer off and then back on. When first turned on, our version always comes up in the monitor. If you have an Apple II Plus System with Autostart ROM, you enter the System Monitor by executing the BASIC statement:

CALL 65385
or
CALL -151

When you are in the System Monitor, the screen will show the asterisk as a prompt signal.

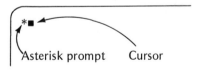

Asterisk prompt   Cursor

To enter the program, first type the starting address in HEX: 300

*300■

Follow this with a colon, which tells the monitor that you want to alter the contents of memory. Follow the colon by each two-digit HEX code for the instructions or data (only one digit is needed if the lead digit is a zero). Separate each code by a blank space. The program can be typed on one complete line as follows:

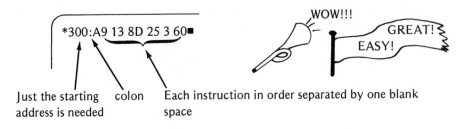

Just the starting
address is needed

colon

Each instruction in order separated by one blank
space

Just as in a BASIC program, the RETURN key is pressed at the end of each complete entry. When the RETURN key is pres ˋ l at the end of the above line, you see:

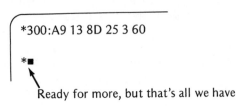

*300:A9 13 8D 25 3 60

*■

Ready for more, but that's all we have

That's all there is to it. If you are not confident that the program has been entered correctly, you can examine memory to verify what you just entered. To show what is in a given block of successive memory locations, type in the starting address of the block and the ending address of the block separated by a period.

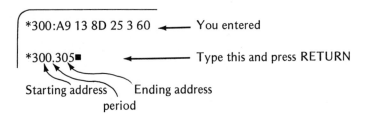

*300:A9 13 8D 25 3 60 ◄——— You entered

*300.305■ ◄————————— Type this and press RETURN

Starting address   Ending address
                period

Then you see:

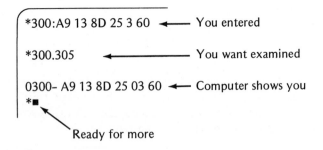

*300:A9 13 8D 25 3 60 ◄——— You entered

*300.305 ◄——————— You want examined

0300- A9 13 8D 25 03 60 ◄— Computer shows you
*■

Ready for more

Yes, the program is there. Now, how easy is it to make the program run? Very easy! Just type: 300G

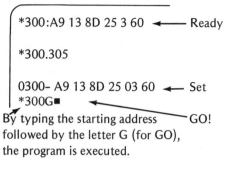

```
*300:A9 13 8D 25 3 60   ◄─── Ready

*300.305

0300- A9 13 8D 25 03 60   ◄─ Set
*300G■                   ◄
```

By typing the starting address ──GO!
followed by the letter G (for GO),
the program is executed.

```
*300:A9 13 8D 25 3 60

*300.305

0300- A9 13 8D 25 03 60
*300G

*■   ◄───
```
Well, what happened? Oh, we didn't ask the computer to display anything, so it just did its job and stored the value 13 in memory location 0325. How can we check it?

To find out if the 13 was really moved to memory location 0325, we must examine that memory location. To look at just one memory location, merely type the address of the location and press the RETURN key.

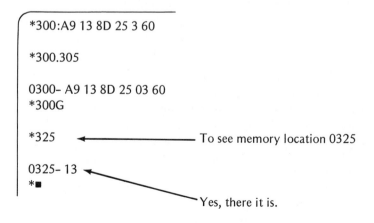

```
*300:A9 13 8D 25 3 60

*300.305

0300- A9 13 8D 25 03 60
*300G

*325   ◄─────────────── To see memory location 0325

0325- 13  ◄
*■
```
─Yes, there it is.

Well, you know how to store some data in memory. That's not very useful by itself, but most problems to be solved by the computer involve moving data back and forth between memory and the accumulator. Let's see how it works in some programs that serve some useful purpose.

We've made it all the way to Chap. 8 without doing a bit of arithmetic. Who ever heard of a computer that couldn't add and subtract?

The 6502 microprocessor includes instructions that are capable of addition and subtraction. Multiplication and division instructions are *not* available, but routines can be created by the programmer to perform those operations. These routines will be discussed in Chap. 12.

Addition and subtraction are performed by two instructions that have several different addressing modes (Immediate, Zero Page, Absolute, etc.). We will be using the Immediate Addressing mode first.

The mnemonic codes for the add and subtract instructions are:

> ADC (ADd to accumulator with Carry)
> and
> SBC (SuBtract from accumulator with borrow)
> Borrow is the inverse of Carry

Remember that the 6502 is an 8-bit microprocessor and can only handle 8 bits (one byte) of data at one time. The addition and subtraction operations are performed in a binary fashion, on one bit at a time.

Example:

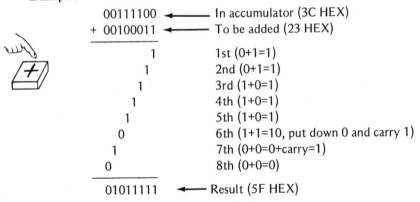

```
  00111100  ◄─────  In accumulator (3C HEX)
+ 00100011  ◄─────  To be added (23 HEX)
──────────
         1          1st (0+1=1)
         1          2nd (0+1=1)
         1          3rd (1+0=1)
         1          4th (1+0=1)
         1          5th (1+0=1)
         0          6th (1+1=10, put down 0 and carry 1)
         1          7th (0+0=0+carry=1)
         0          8th (0+0=0)
──────────
  01011111  ◄─────  Result (5F HEX)
```

Let's try our example in a short machine language program. These are the instructions that we will need.

1. 18 CLC (CLear Carry flag — or carry bit, Implied mode)
   Op
   code mnemonic code

This is a new instruction that is necessary to make sure that a zero is placed in the carry bit of the *status register.* If the carry bit happened to be set to one, we would get an incorrect result (one too large).

2. A9 LDA (LoaD the Accumulator, Immediate mode)
Op
code mnemonic code
You have used this instruction before. It puts the first value to be added (3C HEX = 00111100 binary) in the accumulator.

3. 69 ADC (ADd to accumulator with Carry, Immediate mode)
Op CODE mnemonic code
Another new instruction. It adds the value immediately following the instruction (23 HEX = 00100011 binary), the value in the accumulator (3C HEX = 00111100 binary), and the value in the carry bit of the status register (0 or 1).

We'll also use the monitor subroutine that displays the contents of the accumulator at the end of the program so that we can see the result of the addition.

This is the program.

300 18	CLC	Clear carry flag
301 A9	LDA 3C	Load 3C in the accumulator
302 3C		
303 69	ADC 23	Add 23
304 23		
305 20	JSR FDDA	Display a hexadecimal byte from the
306 DA		accumulator
307 FD		
308 60	RTS	Return to monitor

Now we're ready to go.
1. Enter the program.

```
*300:18 A9 3C 69 23 20 DA FD 60

*■
```

2. Run the program starting at 300.

```
*300:18 A9 3C 69 23 20 DA FD 60

*300G
5F
*■        3C+23 = 5F
```

165

Try adding some other pairs of HEX numbers with the addition program. The HEX values should be substituted in the original program at memory locations 302 and 304.

To change a given memory location, type in the address followed by a colon and the new value.

```
:
*300G
5F
*302:28  ◄─────── First change

*304:1E  ◄─────── Second change

*■
```

Here are some examples you might try.
Examples and results you should obtain:

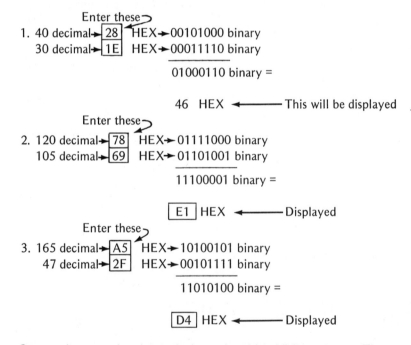

Enter these ⤸
1. 40 decimal ➤ 28   HEX ➤ 00101000 binary
   30 decimal ➤ 1E   HEX ➤ 00011110 binary
   ─────────────────────
   01000110 binary =

   46 HEX ◄─────── This will be displayed

Enter these ⤸
2. 120 decimal ➤ 78   HEX ➤ 01111000 binary
   105 decimal ➤ 69   HEX ➤ 01101001 binary
   ─────────────────────
   11100001 binary =

   E1 HEX ◄─────── Displayed

Enter these ⤸
3. 165 decimal ➤ A5   HEX ➤ 10100101 binary
    47 decimal ➤ 2F   HEX ➤ 00101111 binary
   ─────────────────────
   11010100 binary =

   D4 HEX ◄─────── Displayed

One caution must be observed when using this addition program. The sum of the two values to be added *must* be less than 256 decimal or it will not fit in the accumulator. Remember, you are using an 8-bit computer.

The accumulator and all memory locations can hold only 8 bits of data. The largest 8-bit binary number is 11111111, which is FF HEX or 255 decimal.

Example:

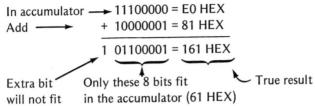

In order to take care of results larger than FF HEX when adding two 8-bit numbers, the 6502 has a way to keep track of that extra bit that won't fit in the accumulator. It uses a special *register*.

THE PROCESSOR STATUS REGISTER

The 6502 microprocessor has a special register called the *processor status register* (status register for short), which keeps track of such things as overflow, carry, negative result, zero result, etc. Each bit in this 8-bit register is assigned a special condition as shown.

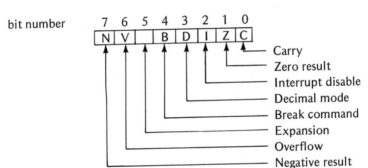

It is this status register that determines whether branches are made or not made when using the instructions:

BMI (Branch on minus) — the N bit = 1
BPL (Branch on plus) — the N bit = 0
BEQ (Branch if equal zero) — the Z bit = 1
BNE (Branch if not equal to zero) — the Z bit = 0

Notice bit zero (labeled C) of the status register. If a carry occurs when an instruction is executed, this bit in the status register is set to a one (1). In our previous example:

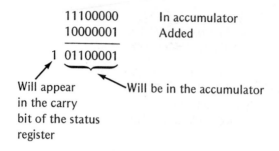

```
11100000        In accumulator
10000001        Added
```

1 01100001

Will appear ⟵Will be in the accumulator
in the carry
bit of the status
register

Even though the extra bit does not appear in the accumulator, it has not been lost. It is in the carry bit of the status register. You, the programmer, must make some provision to test the carry bit to see if a carry has occurred. The 6502 instruction set provides for a way to do this. In fact, there are two instructions that may be used.

B0   BCS (Branch on Carry Set)

Op code

When this instruction is executed, a branch is taken the specified number of steps forward or backward *if the carry bit has been set.*

90   BCC (Branch on Carry Clear)

Op code

When this instruction is executed, a branch is taken the specified number of steps forward or backward *if the carry bit has not been set (or has been cleared).*

Our first addition program worked like this:

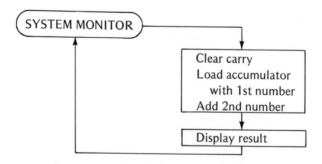

To take care of the carry created by a sum greater than FF, we must modify the program's flow.

The modified addition program will work like this:

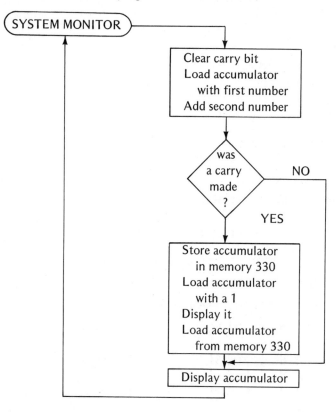

Two possibilities exist when the addition has been made. The action taken depends upon whether or not the carry bit has been set.

1. NO CARRY   32
                 +28
                 ─────
                  5A

C $\boxed{0}$ $\boxed{01011010}$ Accumulator

ANSWER IMMEDIATELY DISPLAYED

2. CARRY   32
                 +E3
                 ─────
                  115

169

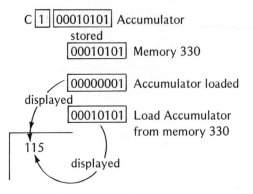

C ⬚1⬚ ⬚00010101⬚ Accumulator
      stored
      ⬚00010101⬚ Memory 330

      ⬚00000001⬚ Accumulator loaded
displayed
      ⬚00010101⬚ Load Accumulator
                  from memory 330

115
      displayed

We will use the Branch on Carry Clear instruction to modify our addition program to take care of sums greater than FF.

MODIFIED ADDITION PROGRAM

1. Clear the Carry bit

300	18	CLC	Clear Carry

2. Load and Add Two Numbers; then Branch if No Carry

301	A9	LDA E0	Load 1st number
302	E0		
303	69	ADC 81	Add 2nd number
304	81		
305	90	BCC 0B	Branch if no carry 11 steps forward
306	0B		

3. If Carry, Store accumulator; Load and Display Carry

307	8D	STA 0330	Save low order part of result
308	30		
309	03		
30A	A9	LDA 01	Load carry
30B	01		
30C	20	JSR FDDA	Display it
30D	DA		
30E	FD		
30F	AD	LDA 0330	Reload low-order part of result
310	30		
311	03		

4. Display Accumulator and Return to Monitor

312	20	JSR FDDA	Display accumulator
313	DA		
314	FD		
315	60	RTS	Go back to Monitor

If the sum of the two numbers is FF or less, no carry will result. Therefore, the accumulator contains the true result. The branch will be taken at 305, and the value in the accumulator will be displayed by the JSR instruction at 312 (Lines 307-311 are skipped).

If the sum is greater than FF, the carry bit will be set. The accumulator will not hold the true result. It will only contain the lower 8 bits of the true result. Since the display subroutine prints the contents of the accumulator, we must first save the lower 8 bits so that the display will first show the bit that was carried. After storing the lower part in memory, the accumulator is loaded with a one. After the one is displayed, the accumulator is reloaded with the lower 8 bits, and it is displayed. The result will appear as one complete number:

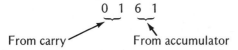

In our example, we know the result will be greater than FF (from our paper-and-pencil result).

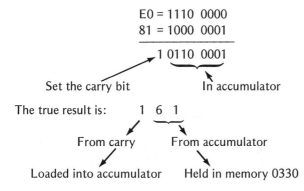

$$E0 = 1110\ 0000$$
$$81 = 1000\ 0001$$
$$1\ 0110\ 0001$$

Set the carry bit   In accumulator

The true result is: 1 6 1

From carry   From accumulator

Loaded into accumulator   Held in memory 0330

Now, since you know the result, enter the program.

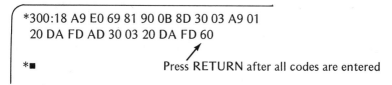

```
*300:18 A9 E0 69 81 90 0B 8D 30 03 A9 01
20 DA FD AD 30 03 20 DA FD 60

*■                    Press RETURN after all codes are entered
```

Now run the program.

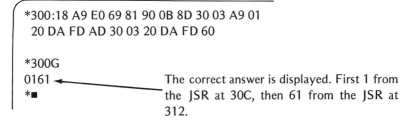

```
*300:18 A9 E0 69 81 90 0B 8D 30 03 A9 01
20 DA FD AD 30 03 20 DA FD 60

*300G
0161                  The correct answer is displayed. First 1 from
*■                    the JSR at 30C, then 61 from the JSR at
                      312.
```

One new instruction was used in the program.

at 30F: LDA 0330   This is the load accumulator from memory using the Absolute Addressing mode. The data is loaded from the specified memory location.

SUBTRACTION

Let's take a look at subtraction now. First consider a binary subtraction as it would be performed with pencil and paper. Remember that binary arithmetic is done in base two. So when a borrow occurs, you borrow a power of two instead of a power of ten, as you would if you used the decimal system.

If a bit is a 0, the borrow makes it 10.

Examples:

Suppose we have the binary number 110. Look at the place values of each bit.

2^2 2^1 2^0
 1   1   0
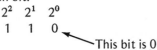
This bit is 0

If a borrow is made to enlarge the 2^0 bit,

2^2 2^1 2^0
 1   1   0
Borrow is made from the 2^1 bit

Think of the result of the borrow to be:

2^2 2^1 2^0
 1   0   10

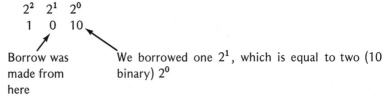

Borrow was made from here

We borrowed one 2^1, which is equal to two (10 binary) 2^0

Subtraction example:

6 decimal – 3 decimal in binary is:

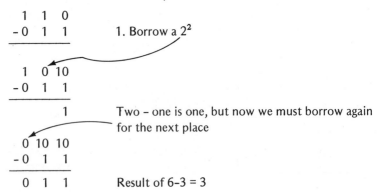

```
   1  1  0
-  0  1  1        1. Borrow a 2²


   1  0 10
-  0  1  1

         1        Two – one is one, but now we must borrow again
                  for the next place
   0 10 10
-  0  1  1

   0  1  1        Result of 6-3 = 3
```

172

It's really just like subtraction in the decimal system, except that you borrow powers of two instead of powers of ten. Here are some examples of subtraction of 8-bit binary numbers.

No borrow

$$10101101 = AD\ HEX = 173\ decimal$$
$$-\ 00100101 = 25\ \ HEX = \ \ 37\ decimal$$

$$10001000 = 88\ \ HEX = 136\ decimal$$

With borrow

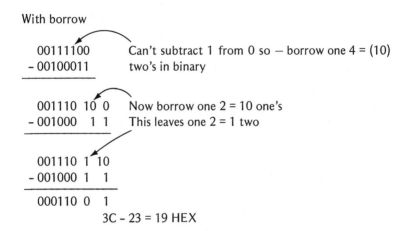

```
  00111100        Can't subtract 1 from 0 so − borrow one 4 = (10)
- 00100011        two's in binary


  001110 10 0      Now borrow one 2 = 10 one's
- 001000   1 1     This leaves one 2 = 1 two


  001110 1 10
- 001000 1   1

  000110 0   1
           3C − 23 = 19 HEX
```

After all this, I must admit that the computer doesn't do subtraction that way. It doesn't have paper and pencil. In fact, it doesn't really know how to subtract at all. It uses a method called *two's complement addition*. It may sound odd to use the addition process to perform a subtraction operation. However, by doing so, the arithmetic unit of the 6502 microprocessor need only contain an adder to perform all of its arithmetic. Therefore, it doesn't have to be so complex as it would have to be if it had an adder *and* a subtracter.

To understand what is meant by *two's complement*, look at the following examples of a binary one's complement.

1. A binary number ⟶ 10011100
   Its one's complement ⟶ 01100011 ⟵——— All 1's become 0's.
   All 0's become 1's.

2. A binary number ⟶ 01010101
   Its one's complement ⟶ 10101010

The one's complement is obtained by changing each bit of the number (a one or a zero) to its opposite (or complement). All 1's are changed to 0's, and all 0's are changed to 1's.

To obtain the two's complement of a binary number, just add one (1) to the one's complement of the number as shown in the following examples.

1. The number ⟶ 10011101
   One's complement ⟶ 01100010
   Add one   + 1
   _____
   Two's complement ⟶ 01100011

2. The number ⟶ 10011100
   One's complement ⟶ 01100011
   Add one   + 1
   _____
   Two's complement ⟶ 01100100

3. The number ⟶ 01010101
   One's complement ⟶ 10101010
   Add one   + 1
   _____
   Two's complement ⟶ 10101011

Now let's see how the computer uses the two's complement in a subtraction problem. Compare it with our paper-and-pencil subtractions above.

Examples:

1.   10101101
      - 00100101◄This number is changed to its
      _____
        11011011 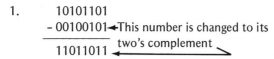 two's complement

Then the two's complement is added to the original number.
     10101101
  + 11011011
  _____
1   10001000

Ignore
Extra bit   88 HEX or 136 decimal

2.   00111100
      - 00100011

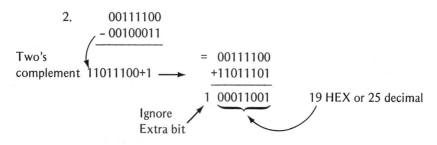

Two's
complement 11011100+1 ⟶   =   00111100
               +11011101
                   _____
           1   00011001   19 HEX or 25 decimal

Ignore
Extra bit

If the computer's method of subtraction is puzzling to you, relax! You don't have to worry about how it does the subtraction. You can check the results by the old paper-and-pencil method.

Let's try a subtraction in a machine language program. By changing two instructions in our original Addition program, we will have:

SUBTRACT TWO NUMBERS

1. REMARK * SET THE CARRY BIT *

300 38   SEC   (SEt the Carry bit)

2. REMARK * LOAD AND SUBTRACT TWO NUMBERS *

301 A9   LDA 3C   (Load the first number)
302 3C

303 E9   SBC 23   (subtract the second number)
304 23

3. REMARK * DISPLAY RESULT AND RETURN TO BASIC *

305 20   JSR FDDA (display the result)
306 DA
307 FD

308 60   RTS   (Go back to Monitor)

In Section 1, the Set Carry Bit instruction is used to place a one (1) in the carry bit of the status register. In subtraction, the carry bit is used to obtain the two's complement of the number to be subtracted. Therefore, SEC (SEt Carry flag) is given *before* the subtraction is performed. The Op code for SEC is 38. The instruction is only used in the Implied mode.

In Section 2, the first number is loaded in the accumulator. Then the SBC (SuBtract with borrow) instruction is used in the Immediate mode (Op code E9). The two's complement of the number immediately following the instruction is added to the number in the accumulator. The result of the subtraction (or two's complement addition) is left in the accumulator.

Section 3 displays the results as before and returns to the System Monitor. Enter the program with the System Monitor.

```
*300:38 A9 3C E9 23 20 DA FD 60

*■
```

Then run the program.

```
*300:38 A9 3C E9 23 20 DA FD 60

*300G
19
*■          The result 19 (HEX), just like pencil and paper
```

Try other numbers at locations 302 and 304. Be sure that the number used at 302 is larger than the number that you are subtracting (at 304) if you want positive results.

O.K. wise guy! What if I don't want positive results?

I thought you'd never ask. Negative results will be discussed in Chap. 9.

We have restricted our discussion so far to positive numbers that can be expressed in 8 bits (one byte). These numbers are less than 256 (100HEX). In the next chapter we'll take a look at negative numbers and at positive numbers that may be larger than 255.

SUMMARY

The System Monitor was introduced along with the following symbols and commands.

*	The System Monitor prompt
*300:A9	Modify a single memory location
*300:A9 13 8D 25 3 60	Modify successive memory locations
	Used in entering new programs
*300	Examine a single memory location
*300.305	Examine memory locations 300 through 305 (HEX)
*300G	Execute the machine language program beginning at memory location 300 (HEX)

You also learned to enter an addition program that added 2 one-byte HEX numbers and displayed the result. The carry bit was used to detect results that were larger than could be held in a single byte.

Subtraction by means of two's complement addition was demonstrated.

The individual bits in the Processor Status Register were discussed.

N	V		B	D	I	Z	C

Several new instructions were introduced.

Mnemonic Code	Addressing Mode	Op Code	Bytes Used	Function
CLC	Implied	18	1	Clear the carry flag
ADC	Immediate	69	2	Add immediate data to accumulator
BCS	Relative	B0	2	Branch on carry set
BCC	Relative	90	2	Branch on carry clear
LDA	Absolute	AD	3	Add contents to memory to accumulator
SEC	Implied	38	1	Set carry flag

EXERCISES

1. Name the mnemonic codes for the instructions Add with carry and Subtract with borrow.
   _____ and _____

2. The Add with carry instruction adds a number to the value in the accumulator. It also adds in what other value?
   _____

3. If the HEX values 35 and 6A are added by the Add Two Numbers Program, what value will be displayed?
   _____

4. If the HEX values 85 and 9A are added by the Add Two Numbers Program, what value will be displayed?
   _____

5. If the Modified Addition Program is used to add the HEX numbers 85 and 9A, what value would be stored in:
   0330_____

6. In exercise 5, what would be displayed after the program has been run?
   _____

7. What is the one's complement of 10110011? _____

8. What is the two's complement of 01101101? _____

9. If the Subtract Two Numbers Program is used to subtract 23 (HEX) from AF (HEX), what would be displayed when the program is run?
   _____

10. What would be the result of A3 – 2F (HEX values)?
    _____

ANSWERS TO EXERCISES

1. ADC and SBC
2. The value in the carry bit
3. 9F (HEX)
4. 1F (HEX) (The actual result is 11F, but the carry bit is not displayed.)
5. 0330 = 1F
6. 011F (HEX)
7. 01001100
8. 10010011
9. 8C (HEX)
10. 74 (HEX)

Chapter 9

Multiple Precision and Negative Numbers

$$\boxed{\text{SM}}$$

In order to handle large numbers, it is necessary to work with values in multiple bytes. We will consider two-byte numbers in this section. If we restrict ourselves to positive numbers, two bytes can provide for numbers as large as:

$$\underbrace{11111111}_{} \quad \underbrace{11111111}_{} = \text{FF FF HEX}$$

Most Significant   Lease Significant
Byte   Byte

$$\text{FF FF HEX} = (15 \times 4096) + (15 \times 256) + (15 \times 16) + 15$$

$$
\begin{aligned}
= \quad &61440 \\
&3840 \\
&240 \\
+ \quad &15 \\
\hline
&65,535 \quad \text{decimal}
\end{aligned}
$$

Largest decimal number for two bytes

Larger values can be obtained by extending the number of bytes as desired.

TWO-BYTE ADDITION

Two Bytes are Better than One

A paper and pencil addition of two-byte numbers will help us decide how to write a program to perform the operation on the computer. Suppose we want to add these two-byte HEX numbers.

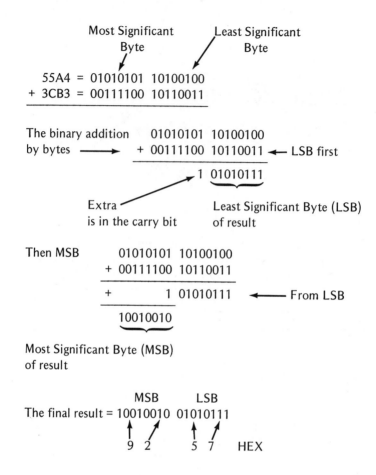

Most Significant   Least Significant
         Byte   Byte

    55A4 = 01010101 10100100
  + 3CB3 = 00111100 10110011

The binary addition   01010101 10100100
by bytes ──────▶   + 00111100 10110011 ◀── LSB first
                              1 01010111

Extra   Least Significant Byte (LSB)
is in the carry bit   of result

Then MSB   01010101 10100100
              + 00111100 10110011
              +   1 01010111   ◀────── From LSB
                10010010

Most Significant Byte (MSB)
of result

                MSB   LSB
The final result = 10010010 01010111
                    9 2   5 7   HEX

Notice that in this example a carry results from the addition of the Least Significant Bytes. The ADC (ADd with Carry) instruction will automatically add in this carry bit to the sum of the Most Significant Bytes. Therefore, it appears that the two-byte numbers are summed by adding:

First, the Least Significant Bytes and
Second, the Most Significant Bytes.

If we draw a flowchart of the operations that must be performed, it will help us write the program step by step.

180

FLOWCHART

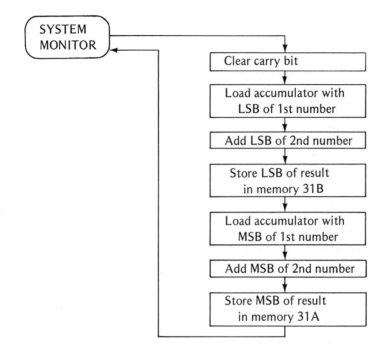

It looks like a very straightforward program. We'll set up a block of memory to store the bytes that are to be added and the bytes of the result of the addition. Since there are 2 bytes for each number, we'll set aside 6 bytes.

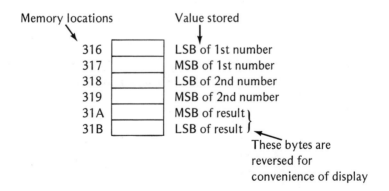

By looking at the flowchart, we can write the program.

TWO-BYTE ADDITION

1. REMARK * CLEAR THE CARRY BIT *

    300 18   CLC

2. REMARK * LOAD, ADD AND STORE LSB *

    301 AD   LDA, 0316 ⟵ Load LSB of 1st number
    302 16
    303 03

    304 6D   ADC, 0318 ⟵ Add LSB of 2nd number
    305 18
    306 03

    307 8D   STA, 031B ⟵ Store result of LSB
    308 1B
    309 03

3. REMARK * LOAD, ADD AND STORE MSB THEN RETURN *

    30A AD   LDA, 0317 ⟵ Load MSB of 1st number
    30B 17
    30C 03

    30D 6D   ADC, 0319 ⟵ Add MSB of 2nd number
    30E 19
    30F 03

    310 8D   STA, 031A ⟵ Store result of MSB
    311 1A
    312 03

    313 60   RTS   ⟵ Go back to Monitor

4. REMARK * DATA *

    314 ∅∅   BRK   Filler
    315 ∅∅   BRK   Filler
    316 A4   ⟵ LSB 1st number
    317 55   ⟵ MSB 1st number
    318 B3   ⟵ LSB 2nd number
    319 3C   ⟵ MSB 2nd number

Notice that we used the LDA and ADC instructions in the Absolute mode this time. The Op code for LDA when used in this mode is AD. The Op code is followed by the least significant byte of the address containing the data to be loaded. The most significant byte of this address follows as the third byte of the instruction.

AD ◄——— Op code for LDA (Absolute mode)
16 ◄——— Least Significant Byte of address
03 ◄——— Most Significant Byte of address

The Op code for ADC in the Absolute mode is 6D. The Op code is also followed by the address containing the number to be added. The Least Significant Byte of the address is given, then the Most Significant Byte.

6D ◄——— Op code for ADC (Absolute mode)
18 ◄——— Least Significant Byte of address
03 ◄——— Most Significant Byte of address

In our paper-and-pencil addition, we calculated a result of 9257 HEX. Let's let the computer have a try at it.

First, enter the program.

*300:18 AD 16 03 6D 18 03 8D 1B 03 AD 17
03 6D 19 03 8D 1A 03 60 00 00 A4 55 B3
3C

*■   All entered

Then run it.

*300:18 AD 16 03 6D 18 03 8D 1B 03 AD 17
03 6D 19 03 8D 1A 03 60 00 00 A4 55 B3
3C

*300G◄————————————————————RUN

*■

Then examine memory locations 31A and 31B to see the results.

> *300:18 AD 16 03 6D 18 03 8D 1B 03 AD 17
> 03 6D 19 03 8D 1A 03 60 00 00 A4 55 B3
> 3C
>
> *300G
>
> *31A.31B
>
> 031A- 92 57 ◄——— There it is — the same as with pencil and paper
> *■

TWO-BYTE SUBTRACTION

Subtraction of two-byte numbers is performed in a similar manner. The Add Two Numbers Program can be modified by three simple changes:

at 300   change 18 (CLC) to 38 (SEC)   ◄——— Set the carry bit

at 304 ⎫
and   ⎬   change 6D (ADC) to ED (SBC) ◄——— Subtract with borrow
at 30D ⎭

The change at 300 sets the carry bit in preparation for the subtraction just as it did in the one-byte subtraction program. The Add with carry instruction (ADC) is replaced by the Subtract with borrow instruction (SBC). The subtract instruction is used in the Absolute mode with the address that contains the number to be subtracted following the Op code.

ED ◄——— Op code for SBC (Absolute mode)
18 ◄——— Least significant byte of address
03 ◄——— Most significant byte of address

Thus, the least significant byte of the value to be subtracted is contained in address 0318 HEX. The most significant byte of the value to be subtracted is contained in address 0319 HEX. It is subtracted from the most significant byte of the first value by the instruction:

ED ◄——— Op code for SBC (Absolute Mode)
19 ◄——— Least Significant Byte of address
03 ◄——— Most Significant Byte of address

You have two choices.
(a) If you still have the two-byte addition program in memory, just make the three changes.

```
*300:38
*304:ED
*30D:ED

*■
```

(b) If you do not have the two-byte program in memory, enter the new program with the changes.

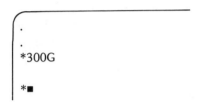

```
*300:38 AD 16 03 ED 18 03 8D 1B 03 AD 17
03 ED 19 03 8D 1A 03 60 00 00 A4 55 B3
3C

*■
```

Then run the program.

```
.
.
*300G

*■
```

Then examine the memory locations that hold the result.

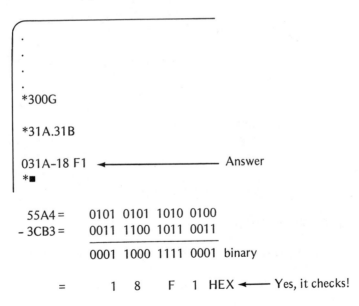

```
.
.
.
.
*300G

*31A.31B

031A-18 F1   ◄─────────────── Answer
*■
```

55A4 =	0101 0101 1010 0100
− 3CB3 =	0011 1100 1011 0011
	0001 1000 1111 0001 binary
=	1 8 F 1 HEX ◄─── Yes, it checks!

185

$$= (1 \times 16^3) + (8 \times 16^2) + (15 \times 16) + 1$$

$$= 4096 + 2048 + 240 + 1$$

$$= 6385 \text{ Decimal}$$

To add or subtract numbers that require more than two bytes, an extension of this two-byte procedure can be made. The operation is always performed from the least significant byte forward (or from right to left).

MULTIPLE-BYTE ADDITION FLOW

1. | Clear carry bit |

2. | Load LSB of 1st number
     Add LSB of 2nd number
     Store result |

3. | Load next byte of 1st number
     Add next byte of 2nd number
     Store result |

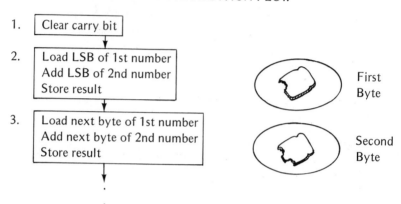

First Byte

Second Byte

4. Repeat Step 3 until all bytes have been stored away.

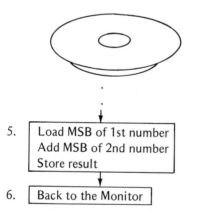

5. | Load MSB of 1st number
     Add MSB of 2nd number
     Store result |

6. | Back to the Monitor |

NEGATIVE NUMBERS

It is possible to look at the way data is represented in the computer in a different way. If signed numbers (those that are either positive, negative, or zero) are to be represented, the computer must have some way to tell them apart.

Consider an 8-bit block of data as being composed of one sign bit and seven data bits.

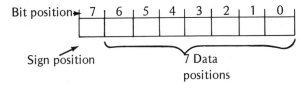

Bit position 7 6 5 4 3 2 1 0

Sign position   7 Data positions

(a) If the sign position holds a zero, the data is considered to be a positive number.

Examples:

0 1 1 1 1 1 1 1 = +127 (64+32+16+8+4+2+1)
0 1 1 1 1 1 1 0 = +126 (64+32+16+8+4+2)
0 1 1 1 1 1 0 1 = +125 (64+32+16+8+4 +1)
0 1 1 1 1 1 0 0 = +124 (64+32+16+8+4   )

.   .   .
.   .   .
.   .   .
.   .   .
.   .   .

0 0 0 0 0 0 1 1 = +3   (+2+1)
0 0 0 0 0 0 1 0 = +2   (+2)
0 0 0 0 0 0 0 1 = +1   (+1)
0 0 0 0 0 0 0 0 = +0   (   )

Zero is considered a positive number by Branch Instructions

(b) If the sign position holds a one (1), the data is considered to be a negative number.

Examples:

1 0 0 0 0 0 0 0 = -128
1 0 0 0 0 0 0 1 = -127
1 0 0 0 0 0 1 0 = -126
1 0 0 0 0 0 1 1 = -125
1 0 0 0 0 1 0 0 = -124

1 1 1 1 1 0 1 1 = -5
1 1 1 1 1 1 0 0 = -4
1 1 1 1 1 1 0 1 = -3
1 1 1 1 1 1 1 0 = -2
1 1 1 1 1 1 1 1 = -1

We have learned to interpret positive binary numbers as positive decimal numbers, but what about these negative critters? They don't look familiar at all. However, it is plain to see that each 8-bit code could represent all the integers from -128 through +127.

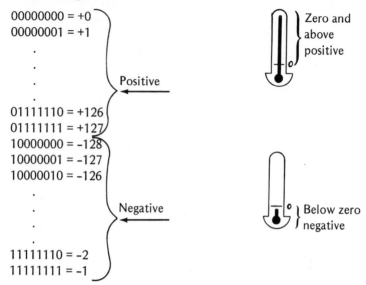

00000000 = +0
00000001 = +1
  .
  .
  .
  .
01111110 = +126
01111111 = +127
10000000 = -128
10000001 = -127
10000010 = -126
  .
  .
  .
11111110 = -2
11111111 = -1

Positive

Negative

Zero and above positive

Below zero negative

Let's take a look at the negatives and see if there is any meaningful relationship to their positive counterparts.

Consider the positive number 126 = 01111110.

Its one's complement = 10000001
Its two's complement = 10000010
Compare the latter with -126 = 10000010

The binary representation of a negative number (-1 through -127) is equal to the two's complement of its positive counterpart.

-127 = the two's complement of +127
-126 = the two's complement of +126
-125 = the two's complement of +125
-2 = the two's complement of +2
-1 = the two's complement of +1

For two-byte numbers, the sign position is considered to be in the *most significant bit* of the *most significant byte.*

Most Significant Byte   Least Significant Byte

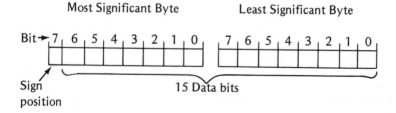

Bit → 7 6 5 4 3 2 1 0   7 6 5 4 3 2 1 0

Sign position

15 Data bits

188

A complete discussion of the arithmetic of signed numbers is beyond the scope of this book. A more thorough discussion of signed numbers and signed number arithmetic can be found in the MOS Technology Programming Manual available in some computer stores or from MOS Technology, Inc., 950 Rittenhouse Road, Norristown, PA 19401.

For our purposes, we must realize that certain branch instructions test the result of numbers to see whether they are negative or positive. This determination depends on whether or not the Negative flag of the Processor Status Register has been set to a 1. The Negative flag is set to 1 when the computer interprets the results of certain instructions as negative numbers (a result of 1 in bit 7). We will stress this fact in the recreational activities that follow.

A NUMBER GUESSING GAME

You probably have seen this game many times in books and magazines. It is usually published in BASIC. We will show a machine language version that makes use of the two-branch instructions that are based on an interpretation of signed numbers. This interpretation hinges on the *negative flag* (or bit) in the Processor Status Register.

BMI	(Branch on result minus)	Branch if the negative flag is
	Op code = 30	set to 1 (negative result)
	Relative Addressing mode	

BPL	(Branch on result plus)	Branch if the negative flag is
	Op code = 10	reset to 0 (positive result)
	Relative Addressing mode	

We will also use the branch on result equal instruction, which makes use of the zero flag in the Processor Status Register.

BEQ	(Branch on result equal)	Branch if the zero flag is
	Op code = F0	set to 1 (result equal zero)
	Relative Addressing mode	

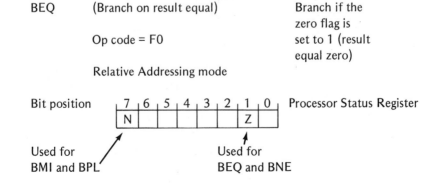

189

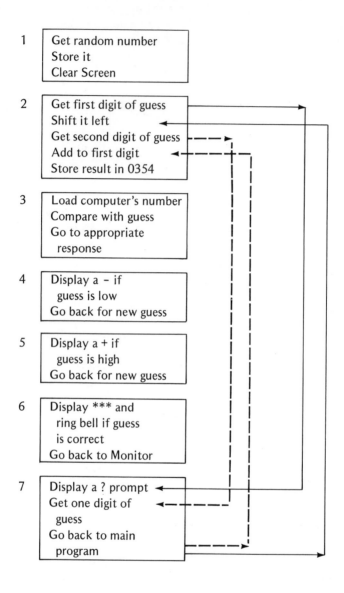

Many useful subroutines are used from the System Monitor by the program. Without these subroutines, the program would take several pages to list and would become quite complex. You should study the Apple II Reference Manual thoroughly so that you can take advantage of these subroutines whenever possible. The manual is available from Apple Computer, Inc., 10260 Bandley Dr., Cupertino, CA 95014. (Apple product number A2L0001A).

Let's look at the program in detail. If you understand how it works, you will be able to modify it as you wish. We have provided the fundamental program, but you may provide numerous additions.

Section 1

```
Get a random number
Store it
Clear the screen
```

300	20 1B FD	JSR FD1B	Get Random number
303	A5 4F	LDA,4F	Read it
305	29 7F	AND 7F	Strip upper bit
307	8D 53 03	STA 0353	Store it
30A	20 58 FC	JSR FC58	Clear screen

We first make use of the KEYIN subroutine at FD1B. It reads the keyboard and waits for a keypress. When a key is pressed, a random number is placed in memory location 004F. The keycode for the character typed is placed in the accumulator, but our program ignores this code. We are interested only in the random number that is generated. The random number is loaded in the accumulator from 004F. It is ANDed with 7F. This restricts the random value to a positive HEX number in the range of 0 through 7F. Remember, the computer would interpret 80 through FF as negative numbers. Let's stay away from those. If we included negatives, the program would get much more complicated.

Remember the AND instruction from Chap. 7? This time we are using it to "strip off" the upper bit of the random number to make sure the computer does not produce a negative number.

Example: Suppose the random number was F3 (a negative).

$$F3 \quad = \quad 1111\ 0011$$
$$\underline{0111\ 1111} \quad AND\ with\ 7F$$
$$0111\ 0011 = 73\ a\ positive\ number$$

The number produced has ones in only the bits where both F3 and 7F have ones.

The random number is then stored in memory location 0353. We will recall it later to compare it to the number guessed. The screen is then cleared, by the monitor routine at FC58, in preparation for the guessing portion of the program.

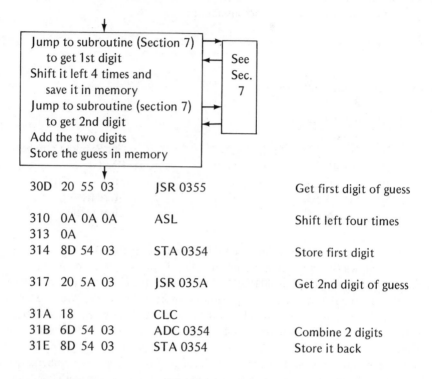

30D	20 55 03	JSR 0355	Get first digit of guess
310	0A 0A 0A	ASL	Shift left four times
313	0A		
314	8D 54 03	STA 0354	Store first digit
317	20 5A 03	JSR 035A	Get 2nd digit of guess
31A	18	CLC	
31B	6D 54 03	ADC 0354	Combine 2 digits
31E	8D 54 03	STA 0354	Store it back

At 30D, a subroutine (see Section 7) is called that displays a question mark as a prompt to let you know that the computer is waiting for your guess (a two-digit HEX number less than 80).

The subroutine allows the entry of one digit of your two-digit guess, modifies its ASCII code, and then returns to 310, where the value is shifted left 4 places.

Suppose that you enter a 5:

7	6	5	4	3	2	1	0
0	0	0	0	0	1	0	1

Accumulator before the shifts

5

7	6	5	4	3	2	1	0
0	1	0	1	0	0	0	0

Accumulator after the shifts

Bits 3,2,1,0 ⎞ 4 zeros inserted
were shifted ⎟
to positions 7,6,5,4
respectively

This result is stored in memory location 0354 as 50 (HEX). At 317, the subroutine (Section 7) is called again to get the second digit of the guess. The subroutine modifies the ASCII code of that digit and returns to the main program at 31A.

The first digit is now added to the second digit.

Suppose that your second digit was 7.

```
0 0 0 0 0 1 1 1        Accumulator (second digit)
                +
0 1 0 1 0 0 0 0        From memory 0354
                =
0 1 0 1 0 1 1 1        The two-digit guess
```

The guess is then stored back in memory location 0354.

Section 3

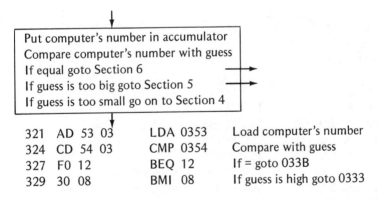

Put computer's number in accumulator
Compare computer's number with guess
If equal goto Section 6
If guess is too big goto Section 5
If guess is too small go on to Section 4

321	AD 53 03	LDA 0353	Load computer's number
324	CD 54 03	CMP 0354	Compare with guess
327	F0 12	BEQ 12	If = goto 033B
329	30 08	BMI 08	If guess is high goto 0333

The computer's number and your guess are compared. If the result is equal, the BEQ instruction at 327 sends the program to 338 (Section 6) to display the victory message. If the guess is too high, the comparison (computer-guess) is negative, and the BMI instruction at 329 sends the program to 333 (Section 5) to display a + sign and go back for a new guess. If the guess is too low, the program proceeds to Section 4.

Section 4

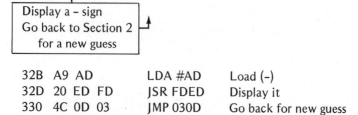

```
32B  A9 AD       LDA #AD      Load (-)
32D  20 ED FD    JSR FDED     Display it
330  4C 0D 03    JMP 030D     Go back for new guess
```

A minus sign is displayed to indicate the guess was too low. The program then jumps back to get the first digit of the new guess.

Section 5

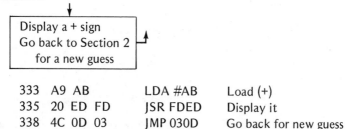

```
333  A9 AB       LDA #AB      Load (+)
335  20 ED FD    JSR FDED     Display it
338  4C 0D 03    JMP 030D     Go back for new guess
```

A plus sign is displayed to indicate the guess was too high. The program then jumps back to get the first digit of the new guess.

Section 6

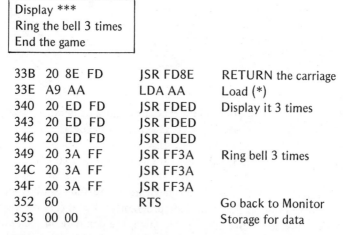

```
33B  20 8E FD    JSR FD8E     RETURN the carriage
33E  A9 AA       LDA AA       Load (*)
340  20 ED FD    JSR FDED     Display it 3 times
343  20 ED FD    JSR FDED
346  20 ED FD    JSR FDED
349  20 3A FF    JSR FF3A     Ring bell 3 times
34C  20 3A FF    JSR FF3A
34F  20 3A FF    JSR FF3A
352  60          RTS          Go back to Monitor
353  00 00                    Storage for data
```

This is the victory message. Three asterisks are displayed followed by three rings of the bell (Monitor subroutine at FF3A). Control is then returned to the Monitor. Location 353 and 354 are used to store the numbers (random and guess).

Section 7

```
         ↓
┌─────────────────────────────┐
│ Display a ? prompt for guess │
│ Get digit and display it     │
│ Make sure it is a HEX digit ├─┐
│ Change to proper form        │ │
│ Return to main program       │ │
└─────────────────────────────┘
```

This subroutine is entered after the random number has been selected in Section 1. A question mark is displayed to prompt you to make your guess. The first digit is displayed after being typed. The subroutine then goes through a series of tests to make sure that the digit has an ASCII code in the range of B0-B9 for the decimal digits 0,1,2,3,4,5,6,7,8,9 or C1-C6 for the letters A,B,C,D,E, F. This allows for the entry of the complete set of HEX digits.

355	A9 BF	LDA #BF	Load (?) as prompt for guess
357	20 ED FD	JSR FDED	Display it
35A	20 35 FD	JSR FD35	Get digit
35D	20 ED FD	JSR FDED	Display it
360	C9 B0	CMP #B0	Tests for legal HEX digits
362	30 15	BMI 15	If low go to 379
364	C9 BA	CMP #BA	
366	30 0E	BMI 0E	In range B0-B9 goto 376
368	C9 C1	CMP #C1	
36A	30 0D	BMI 0D	Between B9 and C1 goto 379
36C	C9 C7	CMP #C7	
36E	10 09	BPL 09	If too high, goto 379
370	29 0F	AND #0F	Strip off upper bits (C)
372	18	CLC	
373	69 09	ADC #09	Change to (A-F)
375	60	RTS	Return to main program
376	29 0F	AND #0F	Strip upper bits (B)
378	60	RTS	Return to main program
379	20 3A FF	JSR FF3A	Ring bell bad input
37C	20 8E FD	JSR FD8E	Carriage return
37F	4C 55 03	JMP 0355	Give another prompt

If a key out of the acceptable range is typed, a bell rings and the computer displays a new question mark prompt. If the keystroke has an ASCII code in the B0-B9 range, the BMI instruction at 366 sends the computer to 376, where the B of the ASCII code is removed by ANDing with 0F. The computer then returns to the main program with the adjusted value in the accumulator. If the keystroke has an ASCII code in the C1-C6 range, the AND instruction at 370 strips off the C. Nine is added to the remaining value to produce a HEX digit A-F. The computer then returns to the main program.

195

Now we're ready to enter the program. Use great care! This is a long program. Take your time. Try entering it in sections and examining memory after each section is entered.

```
*300:20 1B FD A5 4F 29 7F 8D 53 03 20 58
 FC 20 55 03 0A 0A 0A 0A 8D 54 03 20 5A
 03 18 6D 54 03 8D 54 03 AD 53 03 CD 54 0
 3 F0                              ←——— Enter

*300.327

0300- 20 1B FD A5 4F 29 7F 8D  ←——————— Check
0308- 53 03 20 58 FC 20 55 03
0310- 0A 0A 0A 0A 8D 54 03 20
0318- 5A 03 18 6D 54 03 8D 54
0320- 03 AD 53 03 CD 54 03 F0

*■
```

Then

```
*328:12 30 08 A9 AD 20 ED FD 4C 0D 03 A9
 AB 20 ED FD 4C 0D 03 20 8E FD A9 AA 20
 ED FD 20 ED FD 20 ED

*328.347

0328- 12 30 08 A9 AD 20 ED FD
0330- 4C 0D 03 A9 AB 20 ED FD
0338- 4C 0D 03 20 8E FD A9 AA
0340- 20 ED FD 20 ED FD 20 ED

*■
```

Then

```
*348:FD 20 3A FF 20 3A FF 20 3A FF 60 00
 00 A9 BF 20 ED FD 20 35 FD 20 ED FD C9
 B0 30 15 C9 BA 30 0E

*348.367

0348- FD 20 3A FF 20 3A FF 20
0350- 3A FF 60 00 00 A9 BF 20
0358- ED FD 20 35 FD 20 ED FD
0360- C9 B0 30 15 C9 BA 30 0E

*■
```

196

```
*368:C9 C1 30 0D C9 C7 10 09 29 0F 18 69
 09 60 29 0F 60 20 3A FF 20 8E FD 4C 55
 03

*368.381

0368- C9 C1 30 0D C9 C7 10 09
0370- 29 0F 18 69 09 60 29 0F
0378- 60 20 3A FF 20 8E FD 4C
0380- 55 03

*■
```

Check over your entries. Make sure that some of those zeros did not turn out to be capital letter O's. Gather up your courage and try a run. Here is one of our typical runs (after we found and corrected all of our typing errors).

```
.
.
.
9 0F 60 20 3A FF 20 8E FD 4C 55 03

*300G
```

When you press the return key, the cursor disappears and nothing seems to happen. The computer is now generating a random number. When you press any key, the process will stop, and the computer will have a random number. So . . . press a key.

1. PRESS ANY KEY.

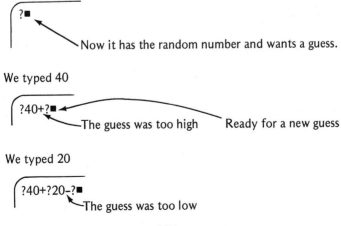

?■
Now it has the random number and wants a guess.

We typed 40

?40+?■
The guess was too high   Ready for a new guess

We typed 20

?40+?20-?■
The guess was too low

We typed 30

```
?40+?20-?30+?■
```
—The guess was too high

We typed 28

```
?40+?20-?30+?28+?■
```
—Still too high

We typed 24

```
?40+?20-?30+?28+?24
***
*■
```
—Three bells rang and 3 asterisks appeared on the screen. The number *was 24*!

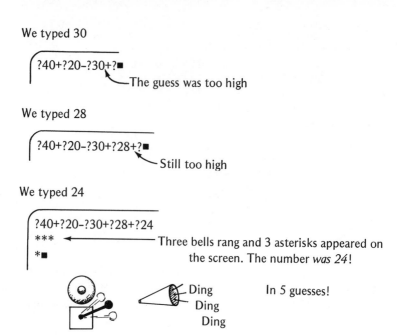

Ding
Ding
Ding

In 5 guesses!

Let's try one more round to see what will happen if we input some non-HEX characters.

Type 300G for another round with a new number.

```
?40+?20-?30+?28+?24
***
*300G
```

Type any key and a random number is again chosen. The screen is cleared and a ? appears.

```
?■
```
—Ready for a new guess

Here are some results of inputs that are not hexadecimal.

```
?N
?■
```
—The N was not accepted. A new ? appears.

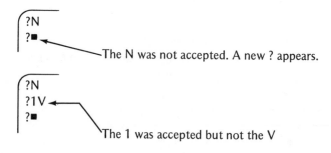

```
?N
?1V
?■
```
The 1 was accepted but not the V

198

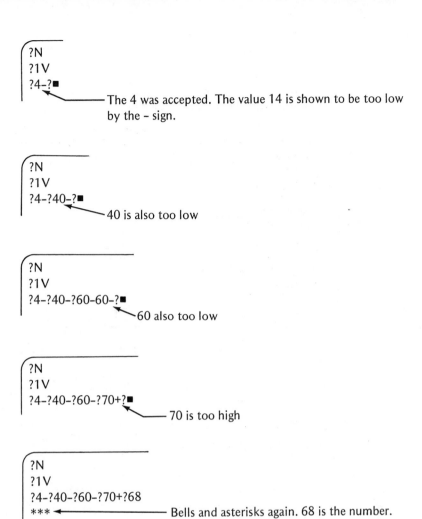

?N
?1V
?4-?■ — The 4 was accepted. The value 14 is shown to be too low by the – sign.

?N
?1V
?4-?40-?■ — 40 is also too low

?N
?1V
?4-?40-?60-60-?■ — 60 also too low

?N
?1V
?4-?40-?60-?70+?■ — 70 is too high

?N
?1V
?4-?40-?60-?70+?68
*** ← Bells and asterisks again. 68 is the number.
*■

Let's check the memory and see if the two numbers really match.

.
.
.
***
*353.354

0353- 68 68 ← Yes they match.

*■

SUMMARY

In this chapter you learned that two-byte addition could be performed by formatting large numbers into two separate bytes. The same proved true for the subtraction of two-byte numbers. This procedure can be extended to higher multiple-byte arithmetic.

Demonstration programs were given for two-byte addition and subtraction. You had a chance to practice examining and modifying memory contents by means of the System Monitor.

You learned that the format for signed numbers is:

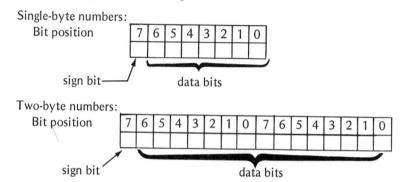

Single-byte numbers:
Bit position

sign bit   data bits

Two-byte numbers:
Bit position

sign bit   data bits

You also learned to interpret negative binary numbers to decimal equivalents by using the two's complement procedure.

A number guessing game used decisions based on signed numbers.

New Instructions Used

Mnemonic Code	Addressing Mode	Op Code	Bytes Used	Function
ADC	Absolute	6D	3	Add contents of memory to accumulator
SBC	Absolute	ED	3	Subtract contents of memory from accumulator
LDA	Zero Page	A5	2	Load accumulator from zero page memory (00XX)
CMP	Absolute	CD	3	Compare accumulator contents and contents of memory

New Subroutines Used

Function	Location in Memory
KEYIN to get a random number	FD1B
CROUT to execute a carriage return	FD8E
BELL1 to ring a bell	FF3A

EXERCISES

1. What is the 4-digit HEX representation of the following two-byte *unsigned* binary value?

   | 0 1 1 0 1 1 1 1 | 1 0 1 0 0 0 1 1 | = _____ _____ _____ _____ (HEX)

   most significant   least significant
        byte   byte

2. The Two-Byte Addition Program added 55A4 and 3CB3 HEX. Show how to modify the program to change these two values to 5A45 and 3B3C HEX.

   * _____

3. If the Two-Byte Addition Program was executed with the modifications of Exercise 2, what result would be displayed by the following command?

   ```
   *300G

   *31A.31B
   ```
   _____

4. In two-byte subtraction, which byte is operated on first? _____
   (most, least)
   significant byte

5. Subtract 03C5 from 25A2 (HEX). Use a computer program, two's complement addition, or pencil-and-paper method.
   Result = _____ (HEX)

6. What is the bit position used to interpret *signed* numbers?
   _____

7. What would be the decimal interpretation of the *signed* number 10111010?
   _____

8. If the computer selects a random HEX number of 6D and you input a guess of 40 when running the Number Guessing Game, what will the display show?

   ?40 _____

9. If a random number of 9E is generated at location 300 of the Number Guessing Game, what number will be stored in memory location 353?
   _____

10. If the first digit of a guess in the Number Guessing Game is 7 and the second digit has *not* been selected, what value is stored in memory location 354? (*Hint:* See Section 2 and Section 7 of the program.)
    _____

ANSWERS TO EXERCISES

1. 6FA3

2.
```
┌─────────────────────────┐        ┌─────────────────
│ *316:5A 45 3B 3C         │  or    │ *316:5A
│                                   │
                                    │ *317:45
                                    │
                                    │ *318:3B
                                    │
                                    │ *319:3C
```

3.
```
┌─────────────────────┐
│ 031A- 95 81
```

4. Least

5. 21DD

6. Bit 7 of the most significant byte

7. -70

8.
```
┌──────────
│ ?40-?
```

9. 1E   (9E ANDed with 7F = 1E   1001 1110
                                               0111 1111
                                               ─────────
                                               0001 1110 = 1E)

10. 70 (the value was shifted left 4 times)

Chapter 10

More Monitor Magic

SM

We have relied on pencil and paper to check the results of hexadecimal additions and subtractions. Computers are made to take over the drudgery of tedious tasks, and pencil-and-paper hexadecimal arithmetic is surely a tedious task. It's also highly subject to errors.

The Monitor will perform simple hexadecimal addition and subtraction of two-digit hexadecimal numbers. You just type in the values separated by the operation symbol. It is not necessary to write a program to do the operation.

HEXADECIMAL ADDITION — IMMEDIATE MODE

Here is the method used. It's almost like using a calculator.

```
*3C+2F      ◄——— You type this
=6B         ◄——————— Computer responds
*■
```

```
*59+C       ◄——— You type this
=65         ◄——————— Computer responds
*■
```

You may notice that our addition examples produce a result that is less than FF. What do you suppose happens if the result is larger than FF? Try it.

```
*FF+13
=12 ◄
*■          The result is less than either addend. Why?
```

Look at the binary addition of FF and 13 to discover the reason.

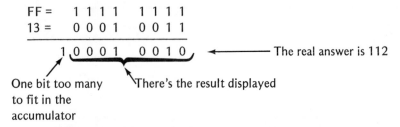

FF = 1 1 1 1   1 1 1 1
13 = 0 0 0 1   0 0 1 1
—————————————————————
      1 0 0 0 1   0 0 1 0 ◄——————— The real answer is 112

One bit too many   There's the result displayed
to fit in the
accumulator

This feature of the monitor is restricted to display the results of the addition of two-digit values whose sum is FF or less. However, you can use the addition feature for sums greater than FF if you keep track of this extra bit.

You can even use the addition feature for multiple-byte addition if you keep track of the extra bit that must be "carried over" to the next place.

Example: Add 35D and 2F5

First, separate the bytes: 3 5D
                              2 F5

Second, add the low-order bytes:

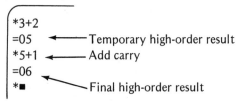

```
*5D+F5
=52   ◄——————— Low-order result, but there was a carry – don't lose it.
*■
```

Third, add the high-order bytes and the carry.

```
*3+2
=05   ◄——————— Temporary high-order result
*5+1  ◄——————— Add carry
=06
*■    ◄——————— Final high-order result
```

Therefore, the final result is: 35D+1F5 = 652

The third step has to be done in two parts since the immediate addition and subtraction will only operate on two values. If you try to add three values, the second value will be ignored. Only the first and last values will be added.

Examples:

```
*3+2+1
=4   ◄——————— Actually 3+1
```

```
*1F+2F+1
=20   ◄——————— Actually 1F+1
```

```
*2A+11+37
=61   ◄——————— Actually 2A+37
```

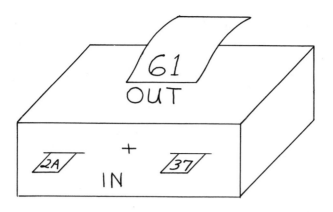

Here are some other examples:

1F30 + 25C8

```
*30+C8
=F8          ◄──── Low order — no carry
*1F+25
=44          ◄──────── High order — no carry
*■
```

Therefore, 1F30+25C8 = 44F8

1F33 + 2FF5

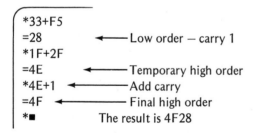

```
*33+F5
=28          ◄──── Low order — carry 1
*1F+2F
=4E          ◄──── Temporary high order
*4E+1    ◄──── Add carry
=4F      ◄──────── Final high order
*■              The result is 4F28
```

It is possible to exceed a two-byte result, as shown in this last addition example.

D14F + E213

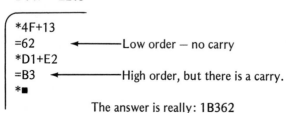

```
*4F+13
=62          ◄──────── Low order — no carry
*D1+E2
=B3      ◄──────── High order, but there is a carry.
*■
```

The answer is really: 1B362

If you are going to use the hexadecimal addition feature of the Monitor when results are larger than a single byte (FF maximum), you must be able to estimate results so that you will know when a carry occurs.

HEXADECIMAL SUBTRACTION

Subtraction may also be performed with similar precautions. Here are some examples.

3D - 28

```
*3D-28 ◄────You type
=15 ◄──────────Computer responds
*
```

A4 - 2D

```
*A4-2D ◄────You type
=77 ◄──────────Computer responds
*
```

It looks easy, but what happens if you try to subtract a large number from a smaller one?

22 - 24 = ??

```
*22-24
=FE ◄────────That's what it says.
*
```

If your algebra is not too rusty, you know that you get a negative value when large positive numbers are subtracted from smaller positive numbers. Could FE be a negative number? Yes. Look back to the negative number table in Appendix B. FE is equivalent to the signed number –2.

You could use subtraction to create a table of negative values for future reference. For example,

```
*0-1           and           *0-4
=FF                          =FC
```

You can omit the 0 as an entry value if you wish. Try entering:

```
*-1            and           *-4
=FF                          =FC
```

Now create a table of negatives.

	Table of Negatives
*-0	
=00	
*-1	
=FF	FF = -1
*-2	
=FE	FE = -2
*-3	
=FD	FD = -3
*-4	
=FC	FC = -4
*-5	
=FB	FB = -5
.	.
.	.
.	.
*-7C	
=84	84 = -7C
*-7D	
=83	83 = -7D
*-7E	
=82	82 = -7E
*-7F	
=81	81 = -7F
*	

Subtraction can come in very handy when calculating the operand used in branch instructions. Turn back to "Description of the Program" in Chap. 7, and check the branch instructions used there.

At 776 and 777 of the Play Your Own Tune Program, we used F9 for a backward branch of -7. At 782 and 783, we used F3 for a backward branch of -13. Let's check these values.

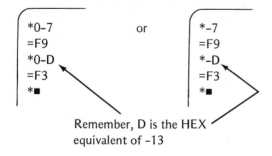

```
*0-7          or     *-7
=F9                  =F9
*0-D                 *-D
=F3                  =F3
*■                   *■
```

Remember, D is the HEX equivalent of -13

They do check.

DECIMAL ARITHMETIC

Are you tired of converting binary to HEX to decimal? If so, the 6502 instruction set includes an instruction to help you out. If you are careful to express the values that you wish to add or subtract as *binary-coded decimal* (BCD) numbers, the Apple can add or subtract those numbers and express the result as a decimal value. What are binary-coded decimal numbers? That's just a fancy name for a binary number that has been separated into two 4-bit parts. These parts are then interpreted as decimal digits.

Examples:

Binary	Binary-coded decimal	Decimal
01011000	0101 1000	58
10010011	1001 0011	93
00010110	0001 0110	16

Since each 4 bits are interpreted as a decimal digit, the binary inputs must be chosen with care.

11001001   =   1100 1001

                                       —— NOT a BCD value

10101011   =   1010 1011

                                       —— NOT BCD values

Each 4-bit part must be one of these:

BCD	DECIMAL
0000	0
0001	1
0010	2
0011	3
0100	4
0101	5
0110	6
0111	7
1000	8
1001	9

The instruction needed to request the computer to perform decimal addition or subtraction is:

SED   (SEt Decimal mode)

Op code = F8
Implied Addressing Mode
One byte long
Status flags affected - D

This instruction sets the decimal flag in the Processor Status Register to 1. Once this instruction has been used, all of the Add and Subtract instructions will be carried out as decimal operations because of the status of the decimal flag. The operation of any of the other instructions is *not* affected. If the SED instruction has been executed in a program, and a binary addition or subtraction is desired, the computer must execute the Clear Decimal Mode instruction.

CLD   (CLear Decimal Mode)

Op code = D8
Implied Addressing Mode
One byte long
Status flags affected - D

This instruction resets the decimal flag in the Processor Status Register to zero.

Suppose that we want to add the decimal numbers 18 and 23. We might use this program.

ADD TWO DECIMAL NUMBERS

300	F8	SED	Set decimal mode
301	18	CLC	Clear the carry bit
302	A9	LDA 23	Load 23 in accumulator
303	23		
304	69	ADC 18	Add 18
305	18		
306	20	JSR FDDA	Display result as two HEX digits
307	DA		
308	FD		
309	60	RTS	Return to Monitor

To enter the program using the Monitor, type:

300:F8 18 A9 23 69 18 20 DA FD 60

following the asterisk prompt. Then execute the program by typing: 300G.

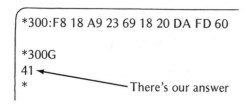

*300:F8 18 A9 23 69 18 20 DA FD 60

*300G
41 ◄
* ————— There's our answer

The decimal result of 18 + 23 is 41. If we had been adding the hexadecimal values of 18 and 23, the result would have been 3B. Remember, 18 and 23 in hexadecimal notation are different values from 18 and 23 in decimal notation. Therefore, 41 decimal and 3B HEX are *not* equivalent values.

Now let's execute the program starting from location 301 (omitting the Set Decimal instruction) and observe the result.

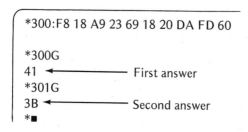

*300:F8 18 A9 23 69 18 20 DA FD 60

*300G
41 ◄————— First answer
*301G
3B ◄————— Second answer
*■

> Once the SED instruction has been executed, all additions in the program are performed in the decimal mode. The CLD (Clear Decimal Mode) instruction must be used to get back to binary addition while the program is running.

When the computer returned to the Monitor after the first run of the above program, the Monitor automatically executed its own CLD instruction. Therefore, when we skipped the SED instruction in the second run, the computer treated the two numbers (18 and 23) as hexadecimal values. The result was 3B. The SED instruction must be executed in every program if you want to use decimal arithmetic. The Monitor will automatically set the decimal bit of the Processor Status Register to 0 (the binary arithmetic mode) when the Monitor is entered.

The advantage of decimal addition is that it relieves you of converting numbers from one base to another for interpretation. You can input decimal values (such as 23 and 18) and obtain decimal results.

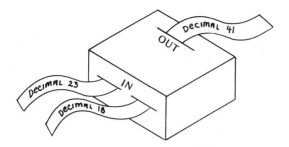

Try the Add Two Decimal Numbers Program with other pairs of decimal values. Substitute them for the values at memory locations 303 and 305.

Example:

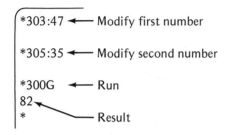

*303:47 ◄─── Modify first number

*305:35 ◄─── Modify second number

*300G ◄─── Run
82
* ─── Result

One caution again — make sure that the sum of the two numbers is less than 100. Any sum whose value is greater than 99 will not fit in the accumulator or any memory location. Remember, this is an 8-bit computer. Here is what will happen to you if you insist on experimenting (we secretly encourage you).

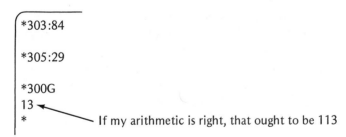

*303:84

*305:29

*300G
13
* ─── If my arithmetic is right, that ought to be 113

Again

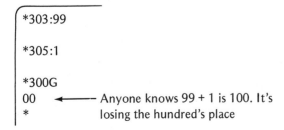

*303:99

*305:1

*300G
00 ◄─── Anyone knows 99 + 1 is 100. It's
* losing the hundred's place

Back to the paper and pencil to see what's happening to our result.

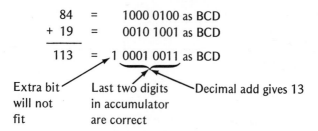

$$
\begin{array}{rcl}
84 & = & 1000\ 0100 \text{ as BCD} \\
+\ 19 & = & 0010\ 1001 \text{ as BCD} \\
\hline
113 & = & 1\ 0001\ 0011 \text{ as BCD}
\end{array}
$$

Extra bit   Last two digits   Decimal add gives 13
will not   in accumulator
fit   are correct

Since the 6502 microprocessor handles blocks of data in 8-bit sizes, some provision must be made for the situation that may result when a sum is larger than can be held in 8 bits. This technique was shown in Chap. 8. We will show two-byte decimal addition later in this chapter. First let's have a look at decimal subtraction.

We'll use some Monitor Magic to move our addition program to a new area of memory so that it will still be available if we need it later.

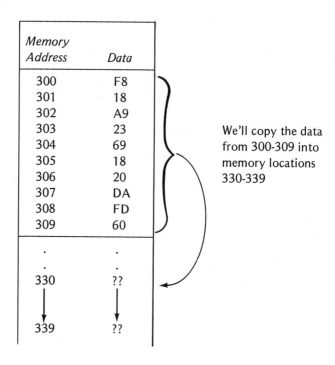

Memory Address	Data
300	F8
301	18
302	A9
303	23
304	69
305	18
306	20
307	DA
308	FD
309	60
.	.
.	.
.	.
330	??
339	??

We'll copy the data from 300-309 into memory locations 330-339

Then we'll alter the original decimal addition program to make it a decimal subtraction program.

1. Move the program.

The Monitor must be told the range of the memory block to be moved (300 through 309 in our case). It must also be told the beginning memory location to which the program is to be moved (330 in our case). The format for this command is:

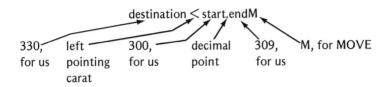

destination ≤ start,endM

330;	left	300,	decimal	309,	M, for MOVE
for us	pointing	for us	point	for us	
	carat				

As seen on the display:

*330<300.309M

Destination   Start   End   MOVE

To see how it works, first examine the original program.

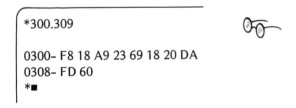

*300.309

0300- F8 18 A9 23 69 18 20 DA
0308- FD 60
*■

Then make the MOVE.

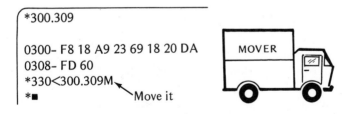

*300.309

0300- F8 18 A9 23 69 18 20 DA
0308- FD 60
*330<300.309M
*■   Move it

MOVER

Then, to make sure the move was successful, we can examine both areas of memory.

```
*300.309
0300- F8 18 A9 23 69 18 20 DA
0308- FD 60
*300<300.309M

*330.339

0330- F8 18 A9 23 69 18 20 DA          Examine 330-339 ⎫
0338- FD 60                                            ⎬  both
*300.309                                               ⎭  alike

0300- F8 18 A9 23 69 18 20 DA          Examine 300-309 ⎭
0308- FD 60
*■
```

A simpler way to do this takes advantage of more Monitor Magic. We can compare two areas of memory and verify that they are the same by one Monitor command called VERIFY. To use the Verify command, the monitor also needs to know a range and a destination. The format used is:

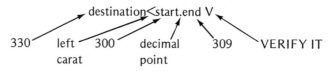

destination<start.end V

330   left   300   decimal   309   VERIFY IT
       carat   point

The Monitor compares the range specified with the range beginning at the destination address. If there are any discrepancies, the address where the difference is found is displayed along with the two unlike values. If no differences are found, nothing is displayed.

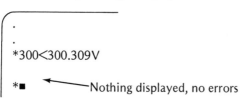

```
.
.
*300<300.309V

*■          Nothing displayed, no errors
```

Let's modify one location so that we can see how discrepancies are displayed.

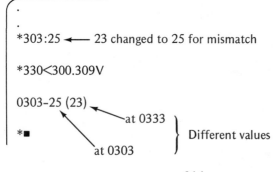

```
.
.
*303:25 ◄── 23 changed to 25 for mismatch

*330<300.309V

0303-25 (23)
              at 0333  ⎫
*■                     ⎬  Different values
        at 0303        ⎭
```

214

The error should then be corrected (whichever version is wrong) and re-verified.

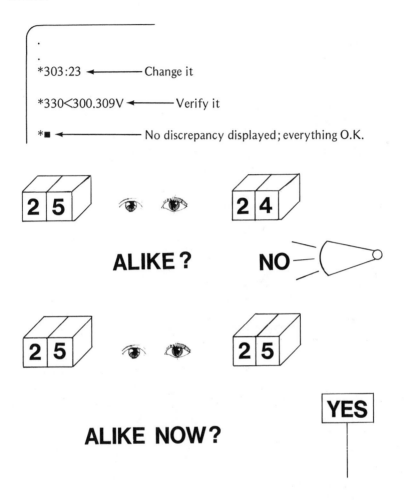

```
        •
        •
*303:23  ◄──────── Change it

*330<300.309V ◄──────── Verify it

*■ ◄──────── No discrepancy displayed; everything O.K.
```

ALIKE ? **NO**

ALIKE NOW? **YES**

2. Change the original program

   Now we will alter the original program for subtraction. We need to change the CLC (18) at location 301 to SEC (38) and ADC (69) at location 304 to SBC (E9).

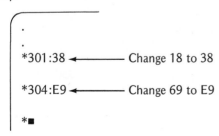

```
        •
        •
*301:38  ◄──────── Change 18 to 38

*304:E9  ◄──────── Change 69 to E9

*■
```

Now examine the modified program.

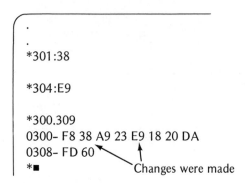

```
         .
         .
*301:38

*304:E9

*300.309
0300- F8 38 A9 23 E9 18 20 DA
0308- FD 60
*■
```
Changes were made

Now run the subtraction program

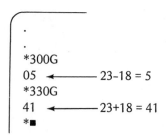

```
      .
      .
*300G
05
*■
```
23–18 = 5 when working with decimal numbers

If you need to run the addition program,

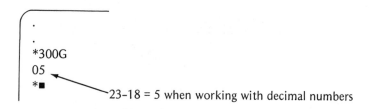

```
      .
      .
*300G
05  ◄———— 23–18 = 5
*330G
41  ◄———— 23+18 = 41
*■
```

Both programs still exist in memory. You can make the choice as to which one is executed.

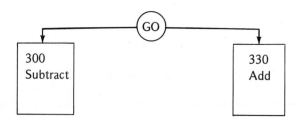

```
                    ┌─(GO)─┐
                    │      │
              ┌─────▼─┐  ┌─▼─────┐
              │ 300   │  │ 330   │
              │ Subtract│ │ Add  │
              └───────┘  └───────┘
```

EXAMINING AND ALTERING REGISTERS

You've seen how to examine and alter memory, but how about the registers? Can they be examined and changed? Yes, you can do both.

To examine the registers, hold down the CTRL key. At the same time, press the E key. Then release both. Press the RETURN key, and the registers will be displayed on the screen. The contents of registers A, X, Y, P, and S will be displayed in that order from left to right. Do you remember what the letters stand for?

A   Accumulator
X   Index register X
Y   Index register Y
P   Processor status register
S   Stack pointer register

The values that we see just after turning on the Apple and pressing CTRL E together followed by RETURN are:

```
*            ◄────CTRL E is not displayed

A=FF X=FF Y=FF P=00 S=FF
*■
```

After you have examined the registers, their contents may be changed (in order from left to right) by typing a colon (:) followed by the new values.
Try these:

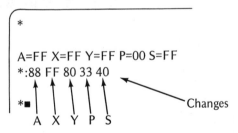

```
*

A=FF X=FF Y=FF P=00 S=FF
*:88 FF 80 33 40
*■ ↑ ↑ ↑ ↑ ↑          Changes
  A X Y P S
```

To find out if they have really been changed, press CTRL E to examine them again.

```
A=FF X=FF Y=FF P=00 S=FF ◄────────Originally
*:88 FF 80 33 40    ◄────────The change

*            ◄────────CTRL E pressed here

A=88 X=FF Y=80 P=33 S=40
*■          Changes have been made
```

217

One of the changes made was to the Processor status register. Its new value is 33. Broken down into the individual status bits we now have:

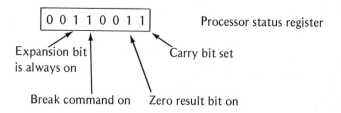

Notice that we have set the carry bit. If an addition is performed now, the carry bit would be included for the ADC instruction. Let's try it.

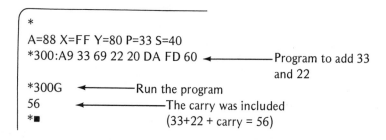

Now let's examine the registers again and then turn off the carry bit by changing the P register (Processor status register). Then we'll add the two numbers again.

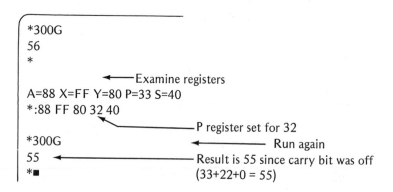

This time we'll load 33 into the accumulator, transfer the result to the X register, add 22 to the accumulator, and display the result. Then we'll take another look at the registers to see how they have changed.

The program:
```
300  A9   LDA 33
301  33
302  AA   TAX   (transfer accumulator to X)
303  69   ADC 22
304  22
305  20   JSR FDDA   Display result
306  DA
307  FD
308  60   RTS         Return to Monitor
```

One of the best methods for finding errors in programs is the Monitor's Single-Step feature. The Single-Step command decodes, displays, and executes one instruction at a time. The instruction is displayed in both machine and assembler codes (the Mini-Assembler will be discussed in Chap. 11).

When the instruction is executed, the contents of the registers are displayed. We'll use the single-step command to watch the registers change as each instruction is executed.

The Single-Step command is an S. To use the command, first type the starting address of the program followed by the S.

Example:

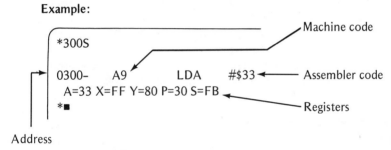

Machine code

*300S

0300-   A9   LDA   #$33 ◄────── Assembler code

A=33 X=FF Y=80 P=30 S=FB

*■

Registers

Address

For each successive instruction, type an S and press the RETURN key, as in the following example.

Enter the program and then single-step through it.

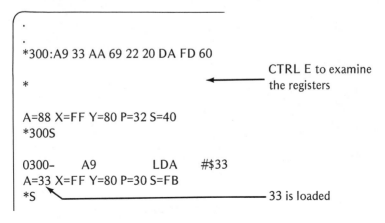

```
.
.
.
*300:A9 33 AA 69 22 20 DA FD 60

*
```
CTRL E to examine
the registers
```
A=88 X=FF Y=80 P=32 S=40
*300S

0300-   A9          LDA     #$33
A=33 X=FF Y=80 P=30 S=FB
*S
```
33 is loaded

219

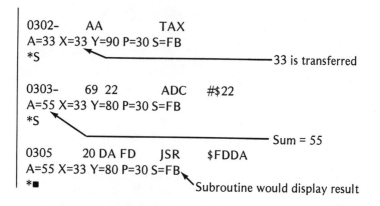

```
0302-    AA        TAX
A=33 X=33 Y=90 P=30 S=FB
*S  ◄——————————————————— 33 is transferred

0303-    69 22     ADC    #$22
A=55 X=33 Y=80 P=30 S=FB
*S  ◄
                ——————————————— Sum = 55
0305     20 DA FD  JSR    $FDDA
A=55 X=33 Y=80 P=30 S=FB
*■              ↖Subroutine would display result
```

By single-stepping through the program you can see the results of executing instructions. Registers affected by each instruction can be seen to change as requested. In this example, the Accumulator and the X register were altered as the program was executed.

The subroutine at FDDA contains many, many steps, so we stopped when we came to that instruction.

You might notice also that the value in the Processor status register was 32 before the first instruction (LDA) was executed. After execution of the LDA instruction, the Processor status register changed to 30. The zero bit has been turned off because 33 is not equal to zero.

Let's now add one instruction, TAY (A8), to transfer the result of the addition to the Y register. We won't display the result this time.

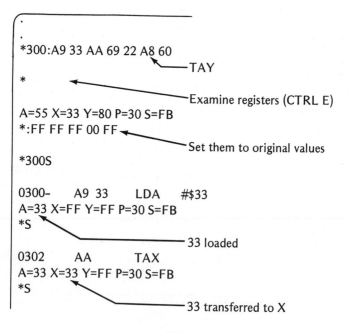

```
   ·
   ·
*300:A9 33 AA 69 22 A8 60
                ↖——TAY
*  ◄
                ↖Examine registers (CTRL E)
A=55 X=33 Y=80 P=30 S=FB
*:FF FF FF 00 FF ◄
                ↖Set them to original values
*300S

0300-    A9 33     LDA    #$33
A=33 X=FF Y=FF P=30 S=FB
*S ↖
                ——— 33 loaded
0302     AA        TAX
A=33 X=33 Y=FF P=30 S=FB
*S ↖
                ——— 33 transferred to X
```

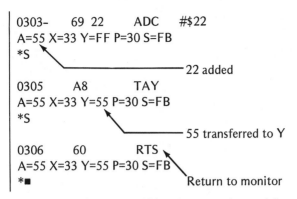

```
0303-    69 22    ADC    #$22
A=55 X=33 Y=FF P=30 S=FB
*S
```
— 22 added

```
0305    A8    TAY
A=55 X=33 Y=55 P=30 S=FB
*S
```
— 55 transferred to Y

```
0306    60    RTS
A=55 X=33 Y=55 P=30 S=FB
*■
```
Return to monitor

So, you see that the X and Y registers can be used for temporary storage. In Chap. 11, we'll show how they are used as index registers for instructions in the Indexed Addressing modes.

Let's try one last program to wind up this chapter. This time we'll increment the X register, compare it with zero, branching back to increment X again if the contents of the X register are not equal to zero.

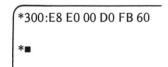

The program
```
300  E8  INX         5
301  E0  CPX 0       4
302  00              3 loop
303  D0  BNE FB      2
304  FB              1 ← FB = -5, check it
305  60  RTS             if you wish on the
                         Apple (0-5=FB)
```

Enter the program

```
*300:E8 E0 00 D0 FB 60

*■
```

Before we run the program, let's put a value of FD in the X register. How long will it be before the contents of the X register reach zero? We'll single-step the program to find out.

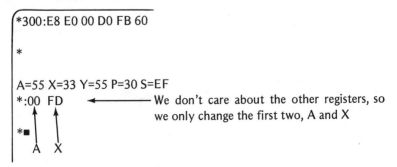

```
*300:E8 E0 00 D0 FB 60

*

A=55 X=33 Y=55 P=30 S=EF
*:00 FD     ←——— We don't care about the other registers, so
                 we only change the first two, A and X
*■
 A  X
```

Next, single-step through the program.

```
*300:E8 E0 00 D0 FB 60

*

A=55 X=33 Y=55 P=30 S=EF
*:00 FD

*300S            ◄────────Request first step

0300-      E8           INX
A=00 X=FE Y=55 P=B0 S=F1        ◄───── X = FD+1=FE
*S                              ◄───── Next step requested

0301-      E0 00        CPX     #$00
A=00 X=FE Y=55 P=B1 S=F1
*S                              ◄───── Next step requested

0303-      D0 FB        BNE     $0300
A=00 X=FE Y=55 P=B1 S=F1
*S                              ◄───── Next step requested

0300-      E8           INX
A=00 X=FF Y=55 P=B1 S=F1        ◄───── X=FE+1=FF
*S                             ◄───── Next step

0301-      E0 00        CPX     #$00
A=00 X=FF Y=55 P=B1 S=F1
*S                             ◄───── Next step

0303-      D0 FB        BNE     $0300
A=00 X=FF Y=55 P=B1 S=F1
*S                             ◄───── Next step

0300-      +8           INX
A=00 X=00 Y=55 P=33 S=F1        ◄───── X=FF+1=00◄─┐
*S                                                │
                             └──── Carry bit on due to ┘

0301-      E0 00        CPX     #$00
A=00 X=00 Y=55 P=33 S=F1
*S                             ◄───── Next step

0303-      D0 FB        BNE     $0300
A=00 X=00 Y=55 P=33 S=F1
*S                             ◄───── Next step

0305-      60           RTS  ◄────── Branch was not taken
A=00 X=00 Y=55 P=33 S=F1             since X register =
*■                                   CPX value (00)
```

SUMMARY

You have had a tour of the Apple System Monitor in this chapter. You have explored some of the features that it has to make machine language programming easier. We hope you will extend these explorations with other experiments of your own until you are thoroughly familiar with the Monitor's capabilities.

You have:

1. Used hexadecimal addition and subtraction in the Immediate mode,

2. Discovered how negative numbers are interpreted using hexadecimal values,

3. Learned how to perform addition and subtraction operations with binary-coded decimal numbers,

4. Learned now to move blocks of data from one memory area to another,

5. Learned how to verify that two blocks of memory are the same, and

6. Learned how to examine and alter registers.

New Instructions

1. SED (SEt Decimal mode) — used to set the decimal flag in the Processor status register to 1. All subsequent add-and-subtract instructions are then executed as if the values to be operated on are binary-coded decimal numbers.

2. CLD (CLear Decimal mode) — resets the decimal flag in the Processor status register to 0. This returns addition and subtraction operations to binary format.

3. TAY (Transfer Accumulator to Y register) — copies the contents of the accumulator into the Y register.

New Monitor Commands and Uses

1. Hexadecimal add and subtract — type in two 2-digit HEX numbers separated by the operation symbol and press RETURN. A 2-digit HEX result is displayed.

2. Move a block of data in memory — provide the Monitor with the address range of the block to be moved and the beginning destination address. The Monitor will then copy the data into the destination area.

   Format: destination start.endM

   Example: *330<300.309M

   —would copy the block of data in memory
   locations 300 through 309 into memory
   locations 330 through 309.

3. Verify two blocks of data — provide the Monitor with the address range of one block of data and the starting address of the second

block of data. The Monitor will compare the two blocks and let you know if a discrepancy exists.

Format: destination start.endM

Example: *330<300.309V
—would compare data in memory
locations 300 through 309 with
data in memory locations 330
through 339.

4. Examine registers — The A,X,Y,P, and S registers may be examined by pressing the CTRL and E keys together followed by a RETURN.

5. Alter registers — The A,X,Y,P, and S registers may be modified by first examining them as in 4 above, then typing a colon followed by the new values, in order, separated by one blank space.

EXERCISES

1. Using hexadecimal addition in the Immediate mode, provide answers to the following:

   a. *2E+35   c. *A4-31

      = _____   = _____

   b. *E5+F   *5A-2E

      = _____   = _____

2. What would be displayed if the following were executed in the Immediate mode?

   a. *D7+4F   b. *24-27

      = _____   = _____

3. Express the following decimal numbers in binary-coded decimal form.

   a. 28 = _____ _____
   b. 37 = _____ _____
   c. 91 = _____ _____

4. If the Add Two Decimal Numbers Program is modified as shown below, fill in the displayed result.

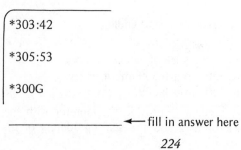

*303:42

*305:53

*300G

_____ ◄—fill in answer here

5. Show how to use the Monitor Move command to move the Add Two Decimal Numbers Program to memory locations 350 through 359.

```
* _____
```

6. Show how to verify that the Move of Exercise 5 was made correctly.

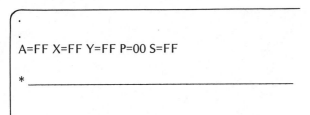

```
.
.
.
* _____
```

7. Describe how to examine the registers.

_____

_____

8. Suppose that you had examined the registers, and the display shows the results below. Show what would be typed to change the accumulator to 00, the X register to 80, and the Y register to 40.

```
.
.
A=FF X=FF Y=FF P=00 S=FF

* _____
```

ANSWERS TO EXERCISES

1. a. =63   c. =73
   b. =F4   d. =2C

2. a. =26   b. =FD
   (carry is not shown,   (FD=-3)
   D7+4F=126)

3. a. 28 = 0010 1000
   b. 37 = 0011 0111
   c. 91 = 1001 0001

4. 95 (42+53=95 in decimal)

5.
```
*350<300.309M
```

6.
```
*350<300.309V
```

7. Press the CTRL and E keys together.
   Then press the RETURN key.

8.

.
.
.

A=FF X=FF Y=FF P=00 S=FF
*:00 80 40

                  (the others do not have to be changed)

Chapter 11

Mini-Assembler and Addressing Modes

MA	SM

There is another program that is part of the Apple Integer BASIC ROM, but is not available in the Apple II Plus systems. This program is called the Apple Mini-Assembler. It is called "mini" because it cannot understand symbolic labels that full-sized assemblers can. It is very useful in creating machine language programs.

In past chapters, we have been showing machine language codes along with their mnemonic codes. The mnemonic code is an abbreviated name for each instruction. We have been translating these mnemonic codes into hexadecimal or binary machine language instructions (Op codes). This process is called *hand assembly*.

Examples:

Mnemonic Code	Addressing Code	Machine Code
LDA	Immediate	A9
ADC	Immediate	69
CLC	Implied	18

Hand assembly is an uninteresting and tedious task that is very prone to small, but disastrous, errors. The length of instructions vary, and branch destinations may be calculated. Some instructions require data as operands, while others require memory addresses or registers. It is easy to pick wrong Op codes or addresses. It is also easy to transpose or mistype digits, etc. It would be much easier for us to assign the job of assembling a program to the computer. The Apple Mini-Assembler can easily take care of assembling programs for us if we write the programs using *assembly language* instructions. This chapter will be devoted to learning the rules for using the Mini-Assembler and the assembly language form for the many addressing modes used.

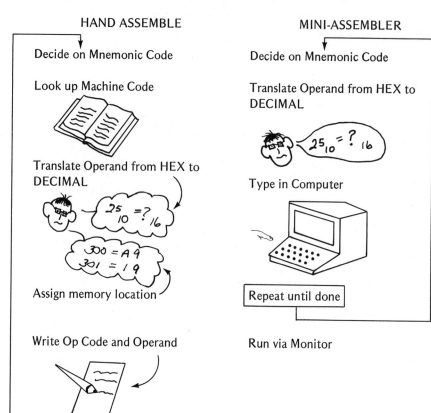

HAND ASSEMBLE

Decide on Mnemonic Code

Look up Machine Code

Translate Operand from HEX to DECIMAL

Assign memory location

Write Op Code and Operand

Repeat until done

MINI-ASSEMBLER

Decide on Mnemonic Code

Translate Operand from HEX to DECIMAL

Type in Computer

Repeat until done

Run via Monitor

Enter program via Monitor

Run via Monitor

USING THE MINI-ASSEMBLER

In order to use the Mini-Assembler, you must know how to access it, and how to get out of it when you have finished assembling your program. If you have the Applesoft II ROM card in your Apple, turn the switch on the back of the computer to Integer BASIC. The Mini-Assembler program is in this ROM. If your machine does not have Integer BASIC, it does not have the Mini-Assembler. This chapter would not then be applicable to your system. Other assemblers are available that can be entered from tape or disk.

To run the Mini-Assembler, type: F666G

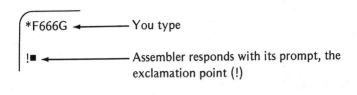

*F666G ◄——— You type

!■ ◄——————— Assembler responds with its prompt, the
exclamation point (!)

Eventually, you'll want to leave the Mini-Assembler and re-enter the Monitor to run the program that you have assembled. This can be done in either of
two ways:

1. Press the RESET key

2. Type the Monitor Command (preceded by a dollar sign): $FF69G

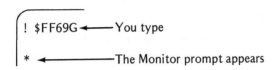

! $FF69G ◄——— You type

* ◄——————— The Monitor prompt appears

After accessing the Mini-Assembler and before returning to the Monitor,
an assembly language program is entered. We'll use the Add Two Decimal Numbers Program from Chap. 10 for a brief demonstration.

1.

*F666G ◄——— Starting in the Monitor, type this

!■ ◄——————— Mini-Assembler prompt appears
Ready to go

2. Type in the address of the first instruction, a colon, and the mnemonic
code for the first instruction. The Mini-Assembler displays each instruction as it is assembled.

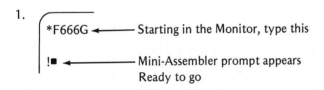

*F666G

!300:SED ◄——— You enter address: instruction

When you press the RETURN key, your assembly instruction disappears, and the assembled machine language code appears.

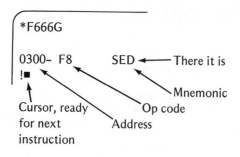

```
*F666G

0300- F8        SED ◄──── There it is
!■ ◄
```

- Cursor, ready for next instruction
- Address
- Op code
- Mnemonic

3. Type only the mnemonic for Clear carry.

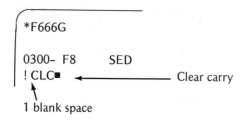

```
*F666G

0300- F8        SED
! CLC■ ◄─────────────── Clear carry
```

1 blank space

Press RETURN

```
*F666G

0300- F8        SED
0301- 18        CLC
!■ ◄────────────────Next?
```

Notice the blank space following the Mini-Assembler prompt. If the blank space is not placed there, the instruction will not be accepted. The Mini-Assembler will show where an error occurs in an improper entry.

Example:

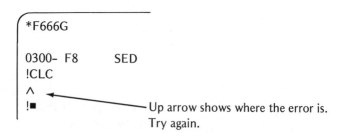

```
*F666G

0300- F8        SED
!CLC
^ ◄
!■ ────────────── Up arrow shows where the error is.
                  Try again.
```

4. So far, both instructions used have been in the Implied mode and need
no operand. The next instruction, LDA, is in the Immediate mode, and
must be followed by the # sign followed by the operand 23 to tell the
computer that this is an immediate operand.

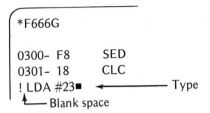

```
*F666G

0300- F8    SED
0301- 18    CLC
! LDA #23■   ◄─────────── Type
  └── Blank space
```

Press RETURN

```
*F666G

0300- F8    SED
0301- 18    CLC
0302- A9 23 LDA #$23
!■
```

5. Next, the ADC instruction followed by #18.

```
  .
  .
  .
! ADC #18■  ◄─────────── Type
```

Press RETURN

```
*F666G

0300- F8    SED
0301- 18    CLC
0302- A9 23 LDA #$23
0304- 69 18 ADC #$18
!■
```

6. Next, the JSR instruction followed by the Absolute address FDDA.

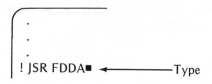

! JSR FDDA■ ◄————————Type

Press RETURN

```
*F666G

0300- F8          SED
0301- 18          CLC
0302- A9 23       LDA #$23
0304- 69 18       ADC #$18
0306- 20 DA FD    JSR $FDDA
!■
```

7. Last, the RTS instruction (Implied mode)

! RTS■ ◄———————— Type

Press RETURN

```
*F666G

0300- F8          SED
0301- 18          CLC
0302- A9 23       LDA #$23
0304- 69 18       ADC #$18
0306- 20 DA FD    JSR $FDDA
0309- 60          RTS
!■
```

8. Now, leave the Mini-Assembler. The program has been assembled.

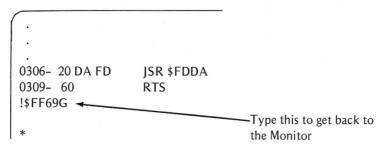

```
      .
      .
      .
0306-  20 DA FD      JSR $FDDA
0309-  60            RTS
!$FF69G ◄───────────────────────────┐
                              Type this to get back to
 *                            the Monitor
```

The assembled program is now in memory. You may list it with the Monitor command L.

The list command of the Monitor works just like the LIST command of BASIC language. If you type:

300L and press RETURN

the Monitor lists the contents of 20 consecutive memory locations starting with 300.

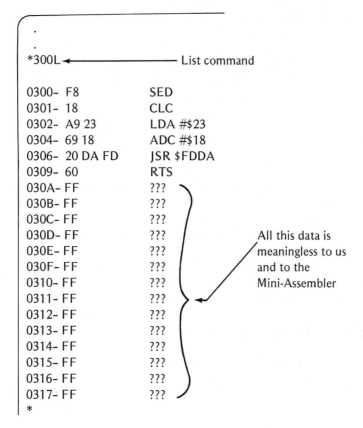

```
      .
      .
*300L ◄─────────── List command

0300-  F8            SED
0301-  18            CLC
0302-  A9 23         LDA #$23
0304-  69 18         ADC #$18
0306-  20 DA FD      JSR $FDDA
0309-  60            RTS
030A- FF             ???
030B- FF             ???
030C- FF             ???
030D- FF             ???         All this data is
030E- FF             ???         meaningless to us
030F- FF             ???         and to the
0310- FF             ???         Mini-Assembler
0311- FF             ???
0312- FF             ???
0313- FF             ???
0314- FF             ???
0315- FF             ???
0316- FF             ???
0317- FF             ???
 *
```

The first few lines are your assembly language program. The rest of the lines are not used by the program. Each time the List command is given, 20 address locations are displayed. For longer programs, 20 more locations will be displayed each time that you press the L key and RETURN.

Now it's time to run the program.

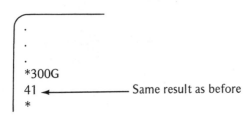

Notice that when using the Mini-Assembler, we didn't have to look up the machine language codes for the instructions. Mnemonic codes are much easier to remember than numeric codes. Remember, though, as we mentioned earlier, that some instructions can be used in several Addressing modes. How does the Mini-Assembler know which mode we want?

In the Add Two Decimal Numbers Program, the choices to be made by the Mini-Assembler were easy. Look at the instructions that were used.

1. SED (Set decimal mode) — this instruction is only used in the Implied mode. No choice necessary.

2. CLD (Clear carry) — this instruction is also used only in the Implied mode. No choice necessary.

3. LDA (Load accumulator) — Notice the pound sign (#) in front of the number 23. That tells the assembler that the code for the Immediate Addressing mode is needed.

4. ADC (Add with carry) — Once again, the # sign is used to denote the Immediate Addressing mode.

5. JSR (Jump to subroutine) — this instruction is only used in the Absolute Addressing mode. No choice necessary.

You have used the Implied, Immediate, Zero Page, and Absolute Addressing modes frequently. We'll now turn our attention to Indexed Addressing, which is quite useful although a little more complex.

INDEXED ADDRESSING

Two of the most frequently used instructions either load the accumulator or store the contents of the accumulator into memory. We'll use these two instructions to demonstrate the Indexed Addressing modes. Here is a list of Indexed modes.

LDA

Assembly Language Form	Addressing Mode	Op Code	Number of Bytes Used
LDA oper, X	Zero Page, X	B5	2
LDA oper, X	Absolute, X	BD	3
LDA oper, Y	Absolute, Y	B9	3
LDA(oper, X)	(Indirect, X)	A1	2
LDA(oper),Y	(Indirect), Y	B1	2

STA

Assembly Language Form	Addressing Mode	Op Code	Number of Bytes Used
STA oper, X	Zero Page, X	95	2
STA oper, X	Absolute, X	9D	3
STA oper, Y	Absolute, Y	99	3
STA(oper, X)	(Indirect, X)	81	2
STA(oper), Y	(Indirect), Y	91	2

ZERO PAGE INDEXING

Because zero page instructions execute quicker than other addressing modes, the Apple computer already uses most of the necessary locations used by these instructions. Zero page memory locations are those from 0000 through 00FF. Only the low-order part of the address is necessary for the computer to recognize the location required. By looking at the Zero Page Memory Map (pages 74 and 75 of the Apple II Reference Manual), you may notice that 0000 through 001F are *not used* by the Monitor or by the Integer BASIC ROM. They *are* used by Applesoft II BASIC. If we stay out of Applesoft II BASIC, we may be able to use that area of memory for demonstrating Zero Page Addressing.

All instructions that use this mode of addressing *except* LDX (Load the X register) and STX (Store the X register) use the X register to modify the instruction's operand (the address used).

LDA oper, X   Load accumulator from the zero
  Op code B5 (Zero page)   page address + contents of the
  2nd byte, operand   X register
    (low order address)

Examples:

1. Contents of X register = 3

    304 LDA 0,X   would load the accumulator from
                               the memory address 0003
                               (0000 + 03)

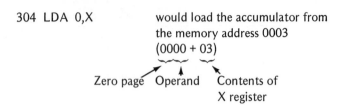

    Zero page Operand   Contents of
                            X register

2. Contents of X register = 2

    307 LDA 3,X   would load the accumulator from
                               memory address 0005
                               (0003 + 02)

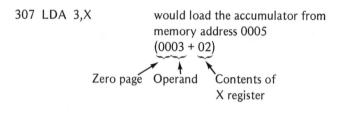

    Zero page Operand   Contents of
                            X register

    STA oper, X   Load accumulator from the zero
      Op code 95 (zero page)   page address + contents of
      2nd byte, operand   X register
      (low order address)

This instruction works just like the LDA oper, X (Zero Page mode) except that the accumulator's contents are stored.

Both types are demonstrated in the following program, which moves the values from memory locations 0005 and 0006 to memory locations 0015 and 0016. We'll use the Mini-Assembler to assemble the program.

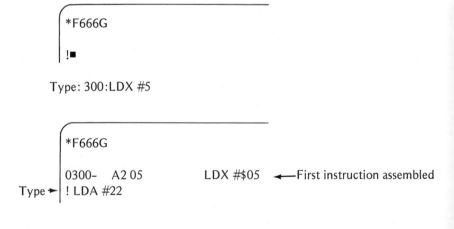

    *F666G

    !■

Type: 300:LDX #5

    *F666G

    0300- A2 05   LDX #$05   ◄——First instruction assembled
Type ► ! LDA #22

236

```
*F666G

0300-   A2 05              LDX #$05
0302-   A9 22              LDA #$22  ◄─── Next instruction added
Type ►  ! STA 0,X
```

```
*F666G

0300-   A2 05              LDX #$05
0302-   A9 22              LDA #$22
0304-   95 00              STA $00,X  ◄─── Next
Type ►  ! LDA #33
```

```
*F666G

0300-   A2 05              LDX #$05
0302-   A9 22              LDA #$22
0304-   95 00              STA $00,X
0306-   A9 33              LDA #$33  ◄─── Next
Type ►  ! STA 1,X
```

```
*F666G

0300-   A2 05              LDX #$05
0302-   A9 22              LDA #$22
0304-   95 00              STA $00,X
0306-   A9 33              LDA #$33
0308-   95 01              STA $01,X  ◄─── Next
Type ►  ! LDA 0,X
```

One new instruction added each time

```
*F666G

0300-   A2 05              LDX #$05
0302-   A9 22              LDA #$22
0304-   95 00              STA $00,X
0306-   A9 33              LDA #$33
0308-   95 01              STA $01,X
030A-   85 00              LDA $00,X
! STA 10,X
```

```
*F666G

0300-   A2 05         LDX #$05
0302-   A9 22         LDA #$22
0304-   95 00         STA $00,X
0306-   A9 33         LDA #$33
0308-   95 01         STA $01,X
030A-   85 00         LDA $00,X
030C-   95 10         STA $10,X
! INX
```

```
*F666G

0300-   A2 05         LDX #$05
0302-   A9 22         LDA #$22
0304-   95 00         STA $00,X
0306-   A9 33         LDA #$33
0308-   95 01         STA $01,X
030A-   85 00         LDA $00,X
030C-   95 10         STA $10,X
030E-   E8           INX
! LDA 0,X
```

```
F666G

0300-   A2 05         LDX #$05
0302-   A9 22         LDA #$22
0304-   95 00         STA $00,X
0306-   A9 33         LDA #$33
0308-   95 01         STA $01,X
030A-   85 00         LDA $00,X
030C-   95 10         STA $10,X
030E-   E8           INX
030F-   85 00         LDA $00,X
! STA 10,X
```

```
F666G

0300-   A2 05        LDX #$05
0302-   A9 22        LDA #$22
0304-   95 00        STA $00,X
0306-   A9 33        LDA #$33
0308-   95 01        STA $01,X
030A-   85 00        LDA $00,X
030C-   95 10        STA $10,X
030E-   E8           INX
030F-   85 00        LDA $00,X
0311-   95 10        STA $10,X
! RTS
```

```
F666G

0300-   A2 05        LDX #$05
0302-   A9 22        LDA #$22
0304-   95 00        STA $00,X
0306-   A9 33        LDA #$33
0308-   95 01        STA $01,X
030A-   85 00        LDA $00,X
030C-   95 10        STA $10,X
030E-   E8           INX
030F-   85 00        LDA $00,X
0311-   95 10        STA $10,X
0313-   60           RTS
! $FF69G  ◄───────────────────── Leave the Mini-Assembler
*
```

Zero Page Indexed instructions were used at 0304, 0308, 030A, 030C, 030F, and 0311. Now run the program. Then examine locations 0005, 0006, 0015, and 0016.

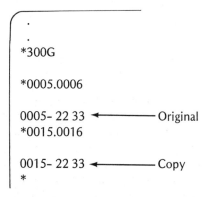

```
    .
    .
*300G

*0005.0006

0005- 22 33  ◄─────────── Original
*0015.0016

0015- 22 33  ◄─────────── Copy
*
```

ABSOLUTE INDEXED ADDRESSING

Either the X or the Y index register can be used to index an absolute address in this mode. You do not have to restrict yourself to zero page memory.

Examples:

LDA 301,X
   Op code BD (Absolute indexed)
   2nd byte, low-order address (10)
   3rd byte, high-order address (03)

This instruction loads the accumulator from the memory address 0310 + contents of the X register. (Y could also be used.)

STA 320,Y
   Op code 99 (Absolute indexed)
   2nd byte, low-order address (20)
   3rd byte, high-order address (03)

This instruction stores the contents of the accumulator into memory address 0320 + contents of the Y register. (X could also be used.)

We'll use these instructions to store some characters from the keyboard into memory and to retrieve them for display on the video screen. We'll use the Mini-Assembler to put the program together.

First we'll store 17 characters from the keyboard in a consecutive memory block using the STA Indexed Addressing mode with X as the index register.

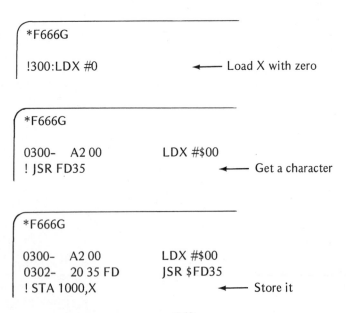

```
*F666G

!300:LDX #0              ◄──── Load X with zero
```

```
*F666G

0300-   A2 00       LDX #$00
! JSR FD35                   ◄──── Get a character
```

```
*F666G

0300-   A2 00       LDX #$00
0302-   20 35 FD    JSR $FD35
! STA 1000,X                 ◄──── Store it
```

```
*F666G

0300-  A2 00       LDX #$00
0302-  20 35 FD    JSR $FD35
0305-  9D 00 10    STA $1000,X
! INX                           ◄──── Increase X by one
```

```
*F666G

0300-  A2 00       LDX #$00
0302-  20 35 FD    JSR $FD35
0305-  9D 00 10    STA $1000,X
0308-  E8          INX
! CPX #11                       ◄──── Done yet?
```

```
*F666G

0300-  A2 00       LDX #$00
0302-  20 35 FD    JSR $FD35
0305-  9D 00 10    STA $1000,X
0308-  E8          INX
0309-  E0 11       CPX #$11
! BNE 302                       ◄──── If not, go back to 302
```

```
*F666G

0300-  A2 00       LDX #$00
0302-  20 35 FD    JSR $FD35
0305-  9D 00 10    STA $1000,X
0308-  E8          INX
0309-  E0 11       CPX #$11
030B-  DO F5       BNE $0302
! JSR FC58                      ◄──── Clear the screen
```

```
*F666G

0300-  A2  00      LDX #$00
0302-  20 35 FD    JSR $FD35
0305-  9D 00 10    STA $1000,X
0308-  E8          INX
0309-  E0 11       CPX #$11
030B-  DO F5       BNE $0302
030D-  20 58 FC    JSR $FC58
!■
```

Let's pause here to see how this part of the program works. Notice that this part contains a loop that is much like a BASIC FOR-NEXT loop. The subroutine at FD35 waits for a character to be typed from the keyboard. The character is then stored by the Absolute Indexed instruction (STA 1000,X). The X register is increased by one and tested to see if it has reached 11 (HEX). If not, a loop is made back to the subroutine for another character. When the seventeenth character has been typed, X will have reached 11. The screen is then cleared by the subroutine at FC58. Not only does the X value control the exit from the loop; it also indexes the memory address at which the character is stored. Thus, the characters are stored in consecutive memory locations like this.

Pass Through the Loop	X reg. (HEX)	Memory Used to Store Character
1	0	1000
2	1	1001
3	2	1002
4	3	1003
.	.	.
.	.	.
15	E	100E
16	F	100F
17	10	1010

Continuing on with the second part of the program, input the following instructions each time you see the Mini-Assembler prompt:

! LDA #0	Reset X to zero
! LDA 1000,X	Load a character from memory
! JSR FDED	Display it
! INX	Get ready for the next one
! CPX #11	Done yet?
! BNE 312	If not, go back to 312
! RTS	If done, go to Monitor

After this, the display will show:

```
*F666G

0300-   A2 00          LDX #$00          ⎫
0302-   20 35 FD       JSR $FD35         ⎪
0305-   9D 00 10       STA $1000,X       ⎪  First part
0308-   E8             INX               ⎬
0309-   E0 11          CPX #$11          ⎪
030B-   D0 F5          BNE $0302         ⎪
030D-   20 58 FC       JSR $FC58         ⎭
0310-   A2 00          LDX #$00          ⎫
0312-   BD 00 10       LDA $1000,X       ⎪
0315-   20 ED FD       JSR $FDED         ⎪  Second part
0318-   E8             INX               ⎬
0319-   E0 11          CPX #$11          ⎪
031B-   D0 F5          BNE $0312         ⎪
031D-   60             RTS               ⎭
!$FF69G        ◄─────────────── End it by leaving the
                                 Mini-Assembler
*
```

The second part of the program also contains a loop that loads a character from memory and displays it. The loop continues until all 17 characters
have been displayed. It then returns to the Monitor. The Indexed Addressing
instruction (LDA 1000,X) is used to load the accumulator on each pass through
the loop. Since the X register was reset to zero at the start of the loop, the
instruction retrieves the previously stored characters in the same order that they
were stored (see table shown earlier in this chapter). Indexed addressing is very
handy to load and store values in blocks of consecutive memory locations.

When you run the program, type in 17 characters from the keyboard
(count spaces as characters). You won't see the characters as they are typed in.
They will be displayed *after* you have entered all 17. Here is a typical run with
the message "ABSOLUTE INDEXING." You may use any 17 character message. Or make a few alterations to the program and fill the screen.

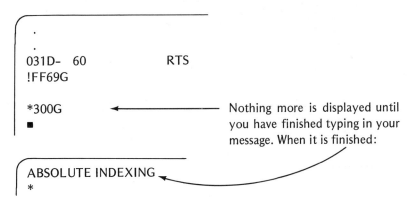

```
    .
    .
    .
031D-   60          RTS
!FF69G

*300G    ◄─────────────── Nothing more is displayed until
■                           you have finished typing in your
                            message. When it is finished:

ABSOLUTE INDEXING
*
```

243

The Y register could have been used instead of the X register for indexing. Either may be used.

STA 1000,X   or   STA 1000,Y
LDA 1000,X   or   LDA 1000,Y

You could also use a combination of the two:

STA 1000,X
LDA 1000,Y

Of course, the proper register must be given the correct initial value and incremented.

INDEXED INDIRECT ADDRESSING

The major use of this mode is in picking up data from a table or list of addresses to perform an operation.

Since there is not much unused space in our zero page memory, we can only present a trivial demonstration of this addressing mode. Once again, the LDA instruction will be used as an example.

The format is:

LDA (oper,X)
Op code A1
2nd byte, offset

The second byte of the instruction (the offset) is added to the contents of the X register (any carry is dropped). The result points to a *location in zero page* that contains the low order part of the effective address from which the data is loaded. The next zero page location holds the high-order part of the effective address.

Example:

Memory location 0019 contains the value 45
Memory location 001A contains the value 10
The X register contains the value 14
The instruction to be executed is:
LDA (05,X)

First, the value in the X register is added to the operand (offset) 14 + 5 = 19. The result is the zero page address that contains the low-order address of the memory location from which the accumulator will be loaded.
Second, the high-order address of the memory from which the data will be loaded is found in the next zero page address (19 + 1 = 1A).

In the example:

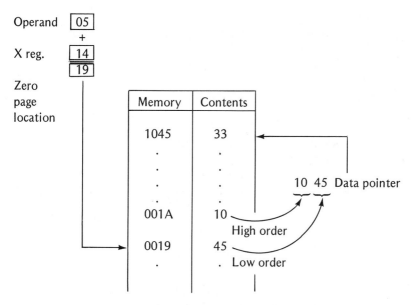

Operand [05]
+
X reg. [14]
[19]

Zero
page   Memory | Contents
location

After LDA (05,X) is executed: Accumulator [33]

Now let's try a short demonstration of the Indexed Indirect Addressing mode for the LDA instruction using the Mini-Assembler to assemble the program. First, type in the instructions after the ! prompt. Each line is assembled as you make your entries, but we will not show the display until all entries have been made.

!300:LDX #14	Put 14 in the X register
! LDA #10	Put 10 in accumulator
! STA 1A	Store it in 001A
! LDA #45	Put 45 in accumulator
! STA 19	Store it in 0019
! LDA #33	Put 33 in accumulator
! STA 1045	Store 33 in 1045
! LDA #0	Put in zero
! LDA (05,X)	Indexed Indirect Addressing mode
! JSR FDDA	Display accumulator
! RTS	

The display:

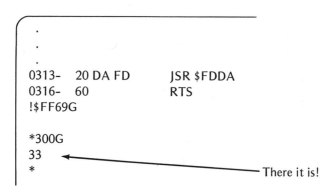

```
*F666G

0300-   A2 14        LDX #$14
0302-   A9 10        LDA #$10
0304-   85 1A        STA $1A
0306-   A9 45        LDA #$45
0308-   85 19        STA $19
030A-   A9 33        LDA #$33
030C-   8D 45 10     STA $1045
030F-   A9 00        LDA #$00
0311-   A1 05        LDA ($05,X)
0313-   20 DA FD     JSR $FDDA
0316-   60           RTS
!$FF69G  ◄──────────────────── Leave the Mini-Assembler

*
```

Run the program. The accumulator is loaded by the Indexed Indirect Addressing mode instruction at 0311. Then the value 33 is displayed.

```
        .
        .
        .
0313-   20 DA FD     JSR $FDDA
0316-   60           RTS
!$FF69G

*300G
33   ◄─────────────────────
*                              ──── There it is!
```

We can see that 33 has been displayed as we expected. How do we know that it was really displayed because of the Indexed Indirect Addressing instruction at location 0311?

If you want to watch each step, single-step through the program until you reach the jump to subroutine instruction at 0313. At that point the 33 should have been moved into the accumulator by the Indexed Indirect Addressing instruction, LDA (05,X).

```
*300S

0300-   A2 14           LDX #$14
 A=00 X=14 Y=FF P=30 S=0C
*S

0302-   A9 10           LDA #$10
 A=10 X=14 Y=FF P=30 S=0C
*S

0304-   85 1A           STA $1A
 A=10 X=14 Y=FF P=30 S=0C
*S

0306-   A9 45           LDA #$45
 A=45 X=14 Y=FF P=30 S=0C
*S

0308-   85 19           STA $19
 A=45 X=14 Y=FF P=30 S=0C
*S

030A-   A9 33           LDA #$33
 A=33 X=14 Y=FF P=30 S=0C
*S

030C-   8D 45 10        STA $1045
 A=33 X=14 Y=FF P=30 S=0C
*S
                              This was done to make
030F-   A9 00           LDA #$00 ◄──── sure the accumulator
 A=00 X=14 Y=FF P=30 S=0C          was cleared of the 33
*S

0311-   A1 05           LDA ($05,X)
 A=33 X=14 Y=FF P=30 S=0C      ＼Accumulator loaded
*S ＼_____ by Indexed Indirect
                                 Addressing
0313-   20 DA FD        JSR $FDDA
 A=33 X=14 Y=FF P=30 S=0C
 *  ◄
                         ─── Stop here
```

That last program wasn't very interesting, was it? This time let's use Indexed Indirect Addressing to access two different lists of data. The first list

will consist of color values, and the second will contain rows at which lines will be plotted.

We'll use the Mini-Assembler to enter the program and the Monitor to enter the data lists.

Start with the Mini-Assembler.

*F666G

!300:JSR FC58■ ◄——— Starting address, colon, and 1st instruction

Press the RETURN key

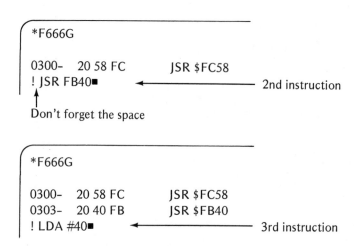

*F666G

0300- 20 58 FC   JSR $FC58
! JSR FB40■ ◄———————————— 2nd instruction
↑
Don't forget the space

*F666G

0300- 20 58 FC   JSR $FC58
0303- 20 40 FB   JSR $FB40
! LDA #40■ ◄———————————— 3rd instruction

Continue in the same manner until all of the following instructions have been entered.

The complete instruction list.

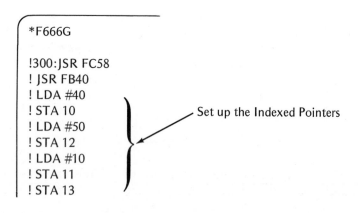

*F666G

!300:JSR FC58
! JSR FB40
! LDA #40
! STA 10
! LDA #50
! STA 12   — Set up the Indexed Pointers
! LDA #10
! STA 11
! STA 13

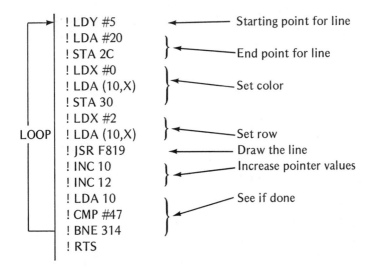

```
         ! LDY #5          <------ Starting point for line
         ! LDA #20         }
         ! STA 2C          } <---- End point for line
         ! LDX #0          }
         ! LDA (10,X)      } <---- Set color
         ! STA 30          }
         ! LDX #2          }
LOOP     ! LDA (10,X)      } <---- Set row
         ! JSR F819        <------ Draw the line
         ! INC 10          }
         ! INC 12          } <---- Increase pointer values
         ! LDA 10          }
         ! CMP #47         } <---- See if done
         ! BNE 314         }
         ! RTS
```

When you have entered all the instructions, the screen will look like this:

```
*F666G

0300-   20 58 FC      JSR $FC58
0303-   20 40 FB      JSR $FB40
0306-   A9 40         LDA #$40
3008-   85 10         STA $10
030A-   A9 50         LDA #$50
030C-   85 12         STA $12
030E-   A9 10         LDA #$10
0310-   85 11         STA $11
0312-   85 13         STA $13
0314-   A0 05         LDY #$05
0316-   A9 20         LDA #$20
0318-   85 2C         STA $20
031A-   A2 00         LDX #$00
031C-   A1 10         LDA ($10,X)
031E-   85 30         STA $30
0320-   A2 02         LDX #$02
0322-   A1 10         LDA ($10,X)
0324-   20 19 F8      JSR $F819
0327-   E6 10         INC $10
0329-   E6 12         INC $12
032B-   A5 10         LDA $10
032D-   C9 47         CMP #$47
032F-   D0 E3         BNE $0314
0331-   60            RTS
!■
```

To enter the data, return to the Monitor. If you try to enter the data lists from the assembler, it will try to interpret the data as instructions. That would foul everything up.

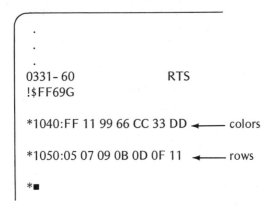

```
    .
    .
    .
0331- 60                    RTS
!$FF69G

*1040:FF 11 99 66 CC 33 DD ◄──── colors

*1050:05 07 09 0B 0D 0F 11 ◄──── rows

*■
```

Now you can run the program.

```
    .
    .
    .
*300G
```

The screen is cleared, and 8 colored lines are picked out of the data lists and displayed on the screen.

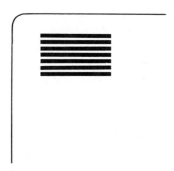

Here is how the values are picked out to draw the lines.

Memory   Pointer

If X=0 ──►   0010   [40] ◄───┐ These values are incremented 1 at a
              0011   [10]   │ time through the loop to point to
                              ╱ the locations for color and row.
If X=2 ──►   0012   [50] ◄──┘
              0013   [10]

250

Color   { 1040 FF
     { 1041 11
     { 1042 99
      etc.

Row   { 1050 05
     { 1051 07
     { 1052 09
      etc.

INDIRECT INDEXED ADDRESSING

This mode differs in its operation from Indexed Indirect Addressing, although their names are so similar as to be confusing.

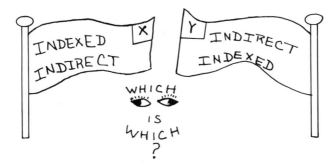

This mode uses the Y register as an index. We'll use the STA instruction to illustrate how it works.

The format is:

STA (oper),Y
Op code 91
2nd byte, zero page address

The second byte of the instruction is a zero page memory address that contains a *base* address. The value of the Y register is added to this base address to form the actual low-order part of the address where the contents of the accumulator are to be stored. The zero page following that given in the second byte provides the high-order part of the storage address.

Example:

Accumulator contains the value 55
Memory location 01 contains the value 32
Memory location 02 contains the value 11
The Y register contains the value 7
The instruction to be executed is:
    STA (01), Y

First, the value 32 is obtained from location 0001.
Second, the contents of the Y register (7) are added. This value (32+7=39) is the low-order part of the storage address.
Third, the value 11 from location 0002 is used as the high-order part of the storage address.
Thus, the contents of the accumulator will be stored in memory location 1139.

In the example:

Accumulator | 55 |

The instruction STA (01),Y is executed:

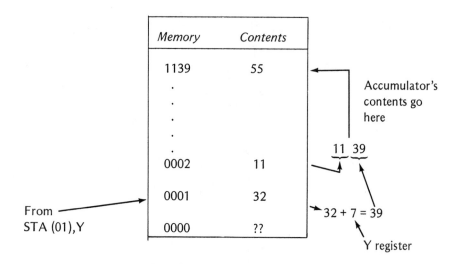

A short demonstration program utilizing the STA (oper),Y instruction follows. Once again we show the entries first.

    *F666G

!300:LDY #7	Load 7 into Y register
! LDA #32	Load accumulator with 32
! STA 1	Store in 0001
! LDA #11	Load 11
! STA 2	Store in 0002
! LDA #55	Load 55
! STA (01),Y	Indirect Indexed Addressing Mode
! RTS	

The display after entering instructions:

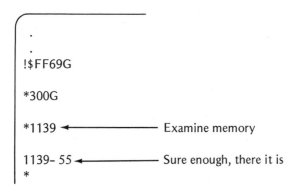

```
*F666G

0300-   A0 07        LDY #$07
0302-   A9 32        LDA #$32
0304-   85 01        STA $01
0306-   A9 11        LDA #$11
0308-   85 02        STA $02
030A-   A9 55        LDA #$55
030C-   91 01        STA ($01),Y
030E-   60           RTS
!$FF69G
                              Once again type this in to
*                             leave Mini-Assembler
```

Run the program. Nothing will be displayed. When the prompt shows at the end of the program, examine memory location 1139.

```
    .
    .
    .
!$FF69G

*300G

*1139 ◄──────────── Examine memory

1139- 55 ◄────────── Sure enough, there it is
*
```

Refer back to the Automated Scale program in Chap. 6. We'll modify that program to provide some changing durations for the notes. The durations and pitch values will be obtained from two data lists. They will be accessed by Indirect Indexed instructions.

MODIFIED AUTOMATED SCALE PROGRAM

*F666G

0300–	20 58 FC	JSR $FC58	
0303–	A0 00	LDY #0	
0305–	B1 03	LDA (03),Y	Load duration from table
0307–	85 01	STA $01	Store it
0309–	B1 05	LDA (05),Y	Load pitch from table
030B–	85 00	STA $00	Store it
030D–	C8	INY	
030E–	98	TYA	Save Y value
030F–	48	PHA	
0310–	C0 09	CPY #09	See if done
0312–	F0 17	BEQ $032B	If so goto end
0314–	AD 30 C0	LDA $C030	
0317–	88	DEY	
0318–	D0 04	BNE $031E	The tweak speaker
031A–	C6 01	DEC $01	part of the program
031C–	F0 08	BEQ $0326	
031E–	CA	DEX	
031F–	D0 F6	BNE $0317	
0321–	A6 00	LDX $00	
0323–	4C 14 03	JMP $0314	
0326–	68	PLA	Get saved Y value back
0327–	A8	TAY	
0328–	4C 05 03	JMP $0305	Get another note
032B–	68	PLA	
032C–	60	RTS	Go back to Monitor

!$FF69G

*1040:FF C8 80 40 C8 40 80 FF   Duration
*1050:85 7F 79 74 6F 6B 67 64   Pitch
*03:40 10 50 10   Pointers for Indirect
*   Indexed Addressing

At the start of the program the values in memory used by the Indirect Indexed Addressing are:

Memory   03=40   Memory   05=50
              04=10   06=10

The Y value is added to each of the low-order parts of the addresses (40 at 0003 and 50 at 0005) to find the correct values of duration and pitch for the notes that are to be played. Since the Y value is incremented each time through the loop, a new pitch and duration are played each time.

Memory	Duration		Memory	Pitch
1040	FF		1050	85
1041	C8		1051	7F
1042	80		1052	79
1043	40		1053	74
1044	C8		1054	6F
1045	40		1055	6B
1046	80		1056	67
1047	FF		1057	64

By changing any of these memory locations, you can vary the pitch and duration. With a little imagination, you can extend these data lists to play a complete song with notes of varying lengths. If you do, don't forget to replace the CPY value in memory location 0311 to reflect the number of notes you wish to play.

When you run the program, the automated scale will be played. However, the length of the notes varies.

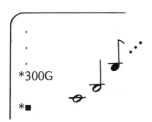

SUMMARY

Congratulations! You are now an assembly language programmer. You have had an introduction to the Apple Mini-Assembler and have explored some of its uses. You can now program in BASIC, 6502 machine language, and assembly language.

We hope you will spend some additional time using the Mini-Assembler. Go back through some of the machine language programs that appeared earlier in the book and enter them by means of the assembler. Try some of your own programs. The more you use assembly language programming, the better you will become and the easier it will be.

In this chapter you have learned how to:

1. Get back and forth between the Mini-Assembler and the System Monitor
2. Use the mnemonic codes of machine language instructions with the Mini-Assembler
3. Enter assembler instructions
4. Use 4 Indexed Addressing modes:
   a. Zero Page Indexed
   b. Absolute Indexed
   c. Indexed Indirect
   d. Indirect Indexed.

New Instructions

1. LDA oper,X — Zero Page Indexed load accumulator — loads the accumulator from the operand's zero page address + the contents of the X register
2. STA oper,X — Zero Page Indexed store accumulator — stores the accumulator's value into the operand's zero page address + the contents of the X register
3. LDA oper,X — Absolute Indexed load accumulator — loads the accumulator from the operand's full address + the contents of the X register (Y can also be used)
4. STA oper,X — Absolute Indexed store accumulator — stores the accumulator's value into the operand's full address + the contents of the X register (Y can also be used)
5. LDA (oper,X) — Indexed Indirect load accumulator — loads the accumulator from a memory location that is indirectly addressed by the operand's offset + the contents of the X register. The result "points to" zero page locations containing the effective address
6. STA (oper),Y — Indirect Indexed store accumulator — stores the value in the accumulator into a memory location that is obtained from the operand's zero page memory (and zero page +1). The contents of the Y register are added to obtain the low-order part of the effective address. Zero page + 1 contains the upper part of the effective address.
7. LDA (oper),Y — Indirect Indexed load accumulator — loads the accumulator from a memory location that is obtained from the operand's zero page memory (and zero page +1). The value in the Y register is added to obtain the low-order part of the effective address. Zero page + 1 contains the high-order part of the effective address.

Mini-Assembler Symbols and Commands

1. F666G — to enter the Mini-Assembler from the Monitor
2. $FF69G — to return to the Monitor from the Mini-Assembler
3. ! — the Mini-Assembler prompt

EXERCISES

1. What is the four-digit hexadecimal command for entering the Mini-Assembler?
   * _____ _____ _____ _____ G

2. What is the Mini-Assembler's prompt symbol?
   _____

3. What is the command to leave the Mini-Assembler and return to the System Monitor?
   ! _____ _____ _____ _____ _____ G

4. The following program has been entered by the Mini-Assembler. Complete the display to show a run.

   *F666G

0300-	F8	SED
0301-	18	CLC
0302-	A9 17	LDA #$17
0304-	69 78	ADC #$78
0306-	20 DA FD	JSR $FDDA
0309	60	RTS

   !$FF69G

   * _____ _____ _____ _____

   _____ _____   Your answers here

   _____

5. A program contains the following two instructions. Explain the result of their execution. Assume that the X register contains 08.

Memory	Op code	Assembler code
0302	A9 22	LDA #$22
0304	95 03	STA $03,X

   _____
   _____

6. Tell what kind of addressing mode would be used for the following:
   a. STA $03,X _____
   b. STA $1033,Y _____
   c. LDA (05,X) _____
   d. STA (07),Y _____

7. How many bytes are used for each of the following types of addressing instructions?
   a. Absolute Indexed _____
   b. Zero Page Indexed _____
   c. Indexed Indirect _____

257

8. The program on page 240-44 allowed you to input 17 characters from the keyboard. Tell which locations must be changed and what the changes would be in order for the program to accept 64 characters.

Memory   Change to

_____   _____

_____   _____

9. Suppose the X register contains 9, the Y register contains 8, and the following values are in the given memory locations:

Memory   Contents
0012   10
0013   11
0014   12

The instruction is executed: LDA (04,X)
From what memory location would the accumulator be loaded?

_____

10. Suppose the same conditions exist as in Exercise 9.
This instruction is executed: STA (12),Y
Into what location would the accumulator's contents be stored?

_____

ANSWERS TO EXERCISES

1. * F 6 6 6 G

2. !

3. ! $ F F 6 9 G

4. * 3 0 0 G
   9 5
   *

5. The value 22 would be loaded into the accumulator and then stored in memory location 000B. (0003+0008=000B)

6. a.   Zero page Indexed   c.   Indexed Indirect
   b.   Absolute Indexed   d.   Indirect Indexed

7. a.   3   b.   2   c.   2

8. Memory   Change to
   a.   030A   40   (40 HEX = 64 decimal)
   b.   031A   40

9. 1211   X register = 9   Plus operand = 4   gives 13
          high-order address obtained from 0014 = 12

10. 1118   10 from location 0012 (operand)
           + 8 from Y register
            18 = low-order address
           11 from location (0012+1) = high-order address

Chapter 12

Putting It All Together

You have learned four methods of entering and executing machine language programs in this book.

1. Directly from BASIC using POKE, CALL, and PEEK
2. By the BASIC Operating System
3. Directly in machine language using the System Monitor
4. By the Mini-Assembler

We'll use each of the four methods to enter and execute an 8-bit multiplication problem in this last chapter.

The 6502 instruction set *does not* contain an instruction for multiplication or division. However, there are many ways that these two operations can be programmed. We will show one that is simple and straightforward.

8-BIT MULTIPLICATION

Remember, the computer does its arithmetic using binary numbers. Let's first look at a pencil-and-paper example of binary multiplication. We'll multiply 18 (decimal) by 58 (decimal) using both decimal and binary multiplication.

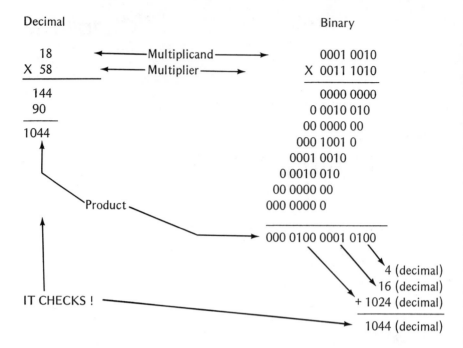

Decimal

			Binary
18	←——Multiplicand——→		0001 0010
X 58	←———Multiplier———→		X 0011 1010

144
90
―――
1044

Product

0000 0000
0 0010 010
00 0000 00
000 1001 0
0001 0010
0 0010 010
00 0000 00
000 0000 0
―――――――――――――
000 0100 0001 0100

4 (decimal)
16 (decimal)
+ 1024 (decimal)
―――――――――――
1044 (decimal)

IT CHECKS !

Notice that our multiplication involves adding the multiplicand every time a 1 appears in the multiplier. Of course, there is a *shift* to the *left* each time a bit of the multiplier is used, just as there is in decimal multiplication. We also proceed from right to left as we "use up" the bits of the multiplier.

The program we will use does much the same thing. The first part of the program will initialize the memories with the appropriate values. We will store these quantities in memory as follows:

Memory Address	Contents
1000	Most Significant Byte of product
1001	Least Significant Byte of product
1002	Multiplicand (12)
1003	Multiplier (3A)

The accumulator will temporarily hold the Least Significant Byte of the product as the program is executed. You may notice that the multiplier is used from left to right (the opposite of the paper-and-pencil method) to simplify the process.

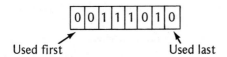

Used first ↗   Used last ↖

The multiplier is shifted left as it multiplies.

A flowchart is shown to clarify the program.

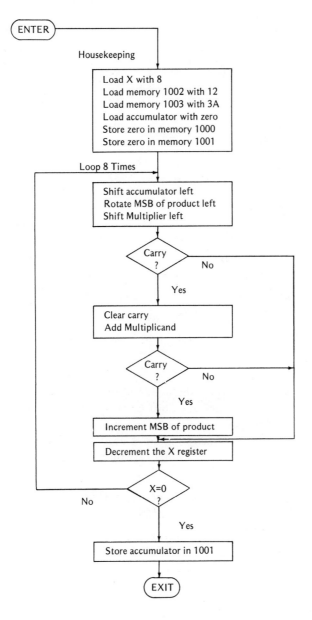

The housekeeping chores at the beginning of the program are easy for us now. You have used each instruction in this section of the program before. They are all either load or store instructions in various addressing modes.

The following table shows the values to be entered in both decimal and hexadecimal forms.

| Memory Address | | Machine | | Assembler |
Dec.	Hex.	Dec.	Hex.	Mnemonic
768	0300	162	A2	LDX #08
769	0301	8	08	
770	0302	169	A9	LDA #12
771	0303	18	12	
772	0304	141	8D	STA $1002
773	0305	2	02	
774	0306	16	10	
775	0307	169	A9	LDA #3A
776	0308	58	3A	
777	0309	141	8D	STA $1003
778	030A	3	03	
779	030B	16	10	
780	030C	169	A9	LDA #00
781	030D	0	00	
782	030E	141	8D	STA $1000
783	030F	0	00	
784	0310	16	10	
785	0311	141	8D	STA $1001
786	0312	1	01	
787	0313	16	10	

The loop section performs the multiplication. Two new instructions appear. One of them, ASL (Arithmetic Shift Left), was discussed in Chap. 3. This time we use it to shift the contents of the accumulator at 788 (decimal). We also use it in the Absolute Addressing mode at 792 (decimal). When used in this mode, the bits of the specified memory are shifted left.

Example:

Memory 1003 before ASL $1003

To carry ◄──────── | 0 | 0 | 0 | 1 | 0 | 0 | 1 | 0 |
bit of
Processor
Status | 0 | 0 | 1 | 0 | 0 | 1 | 0 | 0 | ◄─0 appears by magic
Register

Memory 1003 after ASL $1003

262

We will make use of the fact that the Most Significant Bit from the shift is moved to the carry bit of the Processor Status Register.

Another new instruction ROL (ROtate one bit Left) is used at 789 (decimal) in the Absolute Addressing mode. This instruction is similar to ASL but different in one important way.

Example:

Memory 1000 before ROL $1000

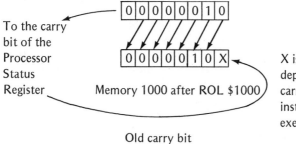

To the carry bit of the Processor Status Register

Memory 1000 after ROL $1000

Old carry bit

X is either 0 or 1 depending on the carry bit when the instruction is executed

As each instruction is executed, the Most Significant Bit moves into the carry bit of the Processor Status Register. In the ASL instruction, the Least Significant Bit is filled with a zero. In the ROL instruction, the Least Significant bit is filled from the carry bit of the status register (either a 1 or a 0).

The instructions derive their names from the action that takes place.

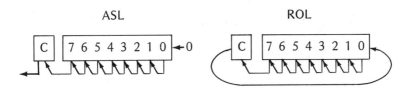

ASL   ROL

The Arithmetic Shift Left instruction merely shifts each bit to the left one place. A zero is shifted into the low-order bit, and the high-order bit shifts into the carry bit. The old carry bit is lost.

The ROtate Left instruction is like a circle. Each bit moves one place around the circle (like Musical Chairs). Hence, the bits are rotated one position to the left.

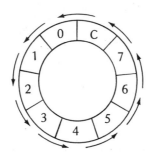

If you rotate left nine times, everything will be right back where it started. If you shift left nine times, you will have zeros in every bit (including the carry bit).

The following table shows both decimal and hexadecimal values to be entered for the loop and exit from the program.

Memory Address		Machine		Assembler
Dec.	Hex.	Dec.	Hex.	Mnemonic
788	0314	10	0A	ASL A
789	0315	46	2E	ROL $1000
790	0316	0	00	
791	0317	16	10	
792	0318	14	0E	ASL $1003
793	0319	3	03	
794	031A	16	10	
795	031B	144	90	BCC $0326
796	031C	9	09	
797	031D	24	18	CLC
798	031E	109	6D	ADC $1002
799	031F	2	02	
800	0320	16	10	
801	0321	144	90	BCC $0326
802	0322	3	03	
803	0323	238	EE	INC $1000
804	0324	0	00	
805	0325	16	10	
806	0326	202	CA	DEX
807	0327	208	D0	BNE $0314
808	0328	235	EB	
809	0329	141	8D	STA $1001
810	032A	1	01	
811	032B	16	10	
812	032C	96	60	RTS

MULTIPLICATION DIRECTLY FROM BASIC

The machine language program can be directly POKEd into memory from BASIC. A FOR-NEXT loop filled with READ and POKE statements will accomplish this. The program is then executed by a CALL statement, and a PRINT PEEK statement is used to display the result. Be sure you are in the Applesoft II BASIC mode.

MULTIPLICATION FROM BASIC

```
10 FOR M = 768 TO 812
20 READ D
30 POKE M,D
40 NEXT M
50 CALL 768
60 PRINT PEEK(4096)*256+PEEK(4097)
70 END
80 DATA 162,8,169,18,141,2,16,169,58,141
90 DATA 3,16,169,0,141,0,16,141,1,16
100 DATA 10,46,0,16,14,3,16,144,9,24,109
110 DATA 2,16,144,3,238,0,16,202,208
120 DATA 235,141,1,16,96
```

After the program has been entered, type RUN to execute it. The following is displayed.

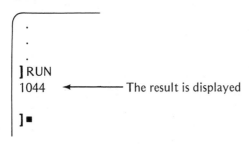

```
 .
 .
 .
] RUN
1044  ◄──────── The result is displayed

] ■
```

Entering the program directly from BASIC has the advantage of speed of entry. A simple FOR-NEXT loop POKEs all the machine language codes into their proper places. The program is then executed by one CALL statement, and the result is displayed by PRINT PEEK.

However, there are disadvantages. Each instruction and address referenced in the program must be converted from hexadecimal notation to its decimal equivalent before the program can be entered. Remember, machine language references are in hexadecimal code, and BASIC uses decimal numbers. The conversion can be time-consuming if the program is long. The process is subject to many human errors. Though seemingly small, these errors can prove disastrous to a program in execution. If mistakes are made, there is no way of debugging the program directly, since you are not using the Apple System Monitor when you are in BASIC.

MULTIPLICATION USING THE BASIC OPERATING SYSTEM

When using the BASIC Operating System, the addresses are entered by the system (except for the starting address). The machine language Op codes are entered in hexadecimal form directly from the reference manual.

The Operating System must be loaded from tape or entered from the keyboard (See Chap. 2). When RUN, the program requests the starting address and the number of bytes. Our starting address is 768, and there are 45 bytes.

STARTING ADDRESS FOR M/L=?768
HOW MANY BYTES?45
PRESS RETURN TO ENTER PROGRAM
768 ■

Now enter the program. The computer will keep track and print each memory location in order. All you have to do is type in the correct hexadecimal code. (See tables shown earlier in chapter for the hexadecimal Op codes to be entered.) After the program has been completely entered, the Operating System displays your entries in blocks of 20 bytes, as follows.

HERE IS YOUR PROGRAM

768 A2
769 08
770 A9
771 12
772 8D
773 02
774 10
775 A9
776 3A
777 8D
778 03
779 10
780 A9
781 00
782 8D
783 00
784 10
785 8D
786 01
787 10
PRESS ANY KEY TO CONTINUE
■

You should then check over this partial listing for any errors. Make a note of the corrections to be made, but do not make the corrections until asked for at the end of the final display block. You are now ready to look at the next block of 20 (or fewer) data bytes.

```
788 0A
789 2E
790 00
791 10
792 0E
793 03
794 10
795 90
796 09
797 18
798 6D
799 02
800 10
801 90
802 03
803 EE
804 00
805 10
806 CA
807 D0
PRESS ANY KEY TO CONTINUE
■
```

Now the last block of data.

```
808 EB
809 8D
810 01
811 10
812 60
PRESS ANY KEY TO CONTINUE
■
```

Now when you press any key, you get a chance to make your changes.

```
        .
      .
    .
  .
IF ANY CHANGES—TYPE ADDRESS
IF NOT — TYPE 99
?■
```

If no changes, type 99 and press any key to RUN.

```
    .
    .
    .
IF ANY CHANGES—TYPE ADDRESS
IF NOT — TYPE 99
?99
PRESS ANY KEY TO RUN■
```

When the program has stopped, type:

PRINT PEEK(4096)*256+Peek(4097)

```
] PRINT PEEK(4096)*256+PEEK(4097)
1044

]■
```

This method overcomes the disadvantage of having to convert the hexadecimal codes to decimal values for BASIC. The Operating System does this for us. All the user has to do is to type in the starting address, the number of bytes, and each hexadecimal data byte.

Of course, we must go to the trouble of loading the BASIC Operating System each time we want to use it. If you have a disk system, this is no big problem. Loading from a cassette recorder is slower, and entering from the keyboard is the slowest of all. The BASIC Operating System is rather cumbersome to use, but it has served the purpose of introducing you to machine language programming in nice, easy steps through BASIC commands and statements.

MULTIPLICATION USING THE SYSTEM MONITOR

This is the most direct way to enter a machine language program. All you have to do is type in the starting address and each hexadecimal value separated by a blank space. Long programs should be broken up into sections of approximately 3 physical line lengths. This time we will use hexadecimal data.

```
*300:A2 08 A9 12 8D 02 10 A9 3A 8D 03 10
A9 00 8D 00 10 8D 01 10 0A 2E 00 10 0E
03 10 90 09 18 6D 02 10 90 03 EE 00 10 C
A D0 EB 8D 01 10 60

*
```

To run the program, you merely type in:

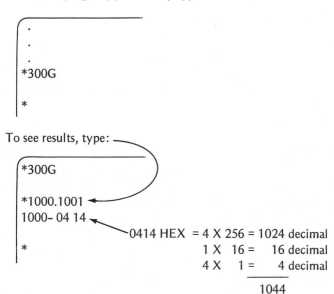

```
.
.
.
*300G

*
```

To see results, type:

```
*300G

*1000.1001
1000- 04 14
                0414 HEX  = 4 X 256 = 1024 decimal
*                         1 X  16 =   16 decimal
                          4 X   1 =    4 decimal
                                     ───────
                                       1044
```

This method allows the direct entry of machine codes, a direct command for execution, and a way to examine the appropriate memory locations to see the results.

The preparation necessary before entry is a disadvantage. Mnemonic codes must be looked up. All branch destinations must be calculated and converted to hexadecimal values. All data must be entered in hexadecimal notation also. Results, too, are in hexadecimal and must be converted to decimal values to be meaningful (unless you have eight fingers on each hand).

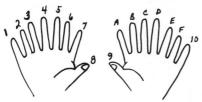

Not many people like to go through all that mathematical calculation, so they use an assembler to create machine language programs.

MULTIPLICATION USING THE MINI-ASSEMBLER

When using the Mini-Assembler, the programmer need only be concerned with the starting address and the mnemonic codes for the instructions. Mnemonic codes are much easier to remember than hexadecimal numbers. After some use, you will find that you don't have to look up the codes. Since they are abbreviations of actual instruction names, they have some meaning.

269

To access the Mini-Assembler, type: F666G

```
*F666G

!■                          Assembler responds with its prompt
```

Type in the starting address, a colon, and the first mnemonic code.

```
*F666G

!300:LDX #8■
```

The Mini-Assembler assembles this instruction and replaces your line with the address, Op code, and mnemonic. The cursor moves to the next line, ready for the next mnemonic code and any operand.

```
*F666G

0300-   A2 08           LDX #$08
!■
```

Continue entering the mnemonic codes with their operands until the program is complete.

```
*F666G

0300-   A2 08       LDX #$08
0302-   A9 12       LDA #$12
0304-   8D 02 10    STA $1002
0307-   A9 3A       LDA #$3A
0309-   8D 03 10    STA $1003
030C-   A9 00       LDA #$00
030E-   8D 00 10    STA $1000
0311-   8D 01 10    STA $1001
0314-   0A          ASL
0315-   2E 00 10    ROL $1000
0318-   0E 03 10    ASL $1003
031B-   90 09       BCC $0326
031D-   18          CLC
031E-   6D 02 10    ADC $1002
0321-   90 03       BCC $0326
0323-   EE 00 10    INC $1000
0326-   CA          DEX
0327-   D0 EB       BNE $0314
0329-   8D 01 10    STA $1001
032C-   60          RTS
!$FF69G ◄
                              To re-enter Monitor
*
```

To run the program, use the Monitor command: 300G

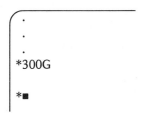

```
    .
    .
    .
*300G

*■
```

To see the result, use the Monitor examine: 1000.1001

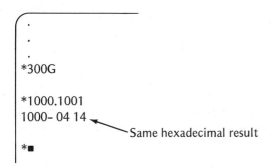

```
    .
    .
    .
*300G

*1000.1001
1000- 04 14
              Same hexadecimal result

*■
```

Most people working with machine language agree that an assembler removes much of the drudgery of machine language programming. It cannot provide execution of programs, but it takes care of assigning Op codes and the operands that go with them.

The Mini-Assembler does rely on the System Monitor for execution of the assembled program and for examination of memory for results (although a display of the results could have been included in the program).

You have seen each of the four methods in action working on the same program. Keep in mind that we provided you with the necessary instruction codes and data for the program. You should try all four methods on a program of your own creation and then decide which method you prefer.

The combination of the Mini-Assembler and System Monitor is hard to beat. The Mini-Assembler does all the detail work, and the Monitor provides the execution and debugging capabilities.

8-BIT DIVISION

Once again, we'll take a look at pencil-and-paper division before looking at the computer's method. Since division is the inverse operation of multiplication, we'll use the same numbers that we used in the multiplication example, with one exception. That exception is made to the dividend so that the division example will not come out even. There will be a remainder.

Example:

1046 (decimal)   ÷   58 (decimal)

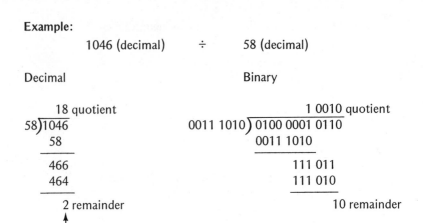

Decimal

```
        18 quotient
  58)1046
       58
      ────
      466
      464
      ────
        2 remainder
```

Binary

```
          1 0010 quotient
  0011 1010) 0100 0001 0110
             0011 1010
             ─────────
              111 011
              111 010
              ───────
                   10 remainder
```

It checks ⟶
⎰ 1 0010 = 12 HEX = 18 dec.
⎱ 10 = 2 HEX = 2 dec.

Just as in multiplication, you can see shifts being made as the division takes place. Place value is very important in this process. Notice that a subtraction is made only if the divisor is smaller than part of the dividend that is being tested. A 1 then is placed in the quotient. If the divisor is larger, a 0 is placed in the quotient.

Our machine language program will operate in much the same way. The first part of the program places the appropriate values in their respective memory locations. The values are stores as follows:

Memory Address	Contents
accumulator	Most Significant Byte of the dividend
1000	Divisor
1001	Least Significant Byte of dividend
1002	Remainder

The accumulator and memory location 1001 hold the original dividend. Each time through the loop, memory location 1001 is shifted left and the accumulator is rotated left. If a carry occurs from memory 1001's shift, it will appear as a 1 in the least significant bit of the accumulator when it is rotated. If no carry occurs from the memory 1001 shift, a zero appears in the least significant bit of the accumulator. Thus, each time through the loop, the dividend is shifted one place from memory 1001 to the accumulator. This lets the computer compare the divisor with the most significant part of the dividend for a trial division.

The division is accomplished by comparing the divisor with the accumulator. Every time the divisor is smaller than or equal to the accumulator, the divisor is subtracted from the accumulator, and memory 1001 is incremented by one. This means a 1 is appearing in the quotient.

If the divisor is larger than the accumulator, no subtraction is made, and memory 1001 is not incremented. This means a 0 appears in the quotient.

As the bits in the accumulator and memory 1001 move to the left, the quotient appears in memory 1001 from the right (0 if divisor did not go into dividend; 1 if divisor did go into dividend).

After the loop is completed (8 passes through), the remainder is placed in memory location 1002. When the program is complete, you'll find the 8-bit quotient in memory location 1001 and the remainder in memory location 1002.

DIVISION FLOWCHART

```
 ( ENTER )──────────────────┐
                            │
   Housekeeping             │
                            ▼
              ┌──────────────────────────────┐
              │ Load X register with 8        │
              │ Load accumulator with divisor │
              │ Store it in memory 1000       │
              │ Load accumulator with Least   │
              │    Significant Byte of dividend│
              │ Store it in memory 1001       │
              │ Load accumulator with Most    │
              │    Significant Byte of dividend│
              └──────────────────────────────┘
                            │
  Loop 8 times   ┌──────────┤
                 │          ▼
                 │  ┌─────────────────────────┐
                 │  │ Shift memory 1001 left    │
                 │  │ Rotate accumulator left   │
                 │  └─────────────────────────┘
                 │          │
                 │          ▼
                 │        ╱ Will it ╲    No
                 │       ╱  divide    ╲──────────┐
                 │       ╲     ?      ╱          │
                 │        ╲          ╱           │
                 │          │ Yes               │
                 │          ▼                    │
                 │  ┌────────────────────────────────┐
                 │  │ Subtract divisor from accumulator│
                 │  │ Increment memory 1001 (quotient) │
                 │  └────────────────────────────────┘
                 │          │◄─────────────────────┘
                 │          ▼
                 │  ┌─────────────────────────┐
                 │  │ Decrement the X register  │
                 │  └─────────────────────────┘
                 │          │
                 │          ▼
                 │        ╱  Is  ╲
                 └───────╱  X=0   ╲
                    No   ╲   ?    ╱
                          ╲      ╱
                            │ Yes
                            ▼
              ┌─────────────────────────┐
              │ Store remainder in 1002   │
              └─────────────────────────┘
                            │
                            ▼
                      ( EXIT )
```

273

The housekeeping chores are similar to those of the multiplication program.

| Memory Address | | Machine | | Assembler |
Dec.	Hex.	Dec.	Hex.	Mnemonic
768	0300	162	A2	LDX #08
769	0301	8	08	
770	0302	169	A9	LDA #3A
771	0303	58	3A	
772	0304	141	8D	STA $1000
773	0305	0	00	
774	0306	16	10	
775	0307	169	A9	LDA #16
776	0308	22	16	
777	0309	141	8D	STA $1001
778	030A	1	01	
779	030B	16	10	
780	030C	169	A9	LDA #4
781	030D	4	04	

The rotate instruction appears in a new form in the loop in this program. We are using ROL A to rotate the accumulator. It works the same way as it did when we rotated a memory location, but this time the accumulator's contents are rotated. The loop is again executed 8 times using the X register as a counter.

Now, the division section.

Memory Address		Machine		Assembler
Dec.	Hex.	Dec.	Hex.	Mnemonic
782	030E	14	0E	ASL $1001
783	030F	1	01	
784	0310	16	10	
785	0311	42	2A	ROL A
786	0312	199	CD	CMP $1000
787	0313	0	00	
788	0314	16	10	
789	0315	144	90	BCC $031D
790	0316	6	06	
791	0317	237	ED	SBC $1000
792	0318	0	00	
793	0319	16	10	
794	031A	238	EE	INC $1001
795	031B	1	01	
796	031C	16	10	
797	031D	196	CA	DEX
798	031E	208	D0	BNE $030E
799	031F	239	EF	
800	0320	141	8D	STA $1002
801	0321	2	02	
802	0322	16	10	
803	0323	96	60	RTS

Take your choice as to how you want to enter and run the program:
1. BASIC
2. BASIC Operating System
3. System Monitor
4. Assembler

We'll use the Assembler.

```
*F666G

0300-    A2 08          LDX #$08
0302-    A9 3A          LDA #$3A
0304-    8D 00 10       STA $1000
0307-    A9 16          LDA #$16
0309-    8D 01 10       STA $1001
030C-    A9 04          LDA #$04
030E-    0E 01 10       ASL $1001
0311-    2A             ROL
0312-    CD 00 10       CMP $1000
0315-    90 06          BCC $031D
0317-    ED 00 10       SBC $1000
031A-    EE 01 10       INC $1001
031D-    CA             DEX
031E-    D0 EF          BNE $030E
0320-    8D 02 10       STA $1002
0323-    60             RTS
!$FF69G

*300G

*1001.1002
1001- 12 02
                        Remainder
*
         Quotient
```

This ends the chapter and the explorations of machine language for this book. There are many more things for you to try. There are some instructions that haven't been covered; but with the knowledge you now have, you will be able to dig everything else out by yourself. The complete list of instructions is given in Appendix D. They may also be found, along with a description of their use, in *MCS6500 Microcomputer Family Programming Manual*, available from MOS Technology, Inc., 950 Rittenhouse Road, Norristown, PA 19401.

SUMMARY

In this chapter you've had a chance to compare four ways to produce a machine language program:

1. Directly from BASIC
2. From the BASIC Operating System
3. From the Apple System Monitor
4. From the Mini-Assembler

Each method has its advantages and disadvantages. Multiplication and division examples were used to demonstrate the different methods.

You learned that

1. Multiplication of two 8-bit numbers produces a 16-bit product

2. The computer can multiply by shifting and rotating data and adding the multiplicand in a predetermined way

3. Each of the four methods produces equivalent results

4. All the methods except the assembler require looking up instructions and/or converting numbers from one base to another

5. The assembler requires the least amount of preparation of the four methods — it assembles a machine language program doing all the necessary calculations and selecting the Op codes from the mnemonics that you provide

6. The computer performs division in a similar way to the common paper-and-pencil method

7. Division of a 16-bit dividend by an 8-bit divisor produces an 8-bit quotient with a remainder

New Instructions

ROL   oper — an Absolute Addressed instruction that rotates each bit in the specified memory location one place to the left. The Most Significant Bit moves into the carry bit, and the carry bit moves into the Least Significant Bit of the specified memory.

ASL oper — an Absolute Addressed instruction that shifts each bit in the specified memory location one place to the left. The Most Significant Bit moves into the carry bit, and a zero is moved into the Least Significant Bit of the specified memory.

ROL A — rotates the bits in the accumulator one place to the left. The Most Significant Bit moves into the carry bit, and the carry bit moves into the Least Significant Bit of the accumulator.

EXERCISES

1. Name the four methods given for entering machine language programs.
   a. _____
   b. _____
   c. _____
   d. _____

2. Explain what happens in the carry bit following the execution of the ASL A instruction.
   The carry bit _____
   _____

3. Explain why the X register was set to 8 at the beginning of the Multiplication programs.

_____

_____

_____

4. Given that memory location 1234 contains the following and the carry bit is set to one,

| 1 | | 0 1 1 1 0 1 0 1 |

    C   memory 1234

show what each contains after a ROL $1234 instruction is executed.

| | | |

    C   memory 1234

5. In what memory locations will the product be found in the Multiplication from BASIC program?

_____ (decimal) and _____ (decimal)

6. If a machine language program is 50 bytes long and it is entered by the BASIC Operating System, the data is displayed in specific-sized blocks. How many blocks of data would be needed to store the 50-byte program?

_____

7. If the Apple System Monitor is used to enter a machine language program, what number system(s) (decimal, hexadecimal, or binary) is(are) used to enter the program?

_____

8. Explain the results of executing the command *F666G.

_____

_____

9. What would be displayed on the screen if the RETURN key were pressed following *F666G?

```
*F666G   _____

_____
```

10. If you wish to leave the Mini-Assembler and return to the System Monitor, what command is typed?

```
.
.
.
! _____
```

11. What memory location is used to hold the quotient in the Division program?
_____ (HEX)

ANSWERS TO EXERCISES

1. a.   Directly from BASIC using POKE, CALL, and PEEK
   b.   The BASIC Operating System
   c.   The System Monitor
   d.   The Mini-Assembler

2. The carry bit (original) is lost. It is replaced by the Most Significant Bit from the accumulator.

3. The X register is used to count the number of passes through the loop. Since we are multiplying by an 8-bit number, there are 8 passes through the loop.

4.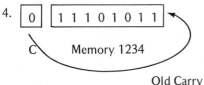

Old Carry

5. 4097 and 4096 (Most and Least Significant Bytes, respectively)

6. 3 (The display shows 20 blocks at a time)

7. hexadecimal only

8. The Mini-Assembler is entered from the Monitor

9.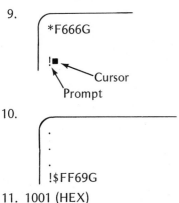

10.

11. 1001 (HEX)

Appendixes

Appendix A contains information that has been used in this book with a page reference for each item. The page reference gives the location of either the first occurrence of the item or an explanation of the item.

Appendix B contains a table of conversions for negative decimal numbers to their hexadecimal equivalents.

Appendix C is an explanation of the memory map used for the video display. Also given are a table of codes used for displaying characters on the screen and a table of color codes used for display of graphics.

Appendix D is a list of 6502 instruction codes.

APPENDIX A-1   BASIC STATEMENTS

Statement	Page	Statement	Page
ASC		LOAD	
CALL		LOGIC	
CHR$		MATH	
COLOR		NEW	
CONT		NORMAL	
DATA		NOTRACE	
FLASH		ON.GOTO	
FOR-NEXT		PDL	
GET		PEEK	
GOSUB		PLOT	
GOTO		POKE	
GR		PRINT	
HLIN		READ	
HOME		RESTORE	
IF.THEN		RETURN	
INPUT		RUN	
INT		SAVE	
INVERSE		SPC	
LEFT$		TEXT	
LET		TRACE	
LIST		VLIN	

APPENDIX A-2 MACHINE LANGUAGE INSTRUCTIONS

Mnemonic Code	Addressing Mode	Page	Mnemonic Code	Addressing Mode	Page
ADC	Absolute		LDA	Index. Ind.	
ADC	Immediate		LDA	Ind. Index.	
AND	Immediate		LDA	Zero Page	
ASL	Absolute		LDA	Zero P. Ind.	
ASL	Accumulator		LDX	Immediate	
BCC	Relative		LDX	Zero Page	
BCS	Relative		LDY	Abs. Index.	
BEQ	Relative		LDY	Immediate	
BMI	Relative		NOP	Implied	
BNE	Relative		PHA	Implied	
BPL	Relative		PLA	Implied	
CLC	Implied		ROL	Absolute	
CLD	Implied		ROL	Accumulator	
CMP	Absolute		RTS	Implied	
CPX	Immediate		SBC	Absolute	
CPY	Immediate		SBC	Immediate	
DEC	Implied		SEC	Implied	
DEX	Implied		SED	Implied	
DEY	Implied		STA	Absolute	
INX	Implied		STA	Abs. Index.	
INY	Implied		STA	Ind. Index.	
JMP	Absolute		STA	Zero Page	
JSR	Absolute		STA	Zero P. Ind.	
LDA	Absolute		TAX	Implied	
LDA	Abs. Ind.		TAY	Implied	
LDA	Immediate		TXA	Implied	

APPENDIX A-3 BUILT-IN SUBROUTINES

Memory Address	Function Performed	Page
F800	Plot a point	
F819	Plot a horizontal line	
F828	Plot a vertical line	
FB40	Set Graphics Mode	
FC58	Clear the screen	
FD1B	Random number	
FD35	Get a keystroke	
FD8E	Carriage return	
FDDA	Display accumulator (HEX)	
FDED	Display accumulator	
FF3A	Ring the bell	

LDA C030 is not really a subroutine, but performs like one. It tweaks (or toggles) the speaker.

APPENDIX A-4 DISPLAY SYMBOLS

Symbol	Function
*	System Monitor Prompt — used for machine language
]	Applesoft II prompt — used for Applesoft II BASIC
>	Integer BASIC prompt — used for Integer BASIC
!	Mini-Assembler prompt — used to assemble machine language programs
■	Cursor — shows next print position to be used (blinks normally)

APPENDIX A-5   PROGRAMS

Title	Language	Page
Add Two Decimal Numbers	A/L	
Add Two Decimal Numbers	M/L	
Add Two Numbers	M/L	
Automated Scale	A/L	
Automated Scale	M/L	
BASIC Operating System	BASIC	
Color Bars	A/L	
Copy Memory Locations	A/L	
Display a Message	M/L	
Display ASCII Codes	M/L	
Display a String of One Letter	M/L	
Display One Letter	M/L	
Division	A/L	
Four-Corner Plot	M/L	
Horizontal Line	M/L	
Indexed Indirect Addressing Demo	A/L	
Indirect Indexed Addressing Demo	A/L	
Increment the X Register	M/L	
Load Accumulator and Store	M/L	
Modified Addition	M/L	
Multiplication from BASIC	M/L	
Multiplication from BASIC Op. Sys.	M/L	
Multiplication from Mini-Assembler	A/L	
Multiplication from System Monitor	M/L	
Number Guessing Game	M/L	
PEEK and POKE Demonstration	BASIC	
Play Your Own Tune	M/L	
Plot a Point	M/L	
POKE and PEEK, Then POKE Again	BASIC	
Rectangle Drawing	M/L	
Running Alphabet	M/L	
Scale with Notes	M/L	
Storing Data from Keyboard	A/L	
Subtract Two Numbers	M/L	
Tone Experiment	M/L	
Two-Byte Addition	M/L	
Two-Byte Subtraction	M/L	
Vertical Line	M/L	

M/L = Machine Language
A/L = Assembly Language
BASIC = Applesoft II BASIC

APPENDIX B   HEX EQUIVALENTS FOR DECIMAL NEGATIVES

Dec.	HEX	Dec.	HEX	Dec.	HEX
-1	FF	-44	D4	-87	A9
-2	FE	-45	D3	-88	A8
-3	FD	-46	D2	-89	A7
-4	FC	-47	D1	-90	A6
-5	FB	-48	D0	-91	A5
-6	FA	-49	CF	-92	A4
-7	F9	-50	CE	-93	A3
-8	F8	-51	CD	-94	A2
-9	F7	-52	CC	-95	A1
-10	F6	-53	CB	-96	A0
-11	F5	-54	CA	-97	9F
-12	F4	-55	C9	-98	9E
-13	F3	-56	C8	-99	9D
-14	F2	-57	C7	-100	9C
-15	F1	-58	C6	-101	9B
-16	F0	-59	C5	-102	9A
-17	EF	-60	C4	-103	99
-18	EE	-61	C3	-104	98
-19	ED	-62	C2	-105	97
-20	EC	-63	C1	-106	96
-21	EB	-64	C0	-107	95
-22	EA	-65	BF	-108	94
-23	E9	-66	BE	-109	93
-24	E8	-67	BD	-110	92
-25	E7	-68	BC	-111	91
-26	E6	-69	BB	-112	90
-27	E5	-70	BA	-113	8F
-28	E4	-71	B9	-114	8E
-29	E3	-72	B8	-115	8D
-30	E2	-73	B7	-116	8C
-31	E1	-74	B6	-117	8B
-32	E0	-75	B5	-118	8A
-33	DF	-76	B4	-119	89
-34	DE	-77	B3	-120	88
-35	DD	-78	B2	-121	87
-36	DC	-79	B1	-122	86
-37	DB	-80	B0	-123	85
-38	DA	-81	AF	-124	84
-39	D9	-82	AE	-125	83
-40	D8	-83	AD	-126	82
-41	D7	-84	AC	-127	81
-42	D6	-85	AB	-128	80
-43	D5	-86	AA		

APPENDIX C-1 VIDEO MEMORY

You discovered in Chap. 5 that the top line (or line 1) of the video display is associated with memory locations 0400 through 0427 hex. You might suspect that the next line would be associated with memory locations 0428 through 044F, but this is not so.

If you go back to the CHARACTER DISPLAY PROGRAM in Chap. 4 and change the instruction at memory locations 775, 776, and 777 to: STA 0428, the program would store a string of A's in those locations.

$$775 \quad 99 \qquad STA\ 0428,Y$$
$$776 \quad 28$$
$$777 \quad 04$$

Here is where the A's would be printed on the display if the program is run with these values.

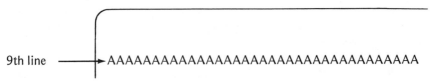

9th line   —————► AAAAAAAAAAAAAAAAAAAAAAAAAAAAAAAAAAAAAAAA

If the value stored in memory location 776 is changed to 50, where do you think the string of A's would appear? If you said the seventeenth line, you were correct.

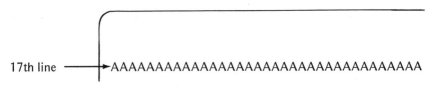

17th line   —————► AAAAAAAAAAAAAAAAAAAAAAAAAAAAAAAAAAAAAAAA

So far, we have found lines 1, 9, and 17.

line 1   0400. 0427

line 9   0428. . . . . .044F

line 17   0450. 0477

By this time, you may have guessed what memory locations are associated with all 24 lines of the video display.

Line 1	0400 → 0427
Line 2	0480 → 04A7
Line 3	0500 → 0527
Line 4	0580 → 05A7
Line 5	0600 → 0627
Line 6	0680 → 06A7
Line 7	0700 → 0727
Line 8	0780 → 07A7
Line 9	0428 → 044F
Line 10	04A8 → 04CF
Line 11	0528 → 054F
Line 12	05A8 → 05CF
Line 13	0628 → 064F
Line 14	06A8 → 06CF
Line 15	0728 → 074F
Line 16	07A8 → 07CF
Line 17	0450 → 0477
Line 18	04D0 → 04F7
Line 19	0550 → 0577
Line 20	05D0 → 05F7
Line 21	0650 → 0677
Line 22	06D0 → 06F7
Line 23	0750 → 0777
Line 24	07D0 → 07F7

Char	Nor.	Fla.	Inv.		Char	Nor.	Fla.	Inv.
	A0	60	20		@	C0	40	00
!	A1	61	21		A	C1	41	01
"	A2	62	22		B	C2	42	02
#	A3	63	23		C	C3	43	03
$	A4	64	24		D	C4	44	04
%	A5	65	25		E	C5	45	05
&	A6	66	26		F	C6	46	06
'	A7	67	27		G	C7	47	07
(	A8	68	28		H	C8	48	08
)	A9	69	29		I	C9	49	09
*	AA	6A	2A		J	CA	4A	0A
+	AB	6B	2B		K	CB	4B	0B
,	AC	6C	2C		L	CC	4C	0C
-	AD	6D	2D		M	CD	4D	0D
.	AE	6E	2E		N	CE	4E	0E
/	AF	6F	2F		O	CF	4F	0F
0	B0	70	30		P	D0	50	10
1	B1	71	31		Q	D1	51	11
2	B2	72	32		R	D2	52	12
3	B3	73	33		S	D3	53	13
4	B4	74	34		T	D4	54	14
5	B5	75	35		U	D5	55	15
6	B6	76	36		V	D6	56	16
7	B7	77	37		W	D7	57	17
8	B8	78	38		X	D8	58	18
9	B9	79	39		Y	D9	59	19
:	BA	7A	3A		Z	DA	5A	1A
;	BB	7B	3B		[	DB	5B	1B
<	BC	7C	3C		\	DC	5C	1C
=	BD	7D	3D		]	DD	5D	1D
>	BE	7E	3E		^	DE	5E	1E
?	BF	7F	3F		—	DF	5F	1F

Char = Character
Nor. = Normal mode
Fla. = Flashing mode
Inv. = Inverse mode

APPENDIX C-3 COLOR CODES FOR LOW RESOLUTION GRAPHICS

Decimal	HEX	Color
0	0	Black
1	1	Magenta
2	2	Dark blue
3	3	Light purple
4	4	Dark green
5	5	Grey
6	6	Medium blue
7	7	Light blue
8	8	Brown
9	9	Orange
10	A	Grey
11	B	Pink
12	C	Green
13	D	Yellow
14	E	Blue/green
15	F	White

The colors may vary somewhat depending on the settings of your TV set.

APPENDIX D 6502 INSTRUCTION CODES

Mnemonic Code	Addressing Mode	Assembler Form	Op Code	No. Bytes	Flags Affected
ADC	Immediate	ADC #oper	69	2	NZCV
	Zero Page	ADC oper	65	2	
	Zero Page,X	ADC oper,X	75	2	
	Absolute	ADC oper	6D	3	
	Absolute,X	ADC oper,X	7D	3	
	Absolute,Y	ADC oper,Y	79	3	
	(Indirect,X)	ADC (oper,X)	61	2	
	(Indirect),Y	ADC (oper),Y	71	2	
AND	Immediate	AND #oper	29	2	NZ
	Zero Page	AND oper	25	2	
	Zero Page,X	AND oper,X	35	2	
	Absolute	AND oper	2D	3	
	Absolute,X	AND oper,X	3D	3	
	Absolute,Y	AND oper,Y	39	3	
	(Indirect,X)	AND (oper,X)	21	2	
	(Indirect),Y	AND (oper),Y	31	2	
ASL	Accumulator	ASL A	0A	1	NZC
	Zero Page	ASL oper	06	2	
	Zero Page,X	ASL oper,X	16	2	
	Absolute	ASL oper	0E	3	
	Absolute,X	ASL oper,X	1E	3	
BCC	Relative	BCC oper	90	2	none
BCS	Relative	BCS oper	B0	2	none
BEQ	Relative	BEQ oper	F0	2	none
BIT	Zero Page	BIT oper	24	2	NZV
	Absolute	BIT oper	2C	3	
BMI	Relative	BMI oper	30	2	none
BNE	Relative	BNE oper	D0	2	none
BPL	Relative	BPL oper	10	2	none
BRK	Implied	BRK	00	1	I

Mnemonic Code	Addressing Mode	Assembler Form	Op Code	No. Bytes	Flags Affected
BVC	Relative	BVC oper	50	2	none
BVS	Relative	BVS oper	70	2	none
CLC	Implied	CLC	18	1	C
CLD	Implied	CLD	D8	1	D
CLI	Implied	CLI	58	1	I
CLV	Implied	CLV	B8	1	V
CMP	Immediate	CMP #oper	C9	2	NZC
	Zero Page	CMP oper	C5	2	
	Zero Page,X	CMP oper,X	D5	2	
	Absolute	CMP oper	CD	3	
	Absolute,X	CMP oper,X	DD	3	
	Absolute,Y	CMP oper,Y	D9	3	
	(Indirect,X)	CMP (oper,X)	C1	2	
	(Indirect),Y	CMP (oper),Y	D1	2	
CPX	Immediate	CPX #oper	E0	2	NZC
	Zero Page	CPX oper	E4	2	
	Absolute	CPX oper	EC	3	
CPY	Immediate	CPY #oper	C0	2	NZC
	Zero Page	CPY oper	C4	2	
	Absolute	CPY oper	CC	3	
DEC	Zero Page	DEC oper	C6	2	NZ
	Zero Page,X	DEC oper,X	D6	2	
	Absolute	DEC oper	CE	3	
	Absolute,X	DEC oper,X	DE	3	
DEX	Implied	DEX	CA	1	NZ
DEY	Implied	DEY	88	1	NZ
EOR	Immediate	EOR #oper	49	2	NZ
	Zero Page	EOR oper	45	2	
	Zero Page,X	EOR oper,X	55	2	

Mnemonic Code	Addressing Mode	Assembler Form	Op Code	No. Bytes	Flags Affected
	Absolute	EOR oper	4D	3	
	Absolute,X	EOR oper,X	5D	3	
	Absolute,Y	EOR oper,Y	59	3	
	(Indirect,X)	EOR (oper,X)	41	2	
	(Indirect),Y	EOR (oper),Y	51	2	
INC	Zero Page	INC oper	E6	2	NZ
	Zero Page,X	INC oper,X	F6	2	
	Absolute	INC oper	EE	3	
	Absolute,X	INC oper,X	FE	3	
INX	Implied	INX	E8	1	NZ
INY	Implied	INY	C8	1	NZ
JMP	Absolute	JMP oper	4C	3	none
	Indirect	JMP (oper)	6C	3	
JSR	Absolute	JSR oper	20	3	none
LDA	Immediate	LDA #oper	A9	2	NZ
	Zero Page	LDA oper	A5	2	
	Zero Page,X	LDA oper,X	B5	2	
	Absolute	LDA oper	AD	3	
	Absolute,X	LDA oper,X	BD	3	
	Absolute,Y	LDA oper,Y	B9	3	
	(Indirect,X)	LDA (oper,X)	A1	2	
	(Indirect),Y	LDA (oper),Y	B1	2	
LDX	Immediate	LDX #oper	A2	2	NZ
	Zero Page	LDX oper	A4	2	
	Zero Page,Y	LDX oper,Y	B6	2	
	Absolute	LDX oper	AE	3	
	Absolute,Y	LDX oper,Y	BE	3	
LDY	Immediate	LDY #oper	A0	2	NZ
	Zero Page	LDY oper	A4	2	
	Zero Page,X	LDY oper,X	B4	2	
	Absolute	LDY oper	AC	3	
	Absolute,X	LDY oper,X	BC	3	

Mnemonic Code	Addressing Mode	Assembler Form	Op Code	No. Bytes	Flags Affected
LSR	Accumulator	LSR A	4A	1	NZC
	Zero Page	LSR oper	46	2	
	Zero Page,X	LSR oper,X	56	2	
	Absolute	LSR oper	4E	3	
	Absolute,X	LSR oper,X	5E	3	
NOP	Implied	NOP	EA	1	none
ORA	Immediate	ORA #oper	09	2	NZ
	Zero Page	ORA oper	05	2	
	Zero Page,X	ORA oper,X	15	2	
	Absolute	ORA oper	0D	3	
	Absolute,X	ORA oper,X	1D	3	
	Absolute,Y	ORA oper,Y	19	3	
	(Indirect,X)	ORA (oper,X)	01	2	
	(Indirect),Y	ORA (oper),Y	11	2	
PHA	Implied	PHA	48	1	none
PHP	Implied	PHP	08	1	none
PLA	Implied	PLA	68	1	NZ
PLP	Implied	PLP	28	1	all
ROL	Accumulator	ROL A	2A	1	NZC
	Zero Page	ROL oper	26	2	
	Zero Page,X	ROL oper,X	36	2	
	Absolute	ROL oper	2E	3	
	Absolute,X	ROL oper,X	3E	3	
RTI	Implied	RTI	40	1	all
RTS	Implied	RTS	60	1	none
SBC	Immediate	SBC #oper	E9	2	NZCV
	Zero Page	SBC oper	E5	2	
	Zero Page,X	SBC oper,X	F5	2	
	Absolute	SBC oper	ED	3	

Mnemonic Code	Addressing Mode	Assembler Form	Op Code	No. Bytes	Flags Affected
	Absolute,X	SBC oper,X	FD	3	
	Absolute,Y	SBC (oper,Y)	F9	3	
	(Indirect,X)	SBC (oper,X)	E1	2	
	(Indirect),Y	SBC (oper),Y	F1	2	
SEC	Implied	SEC	38	1	C
SED	Implied	SED	F8	1	D
SEI	Implied	SEI	78	1	I
STA	Zero Page	STA oper	85	2	none
	Zero Page,X	STA oper,X	95	2	
	Absolute	STA oper	8D	3	
	Absolute,X	STA oper,X	9D	3	
	Absolute,Y	STA oper,Y	99	3	
	(Indirect,X)	STA (oper,X)	81	2	
	(Indirect),Y	STA (oper),Y	91	2	
STX	Zero Page	STX oper	86	2	none
	Zero Page,Y	STX oper,Y	96	2	
	Absolute	STX oper	8E	3	
STY	Zero Page	STY oper	84	2	none
	Zero Page,X	STY oper,X	94	2	
	Absolute	STY oper	8C	3	
TAX	Implied	TAX	AA	1	NZ
TAY	Implied	TAY	A8	1	NZ
TYA	Implied	TYA	98	1	NZ
TSX	Implied	TSX	BA	1	NZ
TXA	Implied	TXA	8A	1	NZ
TXS	Implied	TXS	9A	1	none

Index